Perl

FOR

DUMMIES®

4TH EDITION

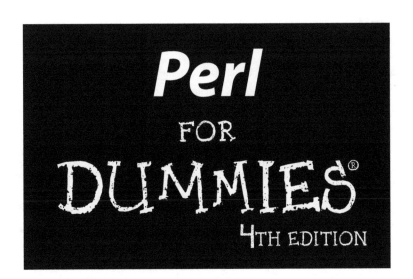

Perl
FOR
DUMMIES®
4TH EDITION

by Paul Hoffman

WILEY

Wiley Publishing, Inc.

Perl for Dummies®, 4th Edition-

Published by
Wiley Publishing, Inc.
111 River St.
Hoboken, NJ 07030-5774
www.wiley.com

For general information on our other products and services, please contact our Customer Care Department within the U.S. at 877-762-2974, outside the U.S. at 317-572-3993, or fax 317-572-4002.

For technical support, please visit www.wiley.com/techsupport.

Wiley also publishes its books in a variety of electronic formats. Some content that appears in print may not be available in electronic books.

Library of Congress Control Number: 2003101830

ISBN-13: 978-0-7645-3750-9

10 9 8 7 6

4B/QW/QT/QT/IN

WILEY

About the Author

Paul E. Hoffman has written more than a dozen computer books, many of them about the Internet (including *Netscape Communicator For Dummies* and *The Internet,* the official book of the Public Television presentation "The Internet Show," both published by Wiley Publishing, Inc.). In fact, he's been active on the Internet for more than 20 years. He is the founder of the VPN Consortium, and has written many of the programs used on that group's Web site. He lives in Santa Cruz, California.

Author's Acknowledgments

The Perl world is full of very helpful people who answer questions for just about anyone. Perl's main developer, Larry Wall, started this trend when he released Perl, and now hundreds of people exist on various mailing lists and Web sites who keep the spirit of cooperation alive. Many of my ideas in this book have come from things that these people have said in different forums over the past many years. Tens of thousands of hours have been spent on making Perl free and useful, and I'm grateful for all this effort by Perl enthusiasts all over the world (and you should be, too!). It is my hope that readers of this book will become enamored not only with Perl, but with creating Perl software that will be freely available.

This is my fourth edition of *Perl For Dummies*, and I'd like to repeat what I said in my very first book. Writing for computer novices is always easier if you have a few of them around asking you questions. My circle of novices and ex-novices keeps me on my toes and reminds me what is not obvious, how frustrating it can be when the system is designed by know-it-all dweebs, and what parts are fun. I am indebted to my friends, my family, and my family-by-choice.

Special thanks to Kala Schrager, the project editor, who spent long hours improving this edition of the book, and for this I am very grateful. Many other folks at Wiley Publishing (and you can find out who they are on the next page) also helped to bring this book to your hands, and I am thankful for their effort and patience.

Publisher's Acknowledgments

We're proud of this book; please send us your comments through our online registration form located at www.dummies.com/register/.

Some of the people who helped bring this book to market include the following:

Acquisitions, Editorial, and Media Development

Project Editor: Kala Schrager

Acquisitions Editor: Terri Varveris

Copy Editor: Rebekah Mancilla

Technical Editor: Steve Seuhring

Editorial Manager: Kevin Kirschner

Media Development Manager: Laura VanWinkle

Media Development Supervisor: Richard Graves

Editorial Assistant: Amanda Foxworth

Cartoons: Rich Tennant (www.the5thwave.com)

Production

Project Coordinator: Nancee Reeves

Layout and Graphics: Seth Conley, Carrie Foster, Michael Kruzil, Jeremey Unger

Proofreaders: Laura Albert, John Greenough; TECHBOOKS Production Services, Inc.

Indexer: TECHBOOKS Production Services, Inc.

Publishing and Editorial for Technology Dummies

Richard Swadley, Vice President and Executive Group Publisher

Andy Cummings, Vice President and Publisher

Mary C. Corder, Editorial Director

Publishing for Consumer Dummies

Diane Graves Steele, Vice President and Publisher

Joyce Pepple, Acquisitions Director

Composition Services

Gerry Fahey, Vice President of Production Services

Debbie Stailey, Director of Composition Services

Contents at a Glance

Table of Contents

Introduction

*A*ssuming that you want to venture into programming, your first step is to pick a specific programming language to start out with. Because you're reading this book, I'm guessing that you're seriously thinking about programming with Perl. I applaud your choice. Like human languages, some programming languages are easier to learn than others. Perl is one of the easiest programming languages to work with, yet it's as powerful as many languages that are much more difficult to master.

The Perl programming language allows you to create fully working computer programs with just a few steps. It's particularly good at common programming tasks, such as reading and writing text files, but it also excels at reducing the work that programmers have to do — more so than other popular languages, such as C and Java.

Who You Are

Your reasons for wanting to learn a programming language probably boil down to the following:

- A fascination with how computers work
- A desire to create your own programs to control your computer
- For professional development (for example, you want to advance to programmer status)

You may also want to get acquainted with a programming language because you work with programmers and you wonder what it is that they do all day. Understanding programming definitely helps you to appreciate what it takes to be a good programmer, even if you don't become one yourself.

If you're interested in discovering how to program (or how others program), *Perl For Dummies,* 4th Edition is for you. If you already know something about programming (but not about Perl), this book is also for you. If you're already an expert programmer, you're still welcome to read this book; you can just skip the basic stuff (you never know what kind of new tips and tricks you'll pick up).

After finding out how to program with Perl, you may decide to go on and become someone who makes a living as a Perl programmer. Or, you may decide that, although programming is interesting, it isn't something that you want to do full time. And, a chance exists (although a slight one) that after you learn how to program in Perl, you may discover that you like programming, but you dislike Perl.

Fortunately, you can also apply most of the Perl programming skills that you can pick up from this book to another programming language later on. Perl is simpler to work with than most other programming languages — and Perl uses many of the same concepts as other languages do, which makes it an excellent introductory language.

What You Need to Know First

This book covers how to use Perl under many different operating systems, such as UNIX, many flavors of Windows (Windows 95/98, Windows NT, Windows 2000, Windows Me, and Windows XP), and Macintosh OS 9 and OS X; in fact, Perl runs on many more operating systems than these. To use this book to learn Perl programming, you need to know at least one of these operating systems. You don't need to know more than one operating system, and very few folks out there know how to use all four. If you're one of those people who's familiar with all four operating systems, you can enjoy the title of Total Computer Dweeb and be comfortable in the fact that few others in the world share your unique skills.

In short, you don't need to know anything about programming up front, or even what Perl is, to get lots of value from this book. However, you do need to know the basics of using your computer system so that you can load Perl and create text files that Perl can use as programs.

What You'll Find in This Book

Because *Perl For Dummies,* 4th Edition is meant for both programming novices and folks who already know something about programming, I arranged the book so that both groups of people can find what they want quickly. You may want to read this book straight through from beginning to end, or you may be one of those folks who enjoys skipping to just what you need. In either case, you need to know how this book is organized.

Part 1: Getting Started with Perl

Part I tells you what programming is all about, what Perl is, what makes it different from other programming languages, and what it means "to program."

This part contains some example programs so that you can see what they look like and how they are put together. You also get some help in installing Perl and running Perl on various operating systems.

Part II: The Basic Perl Programming Ingredients

In Part II, I cover the basic elements of programming with Perl — including techniques for working with text and numbers, plus in-the-trenches programming stuff like lists, strings, operators, loops, and conditional statements. When you're done perusing this part, you can probably write a few short programs of your own.

Part III: The Nuts and Bolts of Perl

This part of the book shows you how to structure a complete Perl program, put together larger and more complex programs, tell Perl to read and write files on your computer, and write programs that know how to talk to a Web server.

Part IV: Advanced Perl Demystified

After you're comfortable with Perl and feeling adventurous, you can dip into this part of the book, which covers a number of advanced Perl topics. Novice programmers aren't expected to use these features immediately, but if you zoom ahead to these chapters (maybe you're saying, "Nah, that's not me," but you may surprise yourself later), you'll find lots of useful information to rev up your Perl programs.

Part V: The Part of Tens

This part of the book contains some nice, quick lists of interesting information about Perl. If you like round numbers, you'll be happy to know that they're all organized in groups of ten.

Part VI: Appendix

Part VI, as you may have guessed, contains the appendix. I list some handy Perl references, such as operators, special variables, and predefined file handles.

A Word about Program Examples

Throughout the book, you can find examples of Perl code that look like the following line:

```
print "Hello, world!\n";
```

You will also see examples of this same kind of typestyle in the body text like this to indicate that this text is a part of a Perl program. You can also find multiple lines of code neatly enclosed in gray boxes. The single lines of code are usually Perl statements (or portions of a statement) and the multiple lines are generally Perl programs. (Yes, you can write an entire program in Perl with just three or four lines.) Not to worry, though. This books tells you all about the difference between statements and programs (and functions and strings and other programming conventions) that are displayed in code font.

Icons Used in This Book

One of the fun things about writing a *For Dummies* book is that you get to use these clever icons to point out items of special interest.

Hopefully, you'll find everything in the book really useful, but these items are especially noteworthy.

This icon alerts you to something that you should definitely watch out for. A couple of important "gotchas" are buried in Perl, and these warnings can help steer you clear of them.

This icon appears next to anything you need to remember later on when you're doing other kinds of stuff with Perl.

Stop here for a side note about something especially high-end. This icon points out technical information that isn't critical to know, but handy nonetheless.

Part I
Getting Started with Perl

The 5th Wave   By Rich Tennant

"IT'S A FOOTBALL/MATH PROGRAM. WE'RE TACKLING MULTIPLICATION, GOING LONG FOR DIVISION, AND PUNTING FRACTIONS."

In this part. . .

You've got to start somewhere, and the beginning is the best place, is it not? In these first few chapters, you find out what a programming language is, what Perl is, how to get Perl up and running on your particular operating system, and what a couple of substantial Perl programs look like.

Chapter 1

Perl's Place in the Programming World

In This Chapter

▶ Understanding programming languages

▶ Comparing Perl to other languages

▶ Using Perl with emerging technologies

*M*any people want to know exactly what makes their computer programs tick. They have a nagging itch to find out what's "under the hood" of their computers, beyond the chips and wires. They want to find out how they can create new and better programs and how it is that programmers can make so much money yet look like they dress in the dark.

Don't assume that everyone who programs or writes books about programming is a young whippersnapper. Without getting too specific, let's just say that my college days are way, way behind me. When I worked with computers back then, I often used punched cards and paper tape — ah, those wonderful pre-PC days.

In pre-PC days, BASIC was the easy language to learn, and serious programmers learned FORTRAN or COBOL to do "real work." But many people discovered that you could accomplish a lot with plain old BASIC. Today, many people have discovered that Perl is a great beginning programming language because it's simple to use and yet you can create powerful programs with little effort. Sure, you can immerse yourself in more difficult languages, such as C++ or Java, but you can probably learn Perl faster and find yourself doing what you want to do just as well, if not better.

Understanding the Purpose of Programming

If you're new to the concept of programming, you may be asking yourself, "Why am I learning how to program?" Sure, programs control computers, but that doesn't mean that everyone should become a programmer.

When personal computers appeared on the scene about 25 years ago, almost no commercial software existed, and the software that did exist was pretty primitive. If you wanted to do anything special, you had to learn to program so that you could create programs to meet your specific needs. By 1981, when the IBM PC came out, plenty of commercial programs were available and users no longer needed to program their computers — the software did it for them.

Today, very few computer users have any real need to write programs. Tens of thousands of programs are available, many for free, and you can find one for just about anything that you want to do with your computer.

Some people think that once they learn to program, they can write any kind of program for their computers. In some cases, people may have some big plans:

- ✔ "I have this great idea for a word processor that's different from the ones I've seen."

- ✔ "I'll create an Internet program that makes Netscape look like a kid's toy!"

- ✔ "There are no good programs that convert English into ancient Greek. I'll create one and make a fortune."

Although such programs are possible, each one would take months or years to create. When you learn to program, you begin by creating simple applications. To create complex programs, you have to practice, practice, and practice, usually full time. In this book, I show you how to cook up lots of simple programs using Perl (but nothing on the order of a word processor, Internet browser, or English-to-ancient-Greek translator, although the latter is certainly possible with Perl).

You may not have to program, but learning the art of programming can open doors for you:

- ✔ **Learning to program is a good way to understand how computer programs work.** Because everything that happens on your computer is controlled by one program or another, learning what it takes to create programs is a good way to find out what makes your computer tick.

✔ **Programming is fun, at least to people like us.** If you enjoy computers and being creative, writing programs can provide great amusement. Programming also appeals to tinkerers, because after you create a program, you can change it a bit here, add a few features there, and just keep on going with it.

✔ **Professional programmers can get paid big bucks, and jobs exist for them all over the world.** Note, however, that most of the programmer jobs you see advertised in the Sunday want ads are for experienced programmers, and the number of entry-level jobs in the field is almost zilch. Still, with a shred of patience and a bit of luck, you can teach yourself programming and turn it into a profession within a few years.

Making Computers Compute

Take a step back to examine what it is that a computer does and what it takes to control a computer. Don't worry, I'll limit the talk about chips and wires and circuit boards to a minimum here. However, you do need a bit of that sort of information because, even though programming is about software, software controls hardware.

A computer is a hardware system that can, well, compute. The main chip in each computer, often called the *central processing unit (CPU)*, takes instructions and data and acts on them, usually to create more data. For example, a CPU can take the data *3* and the data *5* and the instruction *add* and respond with *8*. If, instead, you give it data like *4* and *6* but still give it the instruction *add*, you get the response *10*. Or, if you still used *3* and *5*, but said *multiply* rather than *add*, you see it come back with *15*. This process of taking input, performing some operation, and providing output is really the basis for all computers. Things get fancy when you start talking about the kinds of instructions and data the CPU can handle.

All data given to a computer's CPU is in number form. You may find that fact hard to believe because you've seen your computer produce letters, pictures, and maybe even sounds and movies, but everything you see on-screen is composed in the computer's mind as numbers. When you use a programming language such as Perl, the language lets you think in terms of letters, but the program actually converts letters to numbers for the CPU.

CPUs can do much more than add and multiply. One common CPU operation is the comparison of two numbers. For example, a CPU instruction may say, "If this number is bigger than 0, do this; otherwise, do that instead." By comparing two numbers and choosing what to do next based on the comparison, the CPU can make decisions about how to work when the numbers aren't known ahead of time.

That's the short-and-sweet introduction to the brain of any computer, including a bit about how it "thinks." Of course, a computer doesn't really think: It reacts. And the way that it reacts is based on the instructions and data given to it. The list of instructions that you give to a CPU is a *program,* and you put together a program with a *programming language.* A programming language, such as Perl, is the means by which you, the programmer, can create a set of CPU instructions.

Translating Your Language into Computer Language

In order to make CPUs run efficiently, the instructions and data that you feed them must be compact and concise. As I mentioned in the section "Making Computers Compute," all data given to a computer's CPU is in number form. However, it would be nearly impossible for you to learn a programming language that only used numbers. Instead, programmers use more human-friendly languages like Perl (or C, or COBOL, or Java, and so on). These languages are called *high-level languages,* and when they run, they're converted into instructions and data to let the CPU know what's happening. These instructions and data are called *machine language,* and even though machine language is a kind of programming language, very few people know how to use it.

Interpreters and compilers

Two main types of programming languages exist — *compiled* and *interpreted,* each of which has its advantages and disadvantages. Probably the best-known compiled language is C. Perl, on the other hand, is an interpreted language.

The main difference between the two is that compiled languages generally run faster. Interpreted languages read a program and turn it into machine language before executing it. Compiled languages already have the machine instructions, so they can start executing from the get-go. Many people, particularly C programmers, contend that compiled programs are better

because they run faster. In our faster-is-better society, this may be a compelling argument.

The speed difference between a compiler and an interpreter is sometimes infinitesimal, and unnoticeable by mere mortals. For instance, even for large and complex Perl programs, an equivalent C program may take one-half of a second less to run. Another difference is that interpreted languages are a bit easier to debug (that is, to find and fix errors), because they are executed step by step, so you can find exactly where a problem occurred and stop right there to fix it.

An important feature of a programming language is how quickly people can learn to create useful programs with it. Other considerations, such as how fast programs run after you write them and how much energy you have to expend to get particular tasks done, are important; however, of first and foremost importance is a language's ease of use. A difficult language may be okay for the top 10 or 20 percent of the programming population, but for the rest of us, a difficult language simply isn't worth all the struggle in the learning department and, therefore, isn't likely to be popular.

Designing Computer Languages

People sometimes think of human languages as appearing out of nowhere and never changing, but that's clearly not the case. Human languages evolve in a number of ways, and so do computer languages. Computer languages are quite different from human languages:

- ✔ The main purpose of human language is person-to-person communication; the main purpose of computer languages is human-to-computer communication.

- ✔ All computer languages have been created within the past 50 years. Because they haven't developed over a long period of time like most human languages, they don't present some of the challenges that many human languages do, such as having too many exceptions to the rules.

- ✔ Computer languages are usually invented by a single person or a small group of people (although larger groups of people may get together later to decide how to modify a language). Because human languages are developed by entire cultures, they're apt to have more quirks and oddities than computer languages.

When people create a new computer language, they have to think long and hard about what they want to do with it, and why their language will be better than the ones already out there. Convincing people to stop using their favorite computer language and switch to a new one can be difficult, so a designer must craft a language to make it as attractive as possible (in other words, they have to make the language powerful, or easy to use, or both).

Sometimes, a language is created to do just one little thing better than any other language does it, and that one thing is really important to a select group of people. For example, engineers who design robots may want their own computer language to be able to describe how to move an arm or a leg and what direction to move it in, but they don't need the ability to perform calculus. Other languages are designed to do all things fairly well, which makes program writing simpler because the programmer can do everything with just a single tool.

Picky languages versus free-form languages

When you first learn a programming language, you're allowed to make minor mistakes along the way. When it comes to actually creating a workable program, however, some languages are very particular about how you write it and will block your progress unless the program is perfect.

Some programming languages, such as C, demand that you're extremely careful about the types of data you're using; if you make a mistake, the program can cause errors without you noticing them. Other languages, such as Perl, are much more lenient; they let you be less specific about the kind of data you're using.

Professional programmers can argue on and on about whether a language should be picky or not. Some say being picky is good because it forces the programmer to dictate exactly what he or she wants, leaving no guesswork for the language. Others say languages should be lenient so that a programmer can write code quickly without having to dot all the *i*'s and cross all the *t*'s.

A programming language can be stringent or lenient in other ways, as well. Some languages require that every line of a program line up with each other in a certain way, and others are much more free-form. By the way, you'll discover that Perl is overall a pretty lenient language. However, if you want Perl to get picky, you can tell it to check your programs for probable errors in order to find the things that you may have done wrong.

You may think that every language should be simple to learn so that more people can use it. However, that's not really necessary because a fair number of simple languages already exist — Perl being one of them. Instead of creating new, easily mastered languages, language designers are targeting specific groups of programmers who will spend the time to work with special features or interesting language forms.

When creating a new computer language, designers must keep a number of considerations in mind:

- ✔ How fast will the language run?
- ✔ How easy is it to extend the language to handle tasks unanticipated by the language's authors?
- ✔ What sort of background do programmers of that language need?
- ✔ What type of computers will run the language?

Because of these design challenges, relatively few computer languages are widely used. Although at least 100 languages have been disseminated over the past 30 years, fewer than a dozen are used by more than a few thousand people.

Appreciating the Benefits of Perl

Computer users can argue *ad nauseum* about which programming language is the best or easiest to use. The fact is, no single language is perfect for every task, and the top three or four languages for most tasks get the job done equally well. For the novice or intermediate programmer, then, the question is not really what is the best program to use, but which is the easiest one to master.

Perl scores high on both the learning-curve and ease-of-use scales. You can write a small Perl program designed to do a simple task after reading just the first few chapters of this book. In fact, if you read through the first part of this book, you'll understand enough about Perl that you can begin to modify programs to your heart's content. One of the common phrases in the world of Perl programmers is "there's more than one way to do it."

Certainly, other languages are easy to learn and use, but they don't have the features that make Perl a great all-around language, such as flexibility with the kinds of data it can handle or its ability to deal with objects. Here's the lowdown on some other languages:

- **BASIC:** Good old BASIC has features similar to the easy features of Perl, but it's not very good for modern programming because of its lack of flexibility.

- **Visual Basic:** Microsoft Visual Basic is not nearly as easy to learn as BASIC, and although it's very powerful, many novices find Visual Basic pretty confusing.

- **C:** Some people think C is easy to learn, but difficult to use unless you're very careful, because you can create C programs that look great on the surface but do harmful things to your computer. C also loses points in the text-handling area — one of the places in which Perl shines.

- **Java:** Boy, it's hard to talk about Java without either the pro-Java or anti-Java zealots attacking you. Speaking frankly, Java is an okay language that suffers from being horribly over-promoted. It has some great features, such as safe execution of programs in secure environments and easy reuse of programs written by other people. Unfortunately, it fails miserably at the feature for which it was most touted; namely, that you can write a program for one type of computer and have the program look and act the same on all other types of computers.

Perl also surpasses other programming languages on some common tasks. With Perl, the tasks of opening a file on your computer, reading it, and making some changes based on what you find in the file is quite easy. Perl can handle text files with aplomb, and has no problems with binary files. Perl is also good at handling text in ways that humans do, such as looking at a sentence and breaking it into words or sorting lines in alphabetical order.

A bit of Perl history

Programming languages have been around for several decades. Perl (short for *Practical Extraction and Report Language*) is one of the youngest of the popular programming languages, debuting in the mid-1980s. The idea for Perl pretty much sprang from the head of one person, Larry Wall, who had a bunch of system-administration tasks to do and no good language to get them all done.

In short, Perl was born out of necessity. Larry Wall needed a language that had the power to open a bunch of text files in different formats, read these different files in one way, and create new files that reported on the original files. He could have used C, a popular language at the time, but C is ornery when dealing with text and is prone to making difficult-to-locate errors if you're not careful.

Perl has been extended to do much more than extract text and then generate a report on it.

Thousands of useful system-administration and Internet tools now rely on Perl to perform tasks such as summarizing log files, taking input from Web users, and displaying parts of databases on the Web. In fact, a few Web server programs are written completely in Perl.

Perl now comes bundled with almost every copy of every flavor of UNIX. For a long time, Perl was mostly a UNIX-only language. Until a few years ago, virtually all work on Perl was done on UNIX. The language has recently become popular on PCs and Macintoshes, in part because it is free and easy to get. Indeed, Perl is the most popular free programming language available for Windows systems and Macs, and as these computers need more and more system administration, Perl's acceptance and use is likely to grow even more.

The ten-second summary of Perl's strongest points is this: Perl works great for reading through text files, summarizing processed files or converting files to a different format, and managing UNIX systems. Other languages strive to be elegant or very small; Perl strives to be complete and easy to use.

Another great reason for using Perl is that it's free. This no-cost policy has prompted many people to help out with the Perl development effort and has resulted in widespread usage of Perl over a relatively short period of time. Perl is also *open source software*, meaning that anyone can look at the internal programming in Perl and correct errors or even extend the language itself. Open source software is considered to be more secure and reliable than software for which you can't check the internals.

Many Versions, One Perl

Throughout this book, I talk about Perl as if it were just one programming language. But, like all software, Perl has gone through many changes since the time Larry Wall conceived it. Fortunately, you need to think about only two major versions of Perl: Perl 5.6 and Perl 5.8. (An older version of Perl, Perl 4, is rarely seen and is mentioned in a few places in this book for those of you using very old copies of Perl.)

Each major version (currently, the major version is Perl 5) has many minor versions; for example, for the last edition of this book, the current version of Perl was 5.6; the current version is now 5.8. All minor versions of a major version act pretty much the same, but higher numbered minor versions usually have a few additions and bug fixes.

Perl version 4 was the stable version of Perl for many years. In fact, a few people still use Perl 4 instead of Perl 5 because they just got so used to it — even though Perl 5 added many advanced features. The final subversion of Perl 4 is "patchlevel 36," but most people just refer to it as version 4.036. Whenever I talk about Perl 4 in this book, I'm referring to Perl version 4.036.

In early 1996, people started making the switch to Perl 5; in early 2000, people started switching to Perl 5.6; now people are switching to Perl 5.8. Perl 5.6 and Perl 5.8 are pretty stable (although not completely bug-free, of course) and can certainly be used for almost any application.

This book is almost exclusively about Perl 5.8, which is not to say that a Perl 5.6 user can't use the programs found here. (Perl 5.7 was only used by the people developing Perl — not by folks like you and me.) In fact, about 95 percent of what's in this book works exactly the same under Perl 5.6 as it does with Perl 5.8, which is a testament to the folks who worked so carefully on the Perl project to engineer a smooth transition from Perl 4 to Perl 5 to Perl 5.6 to Perl 5.8.

However, a few things in Perl 5.8 just plain didn't exist in Perl 4, and of course, I cover them in this book. For example, Chapter 19 covers object-oriented Perl, a feature that doesn't exist in Perl 4. I sprinkle descriptions of a few smaller, but nevertheless handy, new features in Perl 5 throughout the book. Similarly, a few things now exist in Perl 5.8 that didn't exist in Perl 5.6, and I cover those as well.

I urge everyone using Perl 5 to upgrade to Perl 5.6 or, preferably, Perl 5.8. Doing so will make your time with this book much easier, and will also give you a much better (and more bug-free!) experience.

Differentiating Between Perl 5 and Perl 5.6

Perl 5.6 took almost four years to come out, so you may be expecting a zillion new features to have been shoved in all over the place. For many programming languages, that would be a reasonable expectation, but not for Perl. The good folks who maintain Perl have stuck to their convictions and kept "creeping featureitis syndrome" to a minimum.

The most visible change, and the one that has garnered the most interest around the world, is Perl's embracing of international characters in general and the Unicode standard in particular. People using just the English language have it easy: They have a small set of characters in their alphabet, and none of those characters have diacritic marks such as acute accents (´) and umlauts (¨). Almost every non-English language, however, uses at least a few characters that are not found in the English alphabet.

Until version 5.6, Perl had no standard way of letting you enter these characters or showing you these characters in your output. With version 5.6, that is fairly easy to do. Perl relies on the Unicode standard, which was created and is maintained by the *Unicode Consortium,* a group of companies and individuals who have been working for over a decade to make all the world's languages easy to handle for all computers. You can find out more about the Unicode standard at `www.unicode.org` and more about how Perl 5.6 uses Unicode in Chapter 5 of this book.

The other improvements in Perl 5.6 aren't nearly as visible to most users. In fact, the creators of Perl 5.6 made a successful effort to mostly add "backend" changes in the new version, and to rely on Perl modules (described in Chapter 19) to add the more visible features. Most of these features are well beyond the scope of this book, but a few that appear include binary numbers and closer integration with Microsoft Windows operating systems.

Exploring the New Features of Perl 5.8

The difference between Perl 5.6 and Perl 5.8 is much smaller than the difference between Perl 5 and Perl 5.6. Whereas Perl 5.6 introduced many new and significant concepts to Perl, Perl 5.8 is mostly an evolutionary revision.

That is not to say that Perl 5.8 isn't important — because it is. For one thing, Perl 5.8 is significantly faster for many programs. It is also more stable than earlier versions of Perl. In addition, it has many new features, including:

  ✔ Improved support of internationalized text (covered in Chapter 5)

  ✔ Additional functions and modules (covered throughout the book)

  ✔ Better accuracy for large numbers (covered in Chapter 6)

All of this adds up to a good reason for you to update to Perl 5.8 if you haven't already.

Chapter 2

Running Perl on Your Computer

. . . .

In This Chapter

- Installing Perl on various platforms
- Running Perl programs
- Getting the latest version of Perl
- Finding out about Perl on other systems

. . . .

*A*ny programming language that runs on a certain type of computer has to be designed for that computer in order to run any programs. For example, in order to read and write files, a language must know precisely how the computer on which it is running reads and writes files.

Technically speaking, a programming language such as Perl runs on an operating system, and not on a computer. Practically every computer built today comes with its own operating system, and some computers can run many optional operating systems. For example, IBM-compatible PCs can run Windows 98, Windows NT, Windows 2000, Windows XP, Linux and other flavors of UNIX, and so on. Perl isn't particular about the computer it's running on — just the computer's operating system.

Perl Isn't Just for UNIX Anymore

Perl was written first and foremost for UNIX and similar operating systems. One of the wonderful things about Perl (or, should I say, "yet another wonderful thing about Perl") is that it tries valiantly to hide any differences among operating systems. Perl for Windows and Perl for the Macintosh have a few features not found on Perl for UNIX, but the vast majority of the interesting stuff in Perl works the same on every operating system. You open files the same way, you do math the same way, and so on.

You do need to be aware of a few important differences between Perl running on UNIX and Perl running on other operating systems. I point out these differences in this book with warnings such as this one (shown in the margin). Ignoring these words of advice can result in programs that don't work the way that you expect.

Most of this book covers the parts of Perl that work the same way on all kinds of computers. Before you can start running Perl programs, however, you need to install Perl on your computer, which requires different steps for each kind of computer. I describe those steps later in this chapter.

Playing the name game

This book describes how to run Perl on many different operating systems: UNIX, all versions of Windows since Windows 95, and Macintosh (Mac OS 9 and Mac OS X):

- **Windows:** Perl for Windows 98, Windows NT, Windows 2000, Windows Me, and Windows XP are actually the same program. In this book, I call the program ActivePerl because that's the name of the commercial version of the program (described a litter later in this chapter).
- **Macintosh:** Perl on the Macintosh is called MacPerl.
- **UNIX:** Perl on UNIX is called, well, just plain Perl.

Getting the latest from the Internet

You can get the latest version of Perl from many sites on the Internet. The central repository for finding where to get Perl is at `www.perl.com`. You can obtain the ActivePerl program for Windows from its developer, ActiveState, at `www.activestate.com`. Similarly, Mac users can get a copy of MacPerl from the Internet by going to `www.macperl.com` and following the directions for downloading MacPerl.

UNIX: Perl's First Home

Because Perl started out as a UNIX application, Perl's integration with UNIX is much tighter than its integration with Windows or the Mac. However, this tight integration doesn't mean that installing and using Perl on UNIX is always a minor task. The following sections of this chapter should help UNIX users to avoid problems with installing Perl on their systems.

Determining whether you need to install Perl on UNIX

If you've used UNIX for any length of time, you know that a zillion variants of UNIX are available. For some folks, the differences don't amount to much.

If you're trying to install a complex program such as Perl, however, those differences can make the installation process utter agony. In my experience, installing Perl can be a cinch or it can be a real mind-bender.

Fortunately, Perl is so popular among UNIX folks that almost every implementation of UNIX now comes with Perl fully installed. A good way to find out whether you already have Perl on your system is to enter the following simple command on the UNIX command line:

```
perl -v
```

If Perl is installed and in your UNIX search path, you get something on-screen that looks like this:

```
This is perl, version 5.8.0 built for i386-bsdos

Copyright 1987-2002, Larry Wall

Perl may be copied only under the terms of either the
Artistic License or the GNU General Public License, which
may be found in the Perl 5.0 source kit.

Complete documentation for Perl, including FAQ lists,
should be found on this system using 'man perl' or
'perldoc perl'. If you have access to the Internet, point
your browser at http://www.perl.com/, the Perl Home Page.
```

Make note of the version number in the first line of the previous message. It should say This is perl, version 5.005 or This is perl, version 5.6.0 or This is perl, version 5.8.0. That means you're running Perl 5, the latest major version of Perl. If the first line says something like This is perl, version 4.0, you're running Perl 4, which is okay (but not great). As I explain in Chapter 1, some of the features described in this book are available only in Perl 5.

A few UNIX systems have both Perl 4 and Perl 5 running simultaneously. Usually, one is invoked as perl and the other as perl4 or perl5. In the text shown previously, perl is Perl 5, and a program called perl4 may be on your UNIX system that will run Perl 4. If running perl gives you Perl 4, you should definitely check whether the command perl5 -v results in the version message for Perl 5.

If you don't have Perl in your UNIX search path when you issue the perl -v command, you see the following message:

```
perl: command not found
```

Not to worry — you may still have Perl on your system, but you should have UNIX do a bit of searching for you by using the whereis command:

```
whereis perl
```

If Perl is in any of the standard places where one may expect to find it, you'll probably get something like this:

```
/usr/bin/perl
/usr/contrib/bin/perl
```

The whereis command sometimes puts the response on a single line.

If you get a blank response from the whereis program, most likely you don't have Perl on your system. You must then resort to the one thing that many of us hate to do: Ask someone else. Your best bet is to ask a system administrator where Perl may be hiding. The administrator may have installed a copy but not made it publicly available, or you may need just one more person (you!) to pester the administrator about installing Perl.

Installing Perl on UNIX

If you're a UNIX system administrator (welcome, oh wizard!), you can probably install Perl with a minimum of muss or fuss if your flavor of UNIX is supported in the Perl build. Unfortunately, it usually isn't. In the past, I installed Perl by using just two commands; but at times, I had to get on the phone with the tech support people at my UNIX vendor to figure out what went wrong.

You can install Perl for other people to use only if you are a system administrator. You can, however, install it for yourself without having system administrator privileges. Perl requires access to some privileged files in order to install it correctly for general use; therefore, you must have system administrator privileges when doing the installation. If you aren't a system administrator with root privileges, you need to ask the person who does have those privileges to do the Perl installation for you.

You first need to get a copy of Perl. The best place to start is www.perl.com, which has links to many places where you can download Perl for free.

You can then install Perl 5.6 or Perl 5.8 with the following seven basic steps:

1. **Use** gunzip **and/or** tar **to uncompress and unpack the** .tar.gz **file.**

   It's a good idea to put the sources in the same place where you put your other program sources (typically in /usr/local/src). Most modern UNIX systems let you use a command like tar -xzf perl.tgz to uncompress and unpack the file.

2. **Read the file called** INSTALL.

This file gives you more information about what you need to install Perl. The file isn't lengthy, and it lists some of the picky details that you need to know for the different flavors of UNIX.

3. **Remove the** `config.sh` **file from the installation directory, if you have one there.**

   The `config.sh` file may be in the installation directory if, for example, you previously tried to install Perl.

4. **Issue the** `sh Configure` **command:**

   This command is a shell script that can figure out lots of information about your system. The script creates the `config.sh` file, which contains dozens of variable definitions for your system.

5. **Issue the** `make` **command.**

   This command compiles and links all the needed files by using the parameters determined in Step 4.

6. **Issue the** `make test` **command.**

   This command performs many tests on the copy of Perl that was made in Step 5. The `make test` command should result in the reply `All tests successful`; if it doesn't, the other messages you get should (hopefully) help you figure out which part of the compilation or linking failed.

   Perl has many parts, and the installer program puts the various Perl files in different places, possibly wiping out previous versions of some system files. Just to be sure, look through the `Makefile` (the file that tells the `make` program what to do) *before* running the `make install` command in Step 7 to be sure everything's going to go where you want it to be.

7. **Last, but certainly not least, issue the** `make install` **command.**

   This command installs all the parts of Perl into the various system directories on your computer.

Running Perl programs under UNIX

Assuming that you have Perl on your system, you can run Perl programs quite easily by using the `perl` command. Perl programs are simply text files, and you can create Perl programs with any text editor, such as vi or emacs.

For example, if you have a Perl program in a file called `proc-invoices`, you can run that program with the following command:

```
perl proc-invoices
```

Perl has many command line options. For example, one of the most useful command line options is `-c`, which tells Perl to not run the program, but to just check it for any syntax errors. Therefore, to check your `proc-invoices` program, you can give the following command:

```
perl -c proc-invoices
```

Under UNIX, Perl acts like a shell interpreter, a subject that's familiar to UNIX-savvy users. The fact that Perl acts as a shell interpreter means that you can write Perl programs invoked from the UNIX command line without starting the command with `perl`. For example, you can run the `proc-invoices` program with the following command:

```
proc-invoices
```

However, in order to make the previous command work, the first line of your Perl program must look something like this:

```
#!/usr/bin/perl
```

The text to the right of the `#!` characters must indicate the location of Perl on your system. Most UNIX systems stash Perl in `/usr/bin/perl`. If your system keeps Perl in a location such as `/usr/contrib/lang/perl`, the first line of your Perl programs is the following:

```
#!/usr/contrib/lang/perl
```

If you use both UNIX and Windows, you may fall into a common trap. In the command window in Windows, don't type the program's extension when you run a program. For example, if you have a program called `procinv.exe`, you would give this command:

```
procinv
```

No actual extensions exist under UNIX. Therefore, if you have a program called `proc-invoices.pl` (`.pl` being the common way of indicating that a file is a Perl program), you have to give the following command:

```
proc-invoices.pl
```

Typing just `proc-invoices` won't work.

ActivePerl on Windows

Installing Perl 5 on any version of Windows since Windows 95 is much easier that installing Perl on UNIX. ActivePerl comes as a *self-installing* program, which means that it comes as a single executable file. When you run that file, it installs all the necessary files in the right places on your hard drive.

Installing ActivePerl under Windows

If you're running under almost any flavor of Windows, go to the Web site for ActiveState at www.activestate.com/Products/ActivePerl. There you will find a form for downloading ActivePerl. After following the directions, you end up with a file called ActivePerl.msi, which is the installer program for ActivePerl.

The ActivePerl installer uses Microsoft's new Windows Installer to help guide you through the installation process. If you use Windows 95, Windows 98, or Windows NT, you may need to download this program before you install ActivePerl (Windows 2000, Windows Me, and Windows XP users don't need this program). The program to install the installer is available from the ActiveState Web site.

Before you run the installer, you may need to take an extra step if you're a Windows 95 user. (Users of Windows 98 and later versions can skip this step.) You have to install the msvcrt.dll file into Windows 95 before you install ActivePerl. The folks at ActiveState tell you how to get this. After you do that, you can then install ActivePerl.

To install Perl, double-click the icon for the ActivePerl.msi file. As the installation program runs, it acts like the installation programs for most other Windows software that you're probably familiar with. Various dialog boxes prompt you for feedback, such as whether you read the license agreement.

One of the important questions that the ActivePerl installer asks you is where you want to put ActivePerl; it suggests the directory C:\perl. Unless you have some strong preference against this location, you should accept this suggestion and install ActivePerl in that spot. Another reason to accept this location: Every Windows example in this book was written with the assumption that Perl is installed in C:\perl.

After you wade through a few more prompts from the installation program, the program installs all the needed files on your hard drive. After it copies all the files, the last prompt asks you whether you want to read the release notes for ActivePerl. If you say yes, the installer program launches your Web browser (such as Netscape Communicator or Internet Explorer) to display the release notes. Feel free to say "no" to the prompt because you can read the release notes later, and you're probably more interested in starting to use Perl than in reading more about it.

Running ActivePerl in a command prompt window

I have some sad news: ActivePerl *isn't* a Windows program. You run it from the command line in a command prompt window. Yes, you read that correctly. That means no menus, no dialog boxes, and lots of typing. At first, I was flabbergasted at this discovery, but I learned to live with it.

First, you need to open a command prompt window manually:

1. **Go to the Start menu, and choose Command Prompt from the Programs item.**

   A black window that's probably not in the directory in which you put ActivePerl appears.

2. **Use the** CD **command to get to your Perl directory.**

   If you followed the installation instructions, this directory is C:\perl.

After reading this section of the chapter, you can see why I use C:\perl as my Perl directory: I can get there with very little typing. However, you can go one step further than that: You can create a shortcut so you don't have to give the CD command every time you start a command prompt window:

1. **Right-click the system's desktop.**

   A contextual menu appears.

2. **Choose New➪Shortcut.**

   A dialog box appears, asking for the command line of the shortcut that you are creating.

3. **Type** C:\Command.com **in the text area for the command line and click Next.**

4. **For the shortcut name, enter** Perl5.

5. **Click Finish.**

   You now have a new icon on your desktop.

6. **Right-click the new icon for a context-sensitive menu.**

7. **Select Properties.**

8. **In the Properties dialog box, click the Program tab.**

9. **In the Working option, enter the name of the directory where you keep ActivePerl; for example,** C:\perl.

   You can specify any other options that you desire under the other tabs in the Properties window.

10. Click OK in the Properties window to make sure that the new settings stick.

Now when you double-click the icon that you created by using the previous steps, the command prompt window starts in your Perl directory.

Because Perl programs are text files, you can create programs with a text editor, such as the Windows Notepad program or the DOS `edit` command. You can also run Perl programs easily by using the `perl` command. For example, if you have a Perl program in the `procinv.pl` file, you can run that program with the following command:

```
perl procinv.pl
```

Perl features a number of command-line options, and one of the most useful of those options is `-c`, which tells Perl to check a program for syntax errors without running the program. So, to check the `proc-invoices` program, you can issue the following command:

```
perl -c procinv.pl
```

You can check the version of ActivePerl that you're running by giving the following command:

```
perl -v
```

The output of this command is shown in Figure 2-1.

```
Perl command prompt                                          _ □ ×

C:\Perl>perl -v

This is perl, v5.8.0 built for MSWin32-x86-multi-thread
(with 1 registered patch, see perl -V for more detail)

Copyright 1987-2002, Larry Wall

Binary build 804 provided by ActiveState Corp. http://www.ActiveState.com
Built 23:15:13 Dec  1 2002

Perl may be copied only under the terms of either the Artistic License or the
GNU General Public License, which may be found in the Perl 5 source kit.

Complete documentation for Perl, including FAQ lists, should be found on
this system using `man perl' or `perldoc perl'.  If you have access to the
Internet, point your browser at http://www.perl.com/, the Perl Home Page.

C:\Perl>_
```

Figure 2-1:
You can check the version of ActivePerl being run.

Perl for Mac Users

Macintosh fans in the audience who read the previous sections of this chapter are probably bored silly by now with all the UNIX and Windows command lines. Fear not: It's your turn. Compared with UNIX, installing Perl for Mac is a breeze.

Running Perl in Mac OS X

If you are one of the millions of Mac users who have installed OS X, Perl is already installed for you. All you need to do is open a Terminal window to use it just like other UNIX users do (as described earlier in this chapter).

Now, admittedly, not every Mac OS X user has used the Terminal window; heck, many users have no idea what it is. To open a Terminal window, simply run the Terminal program, which you can find in the Utilities folder in the computer's Applications folder.

For more information on running the Terminal program, see *Mac OS X For Dummies*, 2nd Edition, by Bob LeVitus (Wiley Publishing, Inc.). That book has hints and tricks for using the Terminal window that will make your time using Perl under OS X more enjoyable.

Installing MacPerl in Mac OS 9

If you are running Mac OS 9 (or even Mac OS 8.5), you can still use Perl. The MacPerl program, available from www.macperl.org, is a fairly complete implementation of Perl 5.6 for the Macintosh. It gives you a graphical interface, just like you would expect from a Mac program. MacPerl has extensions that let you create Mac programs with dialog boxes, windows, menu interaction, and so on.

You can even run MacPerl under OS X if you want to use the extensions. When using OS X, MacPerl runs in the OS X "classic environment," which means that your programs don't look as nice as OS X programs but they still run fine.

To install MacPerl, do the following:

1. **Go to www.macperl.com to get the latest version of the MacPerl program.**

2. **After you download the installer program to your hard drive, double-click the MacPerl Installer to run it.**

You're asked where you want the MacPerl folder, and about 800 files associated with Perl (including the online documentation), to be installed on your computer.

The result of the installation is a folder similar to the one shown in Figure 2-2.

Figure 2-2:
The
MacPerl
folder.

Running MacPerl programs

MacPerl is a program that runs Perl programs. This means that when you run MacPerl, you tell it which Perl programs you want to run. The MacPerl program itself has a nominal user interface. In fact, when you start MacPerl, it doesn't even open up any windows.

MacPerl programs are plain text files, so you can create them with any text editor, such as SimpleText or BBEdit. MacPerl also has a basic text editor built into it.

To create a new text file in MacPerl, follow these steps:

1. **Choose File⇨New.**

2. **Enter and edit your program.**

3. **Choose File⇨Save.**

   You can also use the Open, Close, Print, Cut, Copy, and Paste commands in the MacPerl editor just like you would in any other Mac program.

To run a Perl program in MacPerl, choose one of the two Run commands from the Script menu:

- ✔ The first Run command runs a program that you have on disk.
- ✔ The second Run command runs the program that you are editing in MacPerl.

If you want to use an editor other than MacPerl's internal editor, you should use the first Run command.

When you run a Perl program, MacPerl opens an empty window for input and output. In this window, you can read messages from MacPerl, and you can also enter your text responses to prompts. (Chapter 3 covers reading and entering text in Perl programs.)

You can also use MacPerl to check for errors in your programs before you run them. Instead of using one of the Run commands, simply use one of the Syntax Check commands in the Script menu.

Working with Perl on the Command Line

When you run Perl from the UNIX or Windows command line, you can include command line options that change the way Perl behaves. These options are also available for MacPerl, but not from the command line, because MacOS 9 has no command line. More than a dozen command line options are available for Perl (UNIX dweebs love their command line options!), but only a few are really interesting to most programmers. I cover a few of those options in this section.

Entering command line options

You can give command line options in one of two ways. The first, of course, is on the command line. As an alternative, you can include a line at the beginning of your program that looks like the command line but starts with #!. For example, you can indicate that you always want to use the -w command line option (which tells Perl to check your program for various programming errors) by inserting #!perl -w as the first line of your program. Mac users, who don't have a command line, will be especially thankful for this option.

As described earlier in this chapter, UNIX users must enter the full path to a Perl program in the command line of their programs. Therefore, instead of entering #!perl -w, for example, a UNIX user enters the following as the first line of the program:

```
#!/usr/bin/perl -w
```

Checking syntax with the -c option

The most common Perl option that you can expect to use is -c, which causes Perl to check the syntax of a program without running it. For you Mac users, the Syntax Check command in MacPerl does the same thing as the -c command line option.

Looking for errors with the -w option

The -w option, which causes Perl to carefully examine your program for a number of programming errors, is similar to the -c option. If it finds any of these errors, it prints them so that you can then edit your program in order to fix it. Using the -w option before you start to use a Perl program helps you to avoid embarrassing problems later.

Identifying versions of Perl with the -v option

The -v option tells you which version of Perl you're running. The -v option also works on ActivePerl and MacPerl. For example, if you include the line

```
#!perl -v
```

at the beginning of a ActivePerl file, Perl prints

```
This is perl, v5.6.1 built for MSWin32-x86-multi-thread
(with 1 registered patch, see perl -V for more detail)

Copyright 1987-2001, Larry Wall

Binary build 613 provided by ActiveState Tool Corp.
http://www.ActiveState.com
Built 17:16:22 Jan  2 2002

Perl may be copied only under the terms of either the
Artistic License or the GNU General Public License, which
may be found in the Perl 5 source kit.

Complete documentation for Perl, including FAQ lists,
should be found on this system using 'man perl' or
'perldoc perl'. If you have access to the
Internet, point your browser at http://www.perl.com/, the
Perl Home Page.
```

Running one-liners with the -e option

Perl has a mode in which you can run one-line programs without having to enter them into a text file. If you use the -e option, Perl assumes that the rest of the command line is a one-line Perl program, not the name of a text file that has a program in it. For example, to find the product of two numbers, you can use the following command:

```
perl -e "print 27.35 * .0825;"
```

Debugging with the -d option

After you get more experience in working with Perl, you may want to use Perl's internal debugging system. The debugger is a program that allows you to find errors in your Perl programs by moving through them step by step. The topic of debugging is beyond the scope of this book, but in case you want to experiment with it, you can turn on the debugger with the -d command line option. For example, to debug the proc-invoices program, simply enter the following line:

```
perl -d proc-invoices
```

Other Perls

The Comprehensive Perl Archive Network (CPAN) contains the Perl language for many operating systems. (I describe CPAN in more detail in the next section.) Perl has been made to run on a wide variety of systems, and implementations of Perl for all the following operating systems are available:

- Acorn
- Amiga
- Atari
- BeOS
- MS-DOS
- MVS
- Novell NetWare

- OS/2
- OS 390
- QNX
- RiscOS
- VMS
- Windows 3.1

Most of the these versions of Perl are a bit outdated and unsupported. Most notably, the Windows 3.1 version is for Perl 4 only and hasn't been updated in more than five years.

Some of the other versions of Perl are up-to-date and well supported; you can use them with abandon. If you want to run Perl on one of the other operating systems listed in this section, take a look at the program files on CPAN to see whether any documentation exists, and if so, look for e-mail contact information for the program.

This book covers Perl running on UNIX, Windows, and Mac OS only. If you use Perl on any other operating system, at least 95 percent of the programs presented in this book should work just fine for you, but I can make no guarantees.

Utilizing the Comprehensive Perl Archive Network

CPAN is a huge network of volunteers who contribute Perl software and organize it into a readily accessible format. This archive literally contains thousands of Perl extensions, modules, and programming examples that have been contributed by people all over the world. To find the CPAN network on the Web, head to `www.cpan.org`.

In Chapters 14 and 15, you will find discussions that use modules that are not built into Perl; you can find every one of them at CPAN. The folks at CPAN give you multiple ways to find modules, but the two most useful are by name and by function. If you want to search for modules on CPAN, go to `search.cpan.org`, which gives you an easy way to not only find the modules, but to read their documentation before downloading them.

It is well worth searching the archive before you write a Perl program, in case all or part of what you want has already been created for you.

Working with the ActivePerl Package Manager

Although it is not properly part of CPAN, the Perl Package Manager (PPM) that comes with ActivePerl is a handy way to get software for ActivePerl. The system is an interface to ActiveState's collection of CPAN modules that have been preconfigured for Windows.

PPM lets you download packages that are maintained by ActiveState from the Internet. If you bought ActivePerl on CD-ROM, it lets you install modules from the CD-ROM. It also lets you automatically update any packages that you have installed if newer versions of those packages are available.

To run PPM, give the ppm command at the command prompt in your command window. The response to the command looks like the following:

```
PPM - Programmer's Package Manager version 3.0.1.
Copyright (c) 2001 ActiveState SRL. All Rights Reserved.

Entering interactive shell. Using Term::ReadLine::Stub as readline library.

Profile tracking is not enabled. If you save and restore profiles manually,
your profile may be out of sync with your computer. See 'help profile' for
more information.

Type 'help' to get started.

ppm>
```

Table 2-1 shows the most useful commands for ppm.

Table 2-1	Useful ppm commands for ActivePerl users
Command	*Description*
quickstart	Describes briefly how to use PPM
help	Lists the ppm commands that are available
help *command*	Gives help on the specified *command*
search *packagename*	Searches for packages in the repository; you can use wildcards in the name
install *packagename*	Installs a specific package from the repository
query *	Lists all PPM packages installed on your computer
remove *packagename* or uninstall *packagename*	Uninstalls a PPM package from your computer
upgrade	Lists the available upgrades for packages that you have already installed
version	Shows the version number for PPM
exit or q or quit	Exits from ppm

Getting Help

Perl is one of the best-documented programming languages available. The documentation comes with the program, and can be called up at any time. The `perldoc` program prints help on almost every conceivable Perl topic. Windows, UNIX, and Mac OS X users can run `perldoc` from the command line, just like you run Perl from the command line.

To see everything that `perldoc` knows about, give the following command:

```
perldoc perl
```

If you are looking for documentation on a particular Perl function (functions are described throughout the book), use `perldoc -f`, followed by the function name.

One of the best places to get started (other than by reading this book!) is the Perl introduction that comes with Perl. To read it, give this command:

```
perldoc perlintro
```

Chapter 3

Diving into the Guts of Perl

*I*t's time to get your hands dirty and dig into the basic elements of a Perl program. This chapter describes what a Perl program looks like and how you enter programs on your computer. Perl programs have a certain structure, and knowing how the elements of the structure fit together gives you the ability to put together programs that are super short, really long, or anything in between.

This chapter also covers how Perl handles the kind of data that are most commonly used in programs. You can consider this chapter an anatomy lesson on the inner workings of a program.

Grabbing a Text Editor

When it comes right down to it, Perl programs are just plain text files. You can write these files using just about any text editor that's handy. UNIX folks usually use *vi* and *emacs,* two popular editors that come with most UNIX systems. Windows users can use the Notepad or WordPad programs that come with Windows, or even the EDIT program that's part of MS-DOS, but many other better editors are available. Macintosh users can use the SimpleText program that comes on the Mac, but, again, many superior editors are available from a variety of sources. The freeware BBEdit Lite and commercial BBEdit Pro editors are particularly useful for Mac programmers.

Feel free to use the text-editing program of your choice to create and edit your Perl programs. However, if you end up doing lots of programming in Perl, definitely consider getting an editor that has extra features for programmers (my favorites are TextPad on Windows and BBEdit Pro on the Macintosh). If you're new to programming with Perl, you can use just about any text editor because your first programs will probably be fairly simple and easy to enter. If you use a word processing program like Word or WordPerfect, you have to always save your programs as text files: Perl can't read the native document formats for word processing programs.

Examining Some Basic Components of a Perl Program

This section of the chapter describes a few basic steps for creating a Perl program. Here, and throughout the rest of the chapter, I use a number of short *code fragments,* which consist of a line or two from a complete Perl program. (The fragments are culled from a program described in Chapter 4, but you don't need to see the entire program to understand how the fragments work.)

Executing a statement

When Perl runs a program, it starts at the top of the program and reads downward line by line, executing each statement that it encounters. A *statement* in Perl is like a command in English: It tells Perl what to do. Take the following line, for example:

```
print "For the file $TheFile:\n";
```

In this example, print is the statement, and the rest of the line tells Perl what to print. Perl contains dozens of kinds of statements. Relating statements to what they can do is the essence of understanding Perl. Following what's going on in a Perl program is fairly easy: Just start reading from the top and go down. (You can read more about statements later in this chapter.)

Making a loop

Perl programs don't always follow a straight line, however. Some statements define *loops,* which are sets of lines that Perl repeats over and over until told to stop. The following example illustrates a single loop. The loop consists of the lines in the block of the while statement; that is, the lines between the { and the }:

```
while(<INFILE>) {
  # Your programming steps go here . . .
} # End of while(<INFILE>) loop
```

After Perl leaves a loop, it starts reading the program again at the next line after the loop.

In Chapter 8, you find out what happens in loops and how to tell Perl when it should stop looping. For now, all you need to know is that when you leave a loop, Perl starts executing statements right after the loop one at a time, just as it did before the loop.

Inserting a comment

In a typical Perl program, only about half of the lines really do anything. The other half are *comments* — stuff that Perl ignores. You may be thinking, "What!? Half of my program is going to be ignored by Perl!? Why bother writing it then?" I'll give you two good reasons to like comments — reasons that hold true for every programming language:

 ✔ Comments help you to read your program later so that you can fix things or use the program for new purposes.

 ✔ Comments enable other people who, for some reason down the road, have to read your program to figure out what the heck you meant when you wrote it.

Writing programs is a bit like arranging the junk in your garage: The organization makes perfect sense when you're stashing the stuff away the first time, but six months later, you can't remember why you put things where you did. Comments are notes to yourself about what's going on in a program so that when you examine your program later, you can make some sense of what you originally intended. And, by leaving comments in your program, you provide clues to other people who also have to understand your program in order to work with it.

Hopefully, you now feel a bit better about what comments are and why they take up half your program. Every line that starts with a # character is a comment. (By the way, this character doesn't have a globally accepted name. In the United States, the symbol is usually called the *pound* character, but in other countries, it's often called the *hash* character.)

A comment tells Perl to ignore everything from the # character all the way to the end of the line. For example, the following lines are all comments:

```
#!/usr/bin/perl -w
# counter1.pl: one way to count the characters, words, and
#  lines in a text file.
```

You can also start a comment on the same line with other Perl statements. When Perl sees a # in the middle of a line, it again assumes that everything from the # character all the way to the end of the line is a comment and ignores it. Therefore, in the following line

```
$TheLine = $_; # Save the line's contents
```

Perl only pays attention to the text up to the ; (semicolon) and ignores the comment.

You may have noticed that program code is loaded with blank lines. Blank lines are also comments, in a way. Perl ignores blank lines so you can have as many or as few of them as you want. You can use blank lines wherever you want in your programs to make the program easier to read. I usually put blank lines between each major section of a program so that when I glance at the program as a whole, I can see where each section starts. For most programmers, blank lines act like part separators. For more information, check out the "Keeping Tabs on Statements: Indenting and Spacing" section later in this chapter.

Creating Perl Programs Using Statements

Perl determines what you want to do with your program through the *statements* that you write. Each statement is constructed like a declarative sentence that tells Perl what to do next. Similar to English, some of these "sentences" are short, others are long, and some just go on and on.

Every Perl statement falls into one of the following three categories:

- A statement containing an active verb that calls for immediate and definite action on the part of the program, such as "display this text" or "add these numbers"
- A conditional test, such as, "if such-and-so is true, then do this"
- A loop, such as, "keep doing this set of things until I tell you to stop"

Almost every Perl program has a combination of direct action statements and conditionals, and many also have loops. Trust me, before you know it, you'll be comfortable with all these statement options.

The majority of statements that you see in Perl programs are direct-action statements, such as the following:

```
open(INFILE, $TheFile) or die "The file $TheFile could " .
   "not be found.\n";
   $LineCount = $LineCount + 1; # This is the easy part!
```

In the preceding example, the actions to be taken are open, die, and =. The = operator is used a great deal in Perl. It's called the *assignment operator,* and you use it to set variables. The = operator may not look like an action verb, such as open or die, but it functions like one. It literally means, "Set the variable on the left of the = to the value on the right of the =". (I cover assignment operator and variables in the section "Working with Variables and Literals.")

Ending statements

Perl has an easy way to tell where one statement ends and the next one begins: when it spots a semicolon (;). That's why you see so many semicolons in the code examples in this book. For example, the following is a single statement that ends with a semicolon:

```
$CharCount = 0;
```

You don't need to squeeze an entire statement into a single line. In fact, doing so is often impossible. Perl keeps reading until it finds a semicolon and then goes back and checks to see that the whole glob reads like a single statement.

Perl enables you to have more than one statement on a line. For example, the following three statements:

```
$CharCount = 0;
$WordCount = 0;
$LineCount = 0;
```

can all fit nicely on one line:

```
$CharCount = 0; $WordCount = 0; $LineCount = 0;
```

In the preceding example, the semicolons essentially act as line breaks. (By the way, the reason I put the three statements on separate lines in the first place is so that they're easier to read when you scan the program. When the choice is between clarity and saving a few lines on a page, opt for clarity.)

Understanding the role of blocks

Conditional and loop statements enable you to include lots of other statements within them. Each set of additional statements is called a *block*. You can recognize a block because it's enclosed within curly braces ({ and }). You can think of a block as a single set of statements that always hangs together, like a mini-program.

So that you know what I'm talking about when I mention certain punctuation marks in statements, *parentheses* refer to (and); *curly braces* (or just *braces*) refer to { and }; *angle brackets* refer to < and >; and *square brackets* refer to [and].

Conditional statements employ blocks to tell Perl what to do if a certain condition is true. For example, consider the sentence, "Unless you phone me before 4 o'clock, I will pick up Chris from the day-care center and start dinner." The condition in the sentence is the phrase "Unless you phone me before 4 o'clock," and the block of statements that follows is "I will pick up Chris from the day-care center and start dinner." The same would be true in Perl: The two things will happen in order, and they won't happen unless the conditional statement is true.

Loops also use blocks. A loop stated in everyday English may say something like, "Until the tree is completely full of leaves, I'll water and fertilize it every week." The loop statement is "Until the tree is covered with leaves," and the block is "I'll water and fertilize it every week." If these were instructions given to Perl, the watering and fertilizing would cycle over and over until the tree was completely leafy.

Blocks have one feature that often confuses users who are new to Perl: You don't need to insert a semicolon after the closing brace of a block. Perl knows that the end of a block (that is, the }) is automatically the end of a statement. For example, in the lines

```
if(substr($TheLine, $CharPos, 1) eq " ")
    { $WordCount = $WordCount + 1 }
```

no semicolon is included after the } because Perl knows that a block is the end of the conditional statement. Some people prefer to end their blocks with semicolons for aesthetic reasons even though they don't have to. You can end the statement with a semicolon if you want:

```
if(substr($TheLine, $CharPos, 1) eq " ")
    { $WordCount = $WordCount + 1 };
```

Give yourself a gold star if you noticed something else odd in this example: There's no semicolon *before* the closing brace (and after + 1). The reason for this is similar to not needing the semicolon after the }. Perl knows that if you're ending a block with a }, you're also ending the last statement in the block, and therefore, it lets you skip the semicolon to close out the last statement in the block. If you want to add it, you can:

```
if(substr($TheLine, $CharPos, 1) eq " ")
    { $WordCount = $WordCount + 1; }
```

Recognizing blocks within blocks

A *block* is a set of statements. Single statements can have blocks within them. Therefore, a block can have blocks within it.

In the following example, the first block is the one associated with the while statement. Within that statement, an until statement exists that contains another block, an if statement:

```
while(<INFILE>) {
    $TheLine = $_; # Save the line's contents
    # More programming statements go here . . .
    until($CharPos == $LineLen) {
        if(substr($TheLine, $CharPos, 1) eq " ")
            { $WordCount = $WordCount + 1 }
        $CharPos = $CharPos + 1;
    } # End of until
} # End of while(<INFILE>) loop
```

Keeping track of nested blocks

It's often tricky for even advanced programmers to keep lots of nested blocks straight in their heads. As you'll soon see, you can organize blocks by indenting any that fall under another block (see the section "Keeping Tabs on Statements: Indenting and Spacing" later in this chapter).

If indentation fails to help you keep track of your blocks, you can always determine which brace goes with which block in the same way that Perl does. You can find the right (ending) brace that matches a particular left (beginning) brace by counting all the left and right braces that follow it — each left brace counts +1, and each right brace –1. When you get to zero again after counting the first left brace, you found the match.

In the preceding example, if you want to find which of the right braces matches the left brace on the while line, you can go through the rest of the program, adding 1 for each left brace and subtracting 1 for each right brace. Here's the same code, with comments added to show you the process:

```
while(<INFILE>) { ###Start at 1
  $TheLine = $_;
  # More programming statements go here . . .
  if($TheLine eq "") { next }; ###+1, -1: total is 1
  #    and more go here . . .
  until($CharPos == $LineLen) { ### +1: total is 2
    if(substr($TheLine, $CharPos, 1) eq " ")
      { $WordCount = $WordCount + 1 }
      ###+1, -1: total is 2
    $CharPos = $CharPos + 1;
  } # End of until ### -1: total is 1
} # End of while(<INFILE>) loop ### -1: total is 0
```

You can see that the last brace, which took the count to 0, is the match of the first one.

Introducing operators and functions

You need to know about two other kinds of Perl items before delving further into the language. *Operators* are symbols that enable you to perform actions on data, such as adding two numbers together. In the following statement,

```
$LineCount = $LineCount + 1; # This is the easy part!
```

the + is an operator that tells Perl to add 1 to the value of $LineCount.

Functions are statements that act like operators, but they have alphabetic names, such as chomp, instead of symbolic names, such as =. The following line describes chomp:

```
chomp($TheLine); # Get rid of the line break
```

Functions have *arguments,* usually shown in parentheses, to tell Perl what the function is operating on. Many functions have more than one argument, and if they do, the arguments are separated by commas. For example, the following line contains the substr function with three arguments:

```
substr($TheLine, $CharPos, 1)
```

Throughout the book, I mix the terms *functions* and *statements.* In Perl programming, no important distinction exists between the two, so you can use the terms interchangeably.

Keeping Tabs on Statements: Indenting and Spacing

Every line in a Perl program doesn't necessarily start at the left margin, as in this example:

```
open(INFILE, $TheFile) or die "The file $TheFile could " .
  "not be found.\n";
```

The indentation of the second line is completely optional. Just as it disregards comments, Perl ignores spaces at the beginning of lines.

Indentation is a good way to make your Perl programs more readable. In the preceding example, the indentation is used to show that the die statement doesn't finish on the first line. If you have to continue a statement to a new line, adding indentation to the second line makes it easier for you to see that the two lines are part of one statement.

To see how indentation comes in handy, compare the following two lines to those in the previous example:

```
open(INFILE, $TheFile) or die "The file $TheFile could " .
  "not be found.\n";
```

If you were scanning down a page and spotted the unindented sample, you may think that the chunk in quotation marks on the second line was a separate statement, when in fact, it's part of the statement from the first line.

Indenting blocks

Indentation is also useful when it comes to managing blocks. Most programmers like to indent every line in a block so that it's easy to see where Perl goes after the block finishes.

The following example illustrates how useful indentation can be in formatting the statements in your programs. The until statement has a block as its argument, and that block is indented four spaces farther to the right than the until statement. Inside the until block is an if statement, and that also has a block, which is indented another four spaces:

```
until($CharPos == $LineLen) {
  if(substr($TheLine, $CharPos, 1) eq " ")
    { $WordCount = $WordCount + 1 }
  $CharPos = $CharPos + 1;
}
```

The preceding example also demonstrates another nice feature of Perl: the option of indenting. You can indent however you like, and if you do it incorrectly, you can still count on a perfectly functional (but possibly hard to read) program.

Perl goes even further in its lenience: You can also start and end a block wherever you want to. You can also put the beginning and ending braces on a line with the rest of the block, or on lines of their own. For example, you can choose to have the block in the following if statement look like this:

```
if(substr($TheLine, $CharPos, 1) eq " ")
  { $WordCount = $WordCount + 1 }
```

Or, you may choose to place the braces so that the block looks like it does in the following example:

```
if(substr($TheLine, $CharPos, 1) eq " ") {
  $WordCount = $WordCount + 1;
} # End of if(substr
```

Some programmers insist that the second option is better than the first because all your blocks will then look the same. That is, the opening { will always be at the end of the line that precedes the block, and the closing } will be on a line by itself (or followed by a comment). To me, the first option is better because it saves on the number of lines in your program and is easier to read. If a block is one statement long, I usually enter it as one line with its braces on that same line. As you gain experience with Perl, you'll probably develop a preference for one style or the other.

In fact, you can even put the whole preceding if statement and its block on one line (which I would have done here were it not for the space limitations of an 8½ x 11 page). Not even my computer screen is wide enough to show the entire statement: The line would be more than 80 characters long. This is why it's nice that Perl enables you to break up lines as needed for such non-programming reasons as "it won't fit in the book" or "it won't fit on my screen" or "I just feel that way right now, so there."

Adding extra spacing for the fun of it

By the way, Perl also ignores extra spacing between each part of a statement. For example, Perl sees the following three statements exactly the same:

```
$CharCount = 0;
$CharCount=0;
$CharCount =    0    ;
```

A Five-Minute Guide to Numbers and Text

Your programs can have many different kinds of data, such as numbers, text, lists, files, and so on. For now, the two most important types of data that you need to think about are numbers and text. (Actually, you deal mostly with three specific types of data — real numbers, integers, and strings — which I get to in a moment.)

Ah, numbers. Remember how much *fun* math was when you were a kid? To this day, I'm still not sure how educators managed to make it so miserable, even for those of us who wanted to enjoy it. Probably 80 percent of all adults still have a mild (or heavy) dislike for math, even though we all use numbers every day in many ways.

Perl happens to love numbers. It can handle all sorts of numbers — and make your use of them a breeze. The two types of numbers that you need to care about most are *integers* and *real numbers*. In case your high school math is too distant a memory, here's a refresher: Integers are numbers that don't have anything following the decimal point, while real numbers are numbers that, well, do have something following the decimal point. (This may be a bit different than the strict definition used by mathematicians.) Therefore, 3 is an integer, and 3.5 is a real number. (You can read more about numbers and Perl in Chapter 6.)

However, the world of data consists of much more than just numbers. There's also text, plus a few other types of data. Text is comprised of individual *characters*. Anything you can type on the keyboard is a character, such as the letter *a*, the letter *b*, a word space, the digit *7*, a hyphen (-), and so on.

In Perl, text appears in strings. A *string* is a gang of characters. An example of a string of five characters is abcde; another one is a2-@c. Perl is especially great with text. You can ask Perl to do things like, "Tell me the fifth character in this string," or "Find the first place in this string that has the letter *j*, and tell me everything that comes after it," or "Split this string into two strings: the stuff before the first space, and the stuff after it," or even "Split this string into a bunch of little strings, each one being the stuff that is between the tab characters." Perl responds with aplomb!

Working with Variables and Literals

Here's a $64,000 question: If you've scanned the sample programs in this book, did you notice all the words with a dollar sign ($) in front of them? Those dollar signs indicate Perl *variables*. If you're familiar with any other programming language, you already know about variables because every language has variables or something just like them. If Perl is your first language, don't worry; variables are fairly easy to understand.

A *variable* is a place to store a value. Think of a variable as a box with a label on it. The box can hold exactly one thing (the variable's value), and it has exactly one name on the label (the variable's name). You can put anything you want in the box, but remembering that the box can contain only one item is important. You can have as many boxes (variables) in your program as you desire.

A *literal,* on the other hand, is simply a value, and literals don't have names. The number 47 is a literal: It means 47 and that can never change. The number doesn't have a name; it's just the value 47. The string Cedar is a literal: It can never be anything other than this one set of characters — C, e, d, a, and r — in exactly that order with no other characters involved.

In Perl, you can tell what is and isn't a variable by looking for the $. Anything with a $ at the beginning of it is a variable name. For example, $TheFile and $TheLine are variables.

Variable names can be as long or as short as you want them to be, but they can't have any spaces in them. They can have uppercase and lowercase letters in them, as well as digits, but they can't start with a digit. You can also use the underscore (_) character in your variable names. The following strings are more examples of variable names:

- ✔ `$Bill`
- ✔ `$BoyIsThisALongVariableName`
- ✔ `$I_BET_this_IS_hard_TO_type`

Perl variable names are *case-sensitive,* meaning that uppercase and lowercase letters in variable names are important to properly identifying the variable. Therefore, the name $FirstCar and the name $firstcar identify two different variables. When you edit programs, be sure to keep in mind how you're entering uppercase and lowercase letters.

You can do two things with a variable: examine its value or change its value. The first time you use a variable, you assign a value to it, usually by using a literal. For example, the following statement

```
$TheFile = "sample.txt";
```

says this to Perl: Give the variable called $TheFile a value of sample.txt.

When you make an assignment such as this one, Perl ignores whatever was in the variable before. If you have not used the variable before, Perl creates it; if you *have* used the variable before, Perl wipes out its old value and inserts the new value.

Going back to the box analogy I used at the beginning of this section, making an assignment is like giving Perl these instructions: "If there isn't already a box with the name $TheFile on it, create the box and put the literal sample.txt into it. If a box with the name $TheFile does exist, dump out its contents and put the literal sample.txt into it."

In addition to changing the value of variables, you can take a look at their values. For example, examine the following statement:

```
if($TheLine eq "") { next };
```

This statement means: Look at the value that's in the variable named $TheLine, and see whether that value equals "". If so, do what's inside the block.

Here's another statement that looks at the value of a variable:

```
print "For the file $TheFile:\n";
```

This statement means: Print the literal For the file (including the space after file) and then look at the value that's inside the variable named $TheFile. Next, print that value, then print the character :, and then go to a new line.

Here's an example in which Perl both looks at one variable, $TheLine, and changes another ($LineLen):

```
$LineLen = length($TheLine);
```

This line means: Look at the variable called $TheLine, find its length, and put the value of its length in the variable called $LineLen.

Your statements can have a combination of assignments, commands that tell Perl to look at the current value of a variable, and literals — all in the same statement. The following example is typical of such a statement:

```
$WordCount = $WordCount + 1;
```

At first, this statement may be a tad perplexing, but it can make good sense. The statement says: First, look at the value of the variable named $WordCount. Next, take that value, add 1, and then place that new value into the variable called $WordCount.

Here's the statement again, this time with its relevant parts underlined:

1. Look at the value of the variable named $WordCount.

   ```
   $WordCount = $WordCount + 1;
   ```

2. Take that value and add 1.

   ```
   $WordCount = $WordCount + 1;
   ```

3. Place that new value into the variable called $WordCount.

   ```
   $WordCount = $WordCount + 1;
   ```

This amounts to a long-winded way of saying, "Make the $WordCount variable 1 higher than it already was."

Assigning variables

Get ready, because I'm about to inform you of the Number One, classic, absolutely supreme mistake that most programmers make at one time or another. The technical term for this goof is "using an unassigned variable," and it's one of the more difficult errors to unearth in a program.

A problem with unassigned variables occurs when you either examine or change a variable that you have not already assigned a value. For example, consider the following statement:

```
$LineLen = length($TheLine);
```

This statement makes sense if you assume that $TheLine has been assigned a value, because then the length function is working on a known object.

However, if `$TheLine` has not been assigned a value, such as in a previous statement that has already been executed, then Perl doesn't know what it's taking the length of. So, Perl silently makes a guess about what you wanted in `$TheLine`, and that guess is almost always wrong.

How can you avoid this all-too-common mistake of unassigned variables? Always check your Perl programs with the `-w` command line option (see Chapter 2 for more information). One of the great blessings of using `-w` is that it can find almost every instance in which you look at or change a variable without having first given the variable a value. Perl is one of the few languages that has this kind of built-in feature, and the result is that if you write a program that uses unassigned variables, you can catch it early and fix it.

Using Perl's special variables

You have literals, whose values never change, and your own variables, whose values change when you tell Perl to change them. And you now know beyond a shadow of a doubt that you need to assign values to your variables before you put them to use in a program. Just when you're comfortable living with this strict warning, now you can meet a class of variables that comes with values already assigned.

Perl's *special variables* are those that Perl gives pre-assigned values. You can treat these special variables like any other variable in a Perl program: You can examine them or assign them values. For example, the variable called `$0` contains the name of the program that you're running.

Perl contains dozens of special variables, most of which are of little interest to novices (or even advanced users). I cover a few of them in this book, but if you want the complete list of special variables, turn to Appendix A.

Default arguments

Many Perl functions enable you to skip having to specify some of their arguments (see the section "Introducing operators and functions" earlier in this chapter for more on arguments). If you don't specify an argument, the function uses its *default* value. This speeds up the typing of your programs but it also makes your programs harder to read because you have to remember the defaults for each function. For this reason, I rarely use the default arguments. Nevertheless, you probably need to know a little bit about default arguments because lots of other programmers use them all the time, so you can expect to see them in Perl programs that others have written.

Almost all the functions that enable you to use default arguments fill in the gaps with the Perl special variable $_. Many statements put values in this special variable, such as reading from a file line-by-line or performing a pattern search. Perl enables you to skip including $_ as an argument in some functions because it's so often the argument of the function.

For example, the lc function, which changes text to lowercase, normally takes one argument: the text that will be changed to lowercase. If you have no arguments to lc, the function returns the lowercase version of the value in $_ instead. Therefore, the following three lines all have the same result:

```
lc($_);
lc();
lc;
```

Although it's easier to enter the second or third statement, the first seems much clearer when you review the program later.

Chapter 4

A Perl Program Tour, Times Two

*O*ne of the best ways to begin programming is to examine a model program that features many of the elements you can expect to use when
you write your own programs. But why stop at one? This chapter takes you
on a journey through two working Perl programs.

As you check out the two examples in this chapter, you can see the steps
involved in creating a Perl program. Even a short Perl program created
with a handful of steps can turn out to be surprisingly powerful.

Examining the Inside of a Sample Program

In Listing 4-1, you can find a program called `counter1.pl`. It's a typical-looking
Perl program, about 40 lines long, and is designed to count the number of
characters, words, and lines in a text file. (Bits and pieces of this program
are excerpted in Chapter 3 in order to demonstrate some basic elements
of programming with Perl.) After I dissect the program, in the next section,
I show you what it looks like when it runs.

Incidentally, you don't have to enter the `counter1.pl` program by hand in
order to experiment with it (Can I hear a collective "Whew!" from the audience?). All the sample programs featured in this book are included on this
book's page on the Dummies Web site. Go to www.dummies.com/extras,

and click on the link for this book. There you will find the longer programs and text examples for easy downloading. You can enter a program and save it to disk, or you can copy it from the Web site to your hard drive.

Listing 4-1:   counter1.pl is a program that counts characters, words, and lines in a text file.

```perl
#!/usr/bin/perl -w

# counter1.pl: one way to count the characters, words, and
#   lines in a text file.

# The name of the file that will be counted
$TheFile = "sample.txt";

# Open the file but quit if it doesn't exist
open(INFILE, $TheFile) or die "The file $TheFile could " .
  "not be found.\n";

# Initialize the counters
$CharCount = 0;
$WordCount = 0;
$LineCount = 0;

while(<INFILE>) {
  $TheLine = $_; # Save the line's contents
  chomp($TheLine); # Get rid of the line break
  $LineCount = $LineCount + 1; # This is the easy part!
  $LineLen = length($TheLine);
  # We now know how many characters (minus the line
  #   break) are on this line
  $CharCount = $CharCount + $LineLen;

  # Do the tricky stuff for counting words on the line

  # The line is empty, so we're done
  if($TheLine eq "") { next };
  # The line has at least one word on it
  $WordCount = $WordCount + 1;
  # Now loop through each character on this line
  #   to look for words
  $CharPos = 0; # Position we are in the line
  # Check for line end; if not, check for a space
  until($CharPos == $LineLen) {
    if(substr($TheLine, $CharPos, 1) eq " ")
      { $WordCount = $WordCount + 1 }
    $CharPos = $CharPos + 1;
  } # End of until
} # End of while(<INFILE>) loop
```

```
# All finished, so print out the results

print "For the file $TheFile:\n";
print "Number of characters $CharCount\n";
print "Number of words     $WordCount\n";
print "Number of lines     $LineCount\n";
```

The very first line in Listing 4-1 tells UNIX Perl where to find the Perl language. This special comment is optional for Windows and Macintosh users, but must appear for UNIX users. (I describe this comment in Chapter 2.) Basically, the first part tells UNIX that the program is a Perl program, and the -w says that Perl should provide warnings if it notices that the program has questionable syntax:

```
#!/usr/bin/perl -w
```

The next set of lines is a comment to myself about the program's purpose and why I wrote it. As silly as it may seem, ten years from now when you're trying to figure out what a particular program does, having an explanation right at the top of the file will prove to be a great time-saver:

```
# counter1.pl: one way to count the characters, words, and
#  lines in a text file.
```

The following lines initialize the $TheFile variable. Because counter1.pl is supposed to examine a file, you need to tell the program the name of the file to examine:

```
# The name of the file that will be counted
$TheFile = "sample.txt";
```

The open statement that follows makes the file named in $TheFile available to Perl. In this case, opening the file makes it readable for use in the program. (Chapters 10 and 11 describe the process of opening files in Perl programs.) The open function takes two *arguments* (that is, pieces of information for the function to work with) — INFILE is the "handle" that you use for the rest of the program, and $TheFile is the name of the file. Later in the program, when you refer to the file, you use its handle instead of its name.

The second part of the open statement is a die statement. In essence, the lines mean "Try to open the file or die if you can't," which is exactly what you want Perl to do when you open files. The die statement tells the program to stop running and display the message on the screen just before it stops:

```
# Open the file but quit if it doesn't exist
open(INFILE, $TheFile) or die "The file $TheFile could " .
  "not be found.\n";
```

You should initialize all of your variables before using them. The following lines contain *counters* that (you guessed it!) count characters, words, and lines. They keep a running total for the entire file:

```
# Initialize the counters
$CharCount = 0;
$WordCount = 0;
$LineCount = 0;
```

The next section in the counter1.pl program (see Listing 4-1) is the while loop. A while statement takes an argument and evaluates whether it is true or false. If the argument is true, Perl goes through the steps in the loop and then tests the argument again. If the argument is false, Perl skips to the first statement after the loop's block.

The following statement notes the beginning of the loop. In this case, the argument is <INFILE>, which means to Perl "Read a line from the file that was opened with the handle called INFILE. If you've read to the end of the file, return false." Thus, the loop keeps going as long as lines are in the file, and skips to the end of the block when no more lines exist:

```
while(<INFILE>) {
```

$_ is a special variable that means "the stuff you just read." The following statement essentially says, "Take the line that you just read from INFILE and put it in the $TheLine variable":

```
$TheLine = $_; # Save the line's contents
```

When you read a line, you also get a *line terminator,* which is a character(s) that tells your computer, "This is the end of a line." The chomp function removes the line terminator from the end of the variable so that all that's left is the text that was on the line, minus the end bit.

chomp is available only in Perl 5 and later versions. The chop function in Perl 4 accomplishes pretty much the same thing, however:

```
chomp($TheLine); # Get rid of the line break
```

Because $LineCount keeps track of how many lines are in the file, I added 1 to the count in the following lines from the program because Perl just read another line. The first time through, Perl assigns $LineCount to the sum of 0 (the value set before the loop) plus 1 — which is, of course, 1. The next time through the loop, Perl sets $LineCount to the sum of 1 (the value from the last round through the loop) plus 1, which adds up to 2. In short, this statement just keeps adding 1 to the previous value of $LineCount:

```
$LineCount = $LineCount + 1; # This is the easy part!
```

The length function (in the following line of the program) looks in a text variable and tells you how many characters are in it:

```
$LineLen = length($TheLine);
```

Because $CharCount (in the next statement) keeps track of the total number of characters, you want to add the length of the line you read from the file (minus the line terminator) to the total count. $CharCount is another kind of counter. Instead of adding 1 each time, as you do with $LineCount, you add the length of the line. For example,

```
# We now know how many characters (minus the line
#  break) are on this line
$CharCount = $CharCount + $LineLen;
```

The more comments (such as the following) that you use in your programs, the better! Comments help you to recall the specifics of your own programs later on, and can certainly help someone else who is reading your program to know what your intentions were:

```
# Do the tricky stuff for counting words on the line
```

The following statement tests whether a line has any text in it. Like the while statement, the if statement takes one argument, a test that evaluates to true or false. Here, I test whether $TheLine equals no text at all; if so, the block executes. In that block, the next statement tells Perl to "skip all the rest of the lines in the current enclosing block," meaning that Perl should go back and try the while test again:

```
# The line is empty, so we're done
if($TheLine eq "") { next };
```

If Perl gets this far, the line has something on it (otherwise, the previous if test would have prevented Perl from getting to this point). Therefore, at least one word is on the line, so the following statement updates the $WordCount variable:

```
# The line has at least one word on it
$WordCount = $WordCount + 1;
```

The third line of the next chunk of code initializes the variable $CharPos, which tells you which character on a line you are on:

```
# Now loop through each character on this line
#  to look for words
$CharPos = 0; # Position we are in the line
```

The next statement walks through the line one character at a time, looking for spaces. The until loop (in the second line of the following chunk of code) is the exact opposite of while: It causes Perl to execute a block in a loop only if its argument is false. Here, the test is, "Am I at the end of the line I read from the file yet? If not, do the block again; otherwise, skip to the end of the block." The end of the block is also the end of the while loop:

```
# Check for line end; if not, check for a space
until($CharPos == $LineLen) {
```

Inside the until loop, the following statement tells Perl to use the substr function to see whether the character it's looking at is a space character. The three arguments to substr mean "look in $TheLine, starting at the position $CharPos from the left side of the string, and look at 1 character." If the character is a space character, then Perl adds 1 to $WordCount because one space is after each word:

```
if(substr($TheLine, $CharPos, 1) eq " ")
  { $WordCount = $WordCount + 1 }
```

The word count is based on the number of spaces that the program sees. At first, this makes good sense, but it can lead to highly inaccurate word counts. What if you have two spaces after some words? What if you have space characters at the end of some lines? What if you indent some lines with spaces? Any of these situations can make the reported word count much higher than what actually appears in the text file.

The following statement tells Perl to add 1 to the variable holding the line's character position:

```
$CharPos = $CharPos + 1;
```

The next statement is the closing brace for the until loop:

```
} # End of until
```

The following statement is the closing brace of the while loop that began much earlier in the program:

```
} # End of while(<INFILE>) loop
```

I admit that the following comment isn't the most earth-shattering, but at least it tells you that you're almost done with the program:

```
# All finished, so print out the results
```

print statements (such as the following) tell Perl to display text on your screen. (Actually, print can do much more than that; see Chapter 5 for more on reading and writing files with the `print` statement.) Here, `print` displays the text `For the file`, followed by a space, followed by the value of the variable `$TheFile`, followed by a colon. The `\n` indicates that after printing this text, Perl displays the next text in the string on the next line of your screen. Printing `\n` is like pressing the Enter key in a word-processing program:

```
print "For the file $TheFile:\n";
```

The next three lines are similar to the first `print` statement: They tell Perl to print some text, the value of a variable, and then go to the next line:

```
print "Number of characters $CharCount\n";
print "Number of words     $WordCount\n";
print "Number of lines     $LineCount\n";
```

You're done! Wait, you say you want to actually do something with this program now, like run it? Of course! You don't write programs just for the fun of it: You also want to do some real work with them.

Running the counter1.pl sample program

Because the `counter1.pl` program I present in the preceding section of this chapter counts characters, words, and lines in a text file, you need to have a text file on hand in order to see how the program works. You can create a file called sample.txt by entering the following chunk of information (which, incidentally, is lifted from another *...For Dummies* book of mine, *Netscape and the World Wide Web For Dummies,* published by Wiley Publishing, Inc.), or you can use any old text file of some length that you happen to have around.

You can also pull `sample.txt` off of the `www.dummies.com/extras` Web site mentioned previously. If you choose to type it yourself, be sure to use the same exact line endings shown here:

```
The Internet is a collection of thousands of computers that
communicate through certain methods that have been agreed
on for many years. The Internet started about 25 years ago
with a small handful of computers run by a few people as an
experiment. The initial results were successful; the
network was useful, so it grew.
In fact, the Internet was partially intended to be an
experiment for how to design a network that could grow
easily, with very little central control. That concept is
still considered radical today, and you find few networks
as loose as the Internet.
```

Okay, I admit that it's not the most breathtaking prose in the world. You just need a short text file to measure.

After you create your own `sample.txt` file (or use the one supplied here), the next step is to run the program, which I describe in the next section.

Because the readers of this book may be using any one of a number of operating systems, in the following sections I explain how to run Perl programs on UNIX, Windows 95/98 or Windows NT, and Mac OS. By the way, if Perl finds errors when it checks your program, skip to the end of this chapter where I describe how to decipher Perl's error messages.

Running the program on UNIX

First off, to run the `counter1.pl` program shown in Listing 4-1 (or any other Perl program, for that matter), be sure that the first line of the program actually points to the location of Perl on your system. If it doesn't, edit that line; otherwise, UNIX hands you a confusing error message. If you're not sure about Perl's location on your system, see Chapter 2 for information on installing Perl on UNIX. The `which` command that comes with most UNIX implementations tells you where a particular program is; the command `which perl` tells you where to find Perl.

To check the program for errors (such as a forgotten semicolon or quotation mark), enter the following command at the UNIX command prompt:

```
perl -c counter1.pl
```

To run the program, enter this command:

```
./counter1.pl
```

This run command tells UNIX to run the `counter1.pl` program from the current directory.

Running the program under Windows 95/98 and Windows NT

To run the sample `counter1.pl` program (or any other Perl program under Windows), first make sure that you have opened an MS-DOS window and are in the Perl directory (for information on how to do that, see Chapter 2). To check the program for errors (such as a misspelled function name), enter the following command:

```
perl -c counter1.pl
```

To run the program, enter this command:

```
perl counter1.pl
```

Running the program on a Macintosh

To run the sample program, or any Perl program, on a Macintosh, launch
MacPerl as you do any other Mac program by double-clicking its icon in the
Finder. To check the program for errors (if you forgot a parenthesis, for exam-
ple), choose Script⇨Syntax Check. To run the program, choose Script⇨Run
Script.

Viewing the program results

Assuming that you copy the sample.txt program from the `www.dummies.com/`
`extras` Web site to your hard drive (or, if you type it by hand, assuming that
you entered everything correctly), you see the following on your screen after
you run the `counter1.pl` program:

```
For the file sample.txt:
Number of characters 562
Number of words      98
Number of lines      12
```

After these four lines are displayed, the program exits. On UNIX,
Windows 95/98, or Windows NT, the operating system prompt appears.
On the Macintosh, MacPerl still runs, waiting for you to give a command
from one of the menus.

The numbers shown in the previous example may not match exactly what
Perl reports to you. If you added extra spaces or lines, or possibly spelled
things different from in the example, the numbers will be slightly different.

Exploring a Program with More Features

If you were intrigued by the sample program in Listing 4-1, I have another
program that you may want to peruse in order to help you get the hang of
working with Perl. The program, `empdata1.pl`, is shown in Listing 4-2.
Remember, if you don't want to type it in yourself, you can find the program
on the `www.dummies.com/extras` Web site.

The structure of `empdata1.pl` is somewhat similar to `counter1.pl` (the first
sample program in this chapter), but it serves a different purpose. The `emp-
data.1` program enables you to look through a small text database in order
to search for certain records. It's representative of the kind of programs that

you will write to look through a file for particular information (the employee database that I use here is, of course, fictitious). I list the program in its entirety first, and cover some of its components later.

Listing 4-2:   The empdata1.pl program lets you query a sample employee database.

```
#!/usr/bin/perl -w

# empdata1.pl: a very simple employee database application.
#  This program reads a text file that is an employee
#  database and lets you query it by ID number.
#
#  Each record is on a single line. Each field in the
#  record is separated by a single tab character
#  ("\t"). The database has four fields:
#  - Last name
#  - First name
#  - ID number
#  - Telephone extension

# The name of the database file
$TheDB = 'edata.txt';

# Open the database file but quit if it doesn't exist
open(INDB, $TheDB) or die "The database $TheDB could " .
  "not be found.\n";

while(1) { # Loop forever
  print "\nDo you want to search by employee ID (I), " .
    " or quit (Q): ";
  $DoSearch = <STDIN>;
  chomp($DoSearch);
  $DoSearch =~ tr/A-Z/a-z/;
  # Check if they want to quit
  if($DoSearch eq 'q') { last }
  # Check if they did *not* say i or I
  unless($DoSearch eq 'i') {
    print "You must enter either I or Q.\n";
    next; # Go out to the while loop
  }

  # Ask them what ID they want to search for
  print "Search for ID number: ";
  $SearchFor = <STDIN>;
  chomp($SearchFor);
  # Go to the top of the database in case this isn't
  #  the first time they are searching
  seek(INDB, 0, 0);
  # Reset the count of successes
```

```
    $SuccessCount = 0;
    # Loop through the records in the file
    while(<INDB>) {
        $TheRec = $_;
        chomp($TheRec);
        ($LastName, $FirstName, $ID, $Tel) =
            split(/\t/, $TheRec);
        if($ID eq $SearchFor) {
            $SuccessCount = $SuccessCount + 1;
            print "$ID: $FirstName $LastName, ext. ".
                "$Tel\n";
        } # End of if
    } # End of while(<INDB>)
    if($SuccessCount == 0) { print "No records found.\n" }
    else { print "$SuccessCount records found.\n" }
} # End of while(1)

print "Program finished.\n";
```

The database used in the program, `edata.txt`, is a simple text file, shown as follows:

```
Anastasio    Trey       12 143
Manzanera    Phil       15 156
Stewart      Dave       17 154
Thompson     Richard    20 112
```

The four columns in the data file list each employee's last name, first name, ID number, and telephone extension.

Although it's short, you may want to copy the edata.txt file from this book's page on the www.dummies.com/extras Web site. If you do type it in, be sure to use a single tab between each column. (Don't use spaces, and don't use more than one tab, or else the empdata1.pl program won't work.)

The gist of the program is that it prompts you for employee numbers and then prints out the information on those employees from the database. It lets you go through this "ask a question, get an answer" loop as many times as you want. After you finish, type **q** or **Q** to exit the program.

Breaking down the sample program

The following preamble that tells UNIX Perl where to find the Perl language is needed only on UNIX computers, but because it's a comment, it doesn't hurt to include it if you're working in Windows or on a Mac:

```
#!/usr/bin/perl -w
```

The following lines are comments that describe in detail what the program does. Whenever you write a program that calls for a data file in a particular format (such as four columns with tabs between them), you should indicate that in the comments right at the top of your Perl program, as shown here:

```
# empdata1.pl: a very simple employee database application.
#  This program reads a text file that is an employee
#  database and lets you query it by ID number.
#
#  Each record is on a single line. Each field in the
#  record is separated by a single tab character
#  ("\t"). The database has four fields:
#  - Last name
#  - First name
#  - ID number
#  - Telephone extension
```

I named the file with its own variable (as you can see in the following lines of code) so that it's easy to change it later. Astute readers may notice that the filename in this program is in single quotation marks instead of the double quotation marks in the open statement in the counter1.pl program earlier in this chapter. (In Chapter 5, you can discover the difference between single quotation marks and double quotation marks in Perl.)

```
# The name of the database file
$TheDB = 'edata.txt';
```

The following lines tell Perl to open the file or quit the program with a helpful message if it can't find the file:

```
# Open the database file but quit if it doesn't exist
open(INDB, $TheDB) or die "The database $TheDB could " .
   "not be found.\n";
```

The following statement may seem a bit strange, but you may encounter occasions when you want Perl to run a loop forever (the value 1 always means true). Of course, the loop won't really go *forever,* but you don't want to insert the test for when it should stop in the while statement. Instead, examine the program a few lines down to determine how to get out of the loop (hint: It's the last statement):

```
while(1) { # Loop forever
```

The following lines tell Perl to print a prompt on your screen. Notice that the prompt doesn't end with \n; this enables you to enter text on the same line as the prompt:

```
print "\nDo you want to search by employee ID (I), " .
   " or quit (Q): ";
```

Perl waits for you to type a line and puts whatever you type into the variable $DoSearch, such as in the next line:

```
$DoSearch = <STDIN>;
```

The following line tells Perl to remove the end-of-line character(s) from $DoSearch:

```
chomp($DoSearch);
```

The next line from the program does a neat little trick: It translates any upper-case characters in $DoSearch into lowercase letters. For example, if you type HOWDY, it changes to howdy. Therefore, if your program tells users to enter I or Q, for example, they may use either uppercase or lowercase letters. Instead of blasting them with an error message for not capitalizing the letters, the program simply doesn't care:

```
$DoSearch =~ tr/A-Z/a-z/;
```

If users type q or Q, the while loop stops. The last statement at the end of the following lines of code tells Perl to jump out at the bottom of the block that you're in. The last statement differs from the next statement found in the counter1.pl program (see Listing 4-1) that causes Perl to start the block again at the top. Using last is the best way to tell Perl to break out of an infinite while loop:

```
# Check if they want to quit
   if($DoSearch eq 'q') { last }
```

If the user doesn't type q or Q or i or I here, then he or she must have entered something incorrectly. The next statement in the last line of the following chunk of code restarts the loop:

```
# Check if they did *not* say i or I
   unless($DoSearch eq 'i') {
      print "You must enter either I or Q.\n";
      next; # Go out to the while loop
   }
```

The user ends up at the next chunk of code if he or she enters an i or I; at this point, the program asks the user which ID number he or she wants:

```
# Ask them what ID they want to search for
   print "Search for ID number: ";
```

Perl then waits for the user to type something on the keyboard, but this time, Perl puts the results in $SearchFor (instead of $DoSearch, as it did earlier in this example program). Don't forget to munch off the end-of-line stuff with `chomp`:

```
$SearchFor = <STDIN>;
   chomp($SearchFor);
```

In the `counter1.pl` program (see Listing 4-1), you examine the text file from top to bottom, just once. In the `empdata1.pl` program, covered in this section of the chapter, you want to examine the file each time a user types an ID number. Therefore, you need to tell Perl to stop reading the file where you are and start at the top again. The `seek` statement (which you can see in the following lines from the program) lets you tell Perl where in the file to start; in this case, the instruction is to start at the top:

```
# Go to the top of the database in case this isn't
#   the first time they are searching
   seek(INDB, 0, 0);
```

Suppose that you want to know how many records are found for each request. The database currently being used in this sample program has one person per ID number. Because you may want to have more than one person per ID later, counting the number of successes can be useful:

```
# Reset the count of successes
   $SuccessCount = 0;
```

The following `while` loop reads each record of the database. The program reads a record, assigns it to a variable, and applies the `chomp` function to remove the end-of-line character or characters from the line. After Perl reads the last record, it jumps outside of the `while`'s block:

```
# Loop through the records in the file
   while(<INDB>) {
      $TheRec = $_;
      chomp($TheRec);
```

The `split` function splits a string into many other strings, based on a separator string. The `\t` special string (formally called an *escape sequence*) tells Perl to look for tab characters. The following statement then tells Perl to fill in the four variables `$LastName`, `$FirstName`, `$ID`, and `$Tel` with the four fields from the record that you just read from the database file:

```
($LastName, $FirstName, $ID, $Tel) =
     split(/\t/, $TheRec);
```

The `if` statement compares the field from the record with the field that the user is looking for. If they match, the block executes. The following statements add 1 to the `$SuccessCount` variable and print out the record:

```
if($ID eq $SearchFor) {
  $SuccessCount = $SuccessCount + 1;
  print "$ID: $FirstName $LastName, ext. ".
    "$Tel\n";
} # End of if
```

The following statement marks the end of the inner `while` block, which means that no additional records are in the database:

```
} # End of while(<INDB>)
```

Next, the program prints the number of records found. The `else` is part of the `if` statement, and executes only if the `if` statement is false:

```
if($SuccessCount == 0) { print "No records found.\n" }
  else { print "$SuccessCount records found.\n" }
```

The program ends up at this point after the user enters q or Q:

```
} # End of while(1)
```

It's always polite to say goodbye when you leave someone. That's true in programming as well, so this program prints a nice message as it is about to finish:

```
print "Program finished.\n";
```

Running the empdata1.pl sample program

You can start the `empdata1.pl` program the same way that you start the `counter1.pl` program, or any Perl program for that matter. (See "Running the `counter1.pl` sample program" earlier in this chapter for the details.)

At the program's first prompt, type **I** or **i** and press Enter or Return.

The key above the right Shift key on your keyboard may be labeled in one of two ways: Enter or Return. In this book, whenever I say "press Enter," I mean to press the key above the right Shift key; not the key on the extreme right of the keyboard on the numeric keypad. This problem is frightfully confusing for many novice computer users, and even advanced folks get it wrong from time to time.

The program then prompts you with

```
Search for ID number:
```

and waits for you to enter something. For this example program, type **15** and press Enter. The program finds the record for ID number 15 (that record starts with "Manzanera"), and gives you the original prompt again.

Play around with the program by entering different characters after the various prompts — and watch the results. Some interesting messages are displayed when you enter something that the program doesn't expect. To leave the program, just type **q** or **Q** when the program prompts you.

Avoiding the Most Common Oversights

Entering a typo or two during the course of writing a Perl program is not uncommon. But when you attempt to run a program containing a text-entry slip-up, Perl gets confused and tells you so by reporting an error. The natural reaction for most people, even those with years of programming experience, is to get worried or angry when an error message pops up.

Don't panic. Take a deep breath. Take another slow, deep breath. Seriously, you won't be able to get to the root of the problem if you're all tense and bothered. Trust me, no matter how many years you spend programming, you always end up finding some errors in the code that you write.

So, now that you are a bit calmer (hopefully!), you can start to appreciate the fact that Perl has more helpful error messages than almost any other programming language. The messages aren't always right on the money, but they can get you pretty close to the spot where the problem lies with minimal searching on your part.

Perl has myriad error messages, but a few definitely crop up more than others, owing to some common typos that everyone seems to make. The following errors are produced by minor text-entry goofs that you can easily avoid. (The examples in this section are taken from the `counter1.pl` program shown in Listing 4-1, with a few errors added to it.)

Forgetting a semicolon

Probably the most common error message that you see when programming in Perl looks something like this:

```
# syntax error, near "open"
File 'counter1.pl'; Line 10
# Execution aborted due to compilation errors.
```

You can look and look at Line 10, the one with the open statement, and you won't see anything wrong with it. The trick here is to examine the statement that comes *before* the open statement and see whether it ends with a semicolon. (Perl knows that a statement ends only when it encounters a semicolon.) In this case, the error is caused by a missing semicolon at the end of Line 7 of the program:

```
$TheFile = "sample.txt"
```

Forgetting a quotation mark

The following sort of error message can be extremely frustrating if you don't know of a quick fix:

```
# Bare word found where operator expected, near
# "open(INFILE, $TheFile) or die "The"
# (Might be a runaway multi-line "" string starting on
# line 7)
File 'counter1.pl'; Line 10
```

This error is similar to forgetting a semicolon; instead, it's a quotation mark that's been accidentally omitted:

```
$TheFile = "sample.txt;
```

In this case, Perl did a good job of guessing by suggesting that a runaway multi-line "" string on Line 7 is the problem, which is precisely right.

Entering one parenthesis too many or too few

When you have loads of opening and closing parentheses in a program, slipping an extra one in by accident is easy. If that's the case, you may see a message from Perl that reads something like this:

```
# syntax error, near ") eq"
File 'counter1.pl'; Line 38
# syntax error, near "}"
File 'counter1.pl'; Line 42
```

Here, Perl can't determine where the error is exactly, but it actually got it right on the first guess: Line 38 contains an extra right parenthesis:

```
    if(substr($TheLine, $CharPos, 1)) eq " ")
```

Having one parenthesis too few in a Perl program can cause harder-to-find problems:

```
# Can't use constant item as left arg of implicit ->,
# near "1 }"
File 'counter1.pl'; Line 39
# Scalar found where operator expected, near "$CharPos"
File 'counter1.pl'; Line 40
# (Missing semicolon on previous line?)
# syntax error, near "$CharPos "
File 'counter1.pl'; Line 40
```

Yarp! All this was produced because the last parenthesis on Line 38 is missing:

```
    if(substr($TheLine, $CharPos, 1) eq " "
```

Another good lesson in hunting down typing errors: Start where Perl says it found an error. If you don't find the error there, go up a line or two and see whether the problem started earlier.

A final word of advice: Trust Perl to find the simple typos for you (where it can), and remember that it's giving you all the help it can, which is more than you can say for many programming languages.

Part II
The Basic Perl Programming Ingredients

In this part. . .

Perl is a fairly easy programming language to learn. By the time you finish the chapters in Part II, you'll have absorbed much of what you need to know in order to write a working Perl program. This part contains information about working with text and numbers, and some programming features that only Perl offers.

Chapter 5

Terrific Text

. . . .

In This Chapter

▶ Using the `print` statement

▶ Understanding strings

▶ Using special characters

▶ Quoting text

▶ Putting strings together and pulling them apart

▶ Changing parts of strings

. . . .

*I*f you've been reading along from the beginning of this book, you've seen only a smattering of what Perl can do. If you've skipped around through the book, that's okay; although you may want to check out the two examples I present in Chapter 4 — they introduce about two dozen different Perl statements, functions, and operators. This chapter and Chapters 6 through 8 examine the major types of data that Perl works on and show you how to use Perl to handle that data. In this chapter in particular, I describe one of Perl's strongest features: text handling.

Even the dweebiest of dweebs among us (yes, even us Perl programmers) use considerably more text than numbers in our daily lives. We talk, we read, we jot down notes, and so on, all day long. In computer terms, you can accomplish four basic tasks with a Perl program in terms of managing text — reading text, writing text, searching through text, and changing text.

I base some of the examples in the following chapters on the two programs I present in Chapter 4. (Again, you may want to give that chapter a go if you haven't already.) I give some examples in which I change one or the other of the two programs from Chapter 4 to do something different or more interesting. I also include many other examples to give you a small taste of how to use Perl's many text-handling features.

Checking Your Work: The print Statement

One of the most common Perl statements — one that you use over and over when you work with Perl — is the print statement. print is the best statement to use when you experiment with Perl features. And checking your work as you proceed is just one use of the print statement; you can actually use it for all kinds of display and output of information.

The print statement takes many forms, but the main one includes the statement followed by an *argument* (a string of text or numbers), as in the following example:

```
print "This is a string!";
print 72;
```

In addition to strings and numbers, you can use a *list* as an argument. (I cover the topic of strings in the next section of this chapter and the topic of lists in Chapter 7.) Another interesting use of the print command is writing to a file. (I tell you how to do that in Chapter 10.)

At any time, you can use the print statement to see the end results of what you're doing. Suppose that you just found out how to add two numbers together with the + operator (see Chapter 6); you can test that operator with a one-line program, such as this one:

```
print 2+3;
```

As you'd expect, the program displays the numeral 5.

You can also get the same result with a two-line program, such as the following:

```
$a = 2 + 3;
print $a;
```

Perl prints 5 on your screen.

Defining Strings

Text items in Perl are called *strings*. A string is zero or more characters put together in a single chunk. A *character* is anything that you can type, such as letters, digits, punctuation, and spaces. Strings appear in variables and just as the text that they contain, in which case they are called *string literals*. An example of a one-character string literal is the letter *d*. An example of a five-character string is *vbn59*. Perl variables (which I define in Chapter 3) can hold strings or numbers.

Differentiating between Visible Characters and Character Values

You probably think of characters as the entities that you see on the screen of your computer or that are printed on the page of this book, but computers (by necessity) have a much more liberal view of what constitutes a character. A computer recognizes many other kinds of characters that don't appear on screen or on printouts, or appear differently on different computers.

In the world of Perl versions 4 and 5, a *character* is an 8-bit byte; in Perl versions 5.6 and 5.8, it's a tad more complicated, as described at the end of this chapter. A *bit* is a single unit of information, a 1 or a 0. A *byte* is the chunk of information that the computer processes. So, how does this bits-and-bytes definition fit your notion of characters?

Translating values to characters

Each byte can have a value in it. The values range from 0 to 255, and standards exist for how some of the values correspond to letters, digits, and punctuation. The standards say stuff like, "The value 65 means *A*," or "The value 97 means *a*." So, if a computer thinks that it's supposed to display a byte and that byte has the value 65, the computer knows that it should display a capital *A*.

It's nothing: Null strings

The length of a Perl string is practically unlimited. That's right, you can make Perl strings as long as you want. Then again, you don't have to give them any length at all. A zero-character string is known as a *null string*. "A textless string — that's odd!" you say?

Here's how it works: If you have a variable called $Short, for example, and that variable has a value that is one character, you can remove the single character from the variable and get a smaller value that has zero characters in it. The variable doesn't disappear because Perl knows how to remove characters while retaining the variable. Similarly, if you want to add to a variable character by character, you can start with no characters and build from there.

One problem with this scheme is that the computer can't display certain character values. A simple example is the value 20, which translates to the space character. (As far as a computer goes, when you press the spacebar on your keyboard, you enter a character and not just a space.)

A more complicated example is the value 13, which means "carriage return." On a computer screen, it can be interpreted as "this is the end of the line." Other examples of nonprinting characters are the value 7 (beep), value 12 (form feed), and value 24 (cancel). A slew of such values represents valid characters, even though they don't result in anything being displayed on-screen.

Recognizing defined and undefined values

The original standard for characters, ASCII, is now a relic, even though it's the basis for all other subsequent character standards. ASCII defined equivalents only for the values 0 to 127, and as you've just seen, not all the equivalents can be viewed. Because characters can have values from 0 to 255, ASCII leaves 128 to 255 undefined.

Because computer geeks hate to leave anything undefined, they have specified what the other 128 values should signify. Unfortunately, different standards groups define the values differently. Every group thinks that its set of value-to-character mappings is best and tries to force other people to conform to it. So far, no one has been successful in creating a consensus on the matter.

For example, when the IBM PC came out in 1981, IBM decided to make its own set of definitions. It decreed that the value 128 meant a capital *C* with a cedilla underneath it (Ç); 129 meant a lowercase u with an umlaut over it (ü); and on and on. Apple, on the other hand, defined 128 as a capital *A* with an umlaut over it (Ä); 129 as a capital *A* with a circle over it (Å); and so on.

Examining the 93 standard visible characters

Remember that with computers, characters are really just numeric values between 0 and 255, and only 93 of them (the values 33 through 126) generally have standard representations. The 93 visible characters are *A* through *Z* (in both uppercase and lowercase), 0 through 9, and these guys:

```
!"#$%&'()*+,-./:;<=>?@[\]^_'{|}~
```

The following code is a program that's designed to display all 93 of the standard visible characters. It uses the % operator (which I explain in Chapter 6), the `for` loop statement (which I describe in Chapter 8), and the `sprintf` function (which I demonstrate in Chapter 9). The program generates two handy tables that display the characters and their corresponding values, as shown in Figure 5-1.

```perl
# chartab1.pl: A program to display character tables

$Column = 1;
$Out = '';
for ($i = 33; $i<=126; $i++) {
    $Out .= sprintf("%3s", $i) . "=" . chr($i) . " ";
    if(($Column % 10) == 0) { $Out .= "\n" }
    $Column += 1;
}

$Out .= "\n\n";
$Column = 1;
for ($i = 33; $i<=126; $i++) {
    $Out .= chr($i). "=" . sprintf("%3s", $i) . " ";
    if(($Column % 10) == 0) { $Out .= "\n" }
    $Column += 1;
}
print $Out;
```

Figure 5-1: Character-value tables output by the chartab1.pl program shown in Listing 5-1.

The upshot is that text strings can contain any kind of characters; not just the ones that you can type. This is useful in many circumstances. For example, maybe you want to display a character that you can't type.

Using special characters in text

Many characters exist that you can type but that you won't see in regular text. Perl defines special character combinations that make it possible to enter these "invisible" characters within a string (see Table 5-1).

Beware MacPerl users! \n means the same thing as the character whose ASCII value is 10, as opposed to the character whose ASCII value is 13 that UNIX Perl users are familiar with. The technical reasons for this difference aside, it can be a real puzzler when you convert programs from one operating system to the other.

Table 5-1	Special Characters in Strings
Character	*Meaning*
\n	Newline
\r	Carriage return
\t	Tab
\f	Formfeed
\b	Backspace
\v	Vertical tab (Perl 5 and later versions)
\a	Bell or beep
\e	Escape

The actions that the print statement takes when displaying these characters varies from operating system to operating system. The only character that works universally the same way is \n, which always (as far as I know) causes the print statement to go to the left margin of a new line.

For example, the statement

```
print "This is on line one.\nThis is on line two.\n";
```

displays

```
This is on line one.
This is on line two.
```

And, the statement

```
$Blue1 = "Sapphire";
$Blue2 = "Azure";
print "$Blue1\n$Blue2\n";
```

displays

```
Sapphire
Azure
```

For those of you who like (okay, *need*) to count in hexadecimal or octal, you also can use special backslash formats to indicate characters in these number systems. (The *decimal* number system is based on 10 digits; the *hexadecimal* system uses 16 digits, and *octal* has only 8 digits.) You can use \x followed by two characters that are the hex value that you want, or you can use just \ with an octal value. For example, you can represent the letter *B* as \x42 in hexadecimal or \102 in octal.

These special characters do *not* work in strings with single quotation marks. Look what happens when you use single instead of double quotes:

```
print 'This is on line one.\nThis is on line two.\n';
```

Executing this statement displays

```
This is on line one.\nThis is on line two.\n
```

Not everything inside single quotation marks is output exactly as you enter it. The two exceptions in Perl are \' and \\. Perl converts a \ inside single or double quotation marks to a single quotation mark and a \\ combination inside either single or double quotation marks to a backslash. This makes sense: You need some way to indicate an apostrophe (') or a backslash (\) inside single quotation marks. For example:

```
print 'Here\'s a backslash: \\.';
```

This program displays

```
Here's a backslash: \.
```

You can use two more tricks with double quotation marks. (These don't work with single quotation marks.) If you want to put a double quotation mark inside your text, use \":

```
$Shout = "Help me!";
print "And then he shouted \"$Shout\" very loudly.\n";
```

When you run this program, Perl displays

```
And then he shouted "Help me!" very loudly.
```

And to prevent Perl from trying to interpret a dollar sign inside double quotation marks, enter it as \$, as in

```
$Sweet = "sugar";
print "\$Sweet is $Sweet.";
```

This displays

```
$Sweet is sugar.
```

Perl also gives you a way to specify a character by its value. Earlier in this chapter, I note that each character has a value from 0 to 255. If you know the value of the character that you want to display, you can use the chr function, whose argument is the value. The chr function takes a number as its argument and returns the character associated with that value. For example,

```
$CapB = chr(66);
print "The letter after A is $CapB.\n";
```

displays:

```
The letter after A is B.
```

Quoting Text

When you want to tell Perl to use a literal string, you use *quoted text*. You enter quoted text in two main ways: with single quotes or with double quotes. For example, you can assign the characters "Help me!" to the variable $Shout, using either of the following statements:

```
$Shout = 'Help me!';
```

```
$Shout = "Help me!";
```

Both of the preceding methods produce the same result (you get Help me! on-screen); under some circumstances, however, whether you use single or double quotes can make a huge difference. Understanding how to use quotation marks is a critical aspect of handling text in Perl.

Contrasting single and double quotes

To summarize the main difference between single and double quotation marks: *Single quotation marks do not interpret, and double quotation marks do.* If you put something in single quotation marks, Perl assumes that you want the exact characters that you place between the marks — except for the slash-single quote (\ ') combination and double-slash (\ \) combination, which I talk about in "Special characters in text," earlier in this chapter. If you place text inside double quotation marks, however, Perl interprets variable names. Perl also interprets special characters inside double-quoted literal strings.

Take a look at the following short program, which uses single quotes in its print statement:

```
$Book = 'Perl For Dummies';
print 'The title is $Book.';
```

When you run the program, Perl displays

```
The title is $Book.
```

Now change the single quotes to double quotes in the print statement:

```
$Book = 'Perl For Dummies';
print "The title is $Book.";
```

When you run the program now, Perl displays

```
The title is Perl For Dummies.
```

In the first program, the single quotes tell Perl not to interpret anything inside the quotation marks. In the second program, Perl sees the double quotes, interprets the variable $Book, and then inserts that into the text.

Note that the period at the end of the print statement appears immediately after the value of $Book. After interpreting the variable $Book, Perl starts looking for text again, finds the period, and prints it.

You can have as many variables as you want inside double-quoted strings. For example:

```
$Word1 = "thank";
$Word2 = "you";
$Sentence = "I just wanted to say $Word1 $Word2.";
print $Sentence;
```

These lines print

```
I just wanted to say thank you.
```

Perl interprets each variable and places it directly in the variable $Sentence. Notice that when the print statement displays the contents of $Sentence, it inserts a space between the two quoted words, just as it should, and the period at the end. Perl picks out just the variables and substitutes for them but leaves other characters, such as spaces, exactly as you enter them.

Using functions to quote text

Although quoting text with single and double quotation marks is easy, having a function to do the same task comes in handy in some situations. Perl has two such functions: q and qq. The q function quotes its argument like single quotation marks, and the qq function quotes its argument like double quotation marks. The main purpose of these functions is to enable you to use single and double quotation marks within strings without having to use the \ ', \\, and \" special characters.

For example, you may want to use q if you have a string that has a bunch of apostrophes. Compare

```
$ISaid = 'This isn\'t Bill\'s shirt, I\'m sure.';
```

with

```
$ISaid = q/This isn't Bill's shirt, I'm sure./;
```

Both lines assign the same string to $ISaid, but the second one is much easier to read (and type).

You can use any character for the beginning and ending quote. The slash (/) character is common, as is the vertical bar (|):

```
$ISaid = q|This isn't Bill's shirt, I'm sure.|;
```

You also can use parentheses, square brackets, angle brackets, and curly braces for the delimiters. If you use the left member of any of these character pairs, Perl knows to look for the right member as the one that signifies the end of the quoted text:

```
$ISaid = q(This isn't Bill's shirt, I'm sure.);
```

```
$ISaid = q<This isn't Bill's shirt, I'm sure.>;
```

Quoting large blocks of text

Another way to quote text is with a *here document,* which is particularly useful if you have many lines in a string. Instead of putting a quotation mark at the beginning and end of the string, you start a here document with << and a string (with no space between the << character combination and the string) and then terminate the quote by putting the string by itself on a line at the end of the quote.

Here's an example that puts four lines of text into a variable called $TheLongString, using the string BLARG as the delimiting string:

```
$TheLongString = <<'BLARG';
This is the first line,
And this is the second,
Which is followed by the third,
And so on, ad nauseum.
BLARG
```

The type of quote that you use for the string tells Perl whether to interpret any variables. If you use <<"BLARG" (instead of <<'BLARG') in the preceding code, Perl substitutes any variable names that you include in the quote into $TheLongString.

Being aware of the @ Gotcha!

Another character must be quoted when you use it: the "@" symbol, often called the "at sign." Earlier in this chapter, you saw that if you wanted a dollar sign ("$") to appear in quoted text, you had to precede it with a backslash ("\") so that Perl didn't think it was the beginning of a variable. Thus, to print out the sentence "Mom, I need $2.50 to buy candy!", you would use:

```
print "Mom, I need \$2.50 to buy candy!";
```

The at sign is similar to the dollar sign in this fashion. Right now, you may wonder why it is special; you'll see in Chapter 7 that you use the at sign to denote array variables in the same way that you use the dollar sign to denote scalar variables. As you will also see in Chapter 7, arrays are different than scalar variables, but they are just as important in your Perl programs and that's why Perl treats the at sign just as seriously as the dollar sign.

Thus, if you want to print out "my email address is chris@example.com", you would use:

```
print "my email address is chris\@example.com";
```

If you don't use the backslash before the at sign, Perl may give you an error, or it may just warn you about it, depending on which version of Perl you are using and whether the name after the at sign had been used in the program. In Perl version 5.6.0 and earlier, if you hadn't used the name after the at sign in your program, you would see an error that said:

```
In string, @example now must be written as \@example
```

However, if you had used that name, Perl would interpret the "@example" as an array.

In Perl version 5.6.1 and 5.8, Perl never gives an error. Instead, it simply gives a warning that says:

```
Possible unintended interpolation of @example in string
```

For example, suppose that you had a statement that said:

```
print "Send me mail at bob@example.com";
```

In Perl 5.6.1 and 5.8, if you had not defined the array @example, that string would be interpreted as "Send me mail at bob.com" because the array would be interpreted as an empty string.

Manipulating Strings

Perl features operators that let you perform operations on strings that are similar to addition, multiplication, and subtraction. These operators don't do math, but they manipulate strings in ways that resemble some basic math functions.

Combining strings

String addition, for example, is simply a matter of taking one string and adding its text to the end of another string. The technical term for string addition is *concatenation;* Perl's concatenation operator is a period.

The following line, for example, displays window on-screen:

```
print "win" . "dow";
```

You can use concatenation in string assignment as well:

```
$Name = "Susan";
$Sentence = "Ask ". $Name . " about the goldfish pond.";
print $Sentence;
```

The result:

```
Ask Susan about the goldfish pond.
```

The need for string concatenation comes up often in Perl programs. It's a handy way to take information from different places and bring it all together into a single string. If you're often using double-quoted strings, though, you probably don't need to use string concatenation. For example, the following two lines have the exact same result:

```
$Sentence = "Ask ". $Name . " about the goldfish pond.";
$Sentence = "Ask $Name about the goldfish pond.";
```

The first line in this example concatenates three strings; the second line uses substitution within a single string.

You can also use string concatenation to accomplish mundane tasks, such as making sure that your program lines don't get too long. For example, consider the statement

```
print "$ID: $FirstName $LastName, ext. ".
   "$Tel\n";
```

I use concatenation here to avoid running over the end of the line. Instead of printing just one string, Perl prints two concatenated strings together.

Perl even gives you a way to concatenate a string to the end of an existing string while saving on some typing. Suppose that you have the string $AllNames, to which you keep adding names. You may have the statement

```
$AllNames = $AllNames . $CurrentName;
```

A shorter way to express the same thing in Perl is

```
$AllNames .= $CurrentName;
```

The .= operator concatenates the string on the right to the end of the string on the left.

Making lots of copies

Just as you can add strings, you can multiply them. The not-so-technical term for this method is *repetition.* Perl uses the x operator for repetition. You use a string on the left of the x and a number on the right, and Perl repeats the string that many times. For example,

```
print 'Q'x10;
```

displays 10 Qs in a row:

```
QQQQQQQQQQ
```

Zapping the end of a string

A simple form of string subtraction is to hack the last character off the end of a string. That's when you use the chop function. The function changes the string into the string minus its last character but returns a value of what got chopped off, which can be tricky. Here's an example:

```
$SixLet = "TUVWXY";
$A = chop($SixLet);
print "\$SixLet is now $SixLet and \$A is now $A.";
```

This code displays

```
$SixLet is now TUVWX and $A is now Y.
```

Programmers typically use chop to remove the newline character from the end of multiple-line input. For example, many programs throughout this book read lines in from a file. The lines always end with the computer's line-ending character. You can use chop to get rid of that character.

The chomp function works like the chop function except it knows that some computers have two-character line endings and therefore "chomps" the correct number of characters. You rarely need to worry about this difference, but if you're munching the ends of lines, using chomp is safer than using chop.

The chomp command is not available to Perl version 4 users.

Performing Simple String Transformations

Perl lets you do more than just shove strings together. Many functions let you change the actual contents of a string. I cover the basic functions here.

Letters come in two varieties: lowercase and uppercase. The lc, lcfirst, uc, and ucfirst functions enable you to force specific cases in your text. The lc and uc functions affect the case of an entire string; the lcfirst and ucfirst functions change just the first letter. (Sorry, Perl 4 users: These functions are available only in Perl 5 and later versions.)

The following code, for example,

```
$Name1 = "AbCdEf";
$Name2 = "GhIjKl";
print lc($Name1) . " -- " . uc($Name2) . "\n";
print lcfirst($Name1) . " -- " . ucfirst($Name2) . "\n";
```

generates this result

```
abcdef -- GHIJKL
abCdEf -- GhIjKl
```

If you really like using backslash characters instead of functions, you can use special characters to achieve much the same effect as the four uppercase/lowercase functions. The special characters \l and \u put the next letter in a string in lowercase or uppercase, respectively, which serves the same purpose as the lcfirst and ucfirst functions. For example,

```
$Name1 = "AbCdEf";
print "\l$Name1\n";
```

displays

```
AbCdEf
```

The \L and \U special characters tell Perl to make all letters that follow them lowercase or uppercase, respectively, until Perl sees the special character \E, which indicates the end of the \L or \U.

For example,

```
$Name1 = "AbCdEf";
print "\L$Name1 AND THEN\E \U$Name1\E\n";
```

displays

```
abcdef and then ABCDEF
```

Getting Information from Strings

Two string functions — length and ord — return information about a string. The length function returns the number of characters in a string. Take, for example, the following code:

```
$LineLen = length($TheLine);
```

Here's another example of the print function at work:

```
$TodaysWord = 'equilibrate';
print length($TodaysWord);
```

This command displays

```
11
```

The ord function tells you the numeric value of a character (the opposite of the chr function, which converts a numeric value into a character — see the section "Special characters in text" earlier in this chapter). For example,

```
print ord('C');
```

displays

```
67
```

If the string that you use as an argument to ord is longer than one character, Perl only looks at the first character in the string when determining the value.

Writing for the World in Perl 5.6 and Perl 5.8

Some readers may have noticed that all the text discussed in this chapter consists only of the characters we see in the English-language alphabet. Of course, people from around the world use characters other than these in their daily writing. Many European countries use most of the same letters as we do in English, but have additional letters such as ä and ñ.

Being able to use international characters is important, even if you only speak English. For example, my maternal grandparents came from Denmark, from a city we in the United States spell "Copenhagen" but Danes spell "København." Wouldn't it be nice (and certainly more polite) to be able to spell that city the way that the people there do? Even in the U.S., many people use non-ASCII characters in their names, so being able to use them in your programming would be useful.

Starting with Perl version 5.6, most programming elements that handle characters treat them as international characters. Many different standards exist for international characters, and the folks who maintain Perl wisely chose the most widespread one: Unicode. This choice allows you to use almost any character that's commonly used in the world today in your Perl programs.

Introducing Unicode and UTF-8

Many tens of thousands of characters are used in the world today. The most common standard for identifying each character and the properties of the characters is *Unicode,* which is supported by the Unicode Consortium.

If you're interested in international writing, you should by all means take a look at Unicode (`www.unicode.org`). The Unicode standard is also available as a printed book that has vast amounts of information on the writing styles of the world and how they're represented in computers.

As you saw earlier in this chapter, each ASCII character has a numeric value that indicates its position in the ASCII character set. In the same way, each Unicode character has a value that points to its position. Because the Unicode character set is much larger than ASCII, the range of values is much larger (in fact, it can go over a million character values).

Many ways exist of representing the Unicode character set in computers. The most popular method today is called *UTF-8 (Unicode Transformation Format 8)*. In UTF-8, each Unicode character is represented in one or more bytes. Because the number of bytes varies, languages such as Perl must be able to predict how many bytes are in each character so that they can perform common tasks, such as finding the next character in a string. Fortunately, UTF-8 makes this process easy for the computer.

Entering UTF-8 in your programs

As I discuss earlier in this chapter, many functions and operators act on characters. If you use Perl 5.6, these functions and operators act just the way you would expect on international characters in UTF-8 — even if those characters take up more than one byte. For example, using the length function on the word *fün* would return 3 even though the character *ü* in UTF-8 takes up two bytes.

Perl 5.6 and Perl 5.8 has much of the Unicode and UTF-8 support already built in. However, Perl 5.6 is a transition step from Perl 5, which had no Unicode, to Perl 5.8 that natively uses Unicode in strings. In Perl 5.6, you must put the Perl statement use utf8 at the beginning of any program that uses Unicode characters in strings. This statement is always safe for any program in which you're using UTF-8 strings. In Perl 5.8, you don't need the use utf8 statement to tell Perl that you have UTF-8 in some of your strings, but it doesn't hurt if the statement is there.

Starting with Perl 5.6, you can also use UTF-8 characters in variable names, if you're so inclined. For example, you can have a variable called $K‼1n. You can use any Unicode character that is alphabetic or numeric, which is the same restriction that you have when you're using ASCII characters in earlier versions of Perl. In both Perl 5.6 and Perl 5.8, if you use UTF-8 characters in your variable names, you must use the use unicode statement in your program.

When you create your Perl programs that include UTF-8 in strings, you have two options: You can either edit using a text editor that can read and write in UTF-8, or you can enter the UTF-8 characters in hexadecimal notation. (I cover hexadecimal notation in Chapter 6, but I show it in this section because few people have text editors that use UTF-8.) Many text editors for Windows, Unix, and the Macintosh support UTF-8, although not all do, so you have to check the editor's documentation before using it.

Hexadecimal notation for UTF-8 consists of the characters \x{} with the hex value of the UTF-8 character in the braces. For example, the character *ñ* has the hex value c3b1 in UTF-8, and is entered in programs as \x{c3b1}. Thus, a program that sets the variable $Tomorrow to the string "mañana" would look like

```
use utf8;  # only needed for Perl 5.6
$Tomorrow = "ma\x{c3b1}ana";
```

If this code had instead been entered in a text editor that uses UTF-8, the program would look like

```
use utf8;  # only needed for Perl 5.6
$Tomorrow = "mañana";
```

Entering UTF-8 using \x{} notation is somewhat difficult in regular programming because few tables give the UTF-8 equivalents for Unicode characters. That is, if you look up characters in the Unicode standard, the values are in UTF-16 format, and not UTF-8. Thus, you need a program that converts between the two formats so that you can enter the values into your programs. As you can imagine, just using a text editor that handles UTF-8 is much easier.

You can use an additional method for entering Unicode characters, but it's particularly cumbersome and is thus rarely used. You can enter a character by its full Unicode name. For example, the full Unicode name for $\tilde{n}$ is "Latin small letter *n* with tilde." To use the names, you must also use the Perl statement use charnames ':full' (you need to use this in both Perl 5.6 and Perl 5.8). Thus, the previous program may also be written as

```
use utf8;  # only needed for Perl 5.6
use charnames ':full';
$Tomorrow = "ma\N{LATIN SMALL LETTER N WITH TILDE}ana";
```

Using international characters

Strings with international characters are treated just like regular characters in Perl 5.6 and Perl 5.8. For example, length("ma\x{c3b1}ana") returns 6. Similarly, ucfirst("ma\x{c3b1}ana") returns mañana. (Chapters 9 and 12 have more string-related functions, and they work just as well on international characters as length and ucfirst do.)

Appreciating the Unicode in Perl 5.8

Not everything is hunky-dory with international strings in Perl 5.6. As I stated earlier, Perl's handling of Unicode was in transition when Perl 5.6 was released. For example, in Perl 5.6, when you read text from a file, Perl thinks of it as ASCII characters (that is, bytes) instead of Unicode characters. This situation is fixed in Perl 5.8. In Perl 5.6, you have to keep track of which strings have been entered by you (and therefore, you know whether they are Unicode) and which have come from file input, and therefore are considered ASCII by Perl; in Perl 5.8, both types of strings are automatically in Unicode.

Perl 5.6 has some other limitations with Unicode that are fixed in Perl 5.8. The two most significant fixes is that you can't use UTF-8 in the keys of hashes (which I cover in Chapter 7) in Perl 5.6, and that UTF-8 only worked sometimes in regular expressions (which I describe in Chapter 12). Another big change is that Perl 5.8 is based on Unicode version 3.2, while Perl 5.6 used Unicode version 3.0. Unicode version 3.2 has tens of thousands more characters than Unicode version 3.0.

Chapter 6

Nifty Numbers

. . . .

In This Chapter

▶ Differentiating between integers and real numbers

▶ Using Perl's math operators

▶ Employing counters for incrementing and decrementing values

▶ Assigning values to variables

▶ Examining numeric functions

▶ Turning numbers into strings

. . . .

*P*art of the reason that computer programs are so good with math is that computers themselves are pretty darn good with math. So people who create programming languages have it pretty easy when it comes to adding a zillion math functions to their programs.

You'll be happy to know that Perl does a whole lot for you in terms of math besides addition, subtraction, multiplication, and division — and it does it with less muss and fuss than languages like C or Java. Unlike those other languages, you don't have to spend as much time rigidly defining your numeric variables and making sure that you only combine two variables of the same type. In, Perl, you can just use a number and go.

Contrasting Integers and Real Numbers

Computers handle two kinds of numbers: *integers* and *real numbers*. (Real numbers are also known as *reals* or *floating-point numbers*.) The basic difference between these two in Perl is that integers have no decimal point or fractions and real numbers do.

If I were writing about almost any programming language other than Perl, I would have to follow the preceding paragraph with pages and pages of description of how the language stores integers in the CPU, how it handles real numbers differently, and so on — enough to make most novice programmers run away screaming or break down in heaving sobs. Fortunately, this book is about Perl.

Perl stores all numerical values internally as real numbers in whatever way that best suits the operating system and CPU. Perl uses floating-point math, which simplifies programming because you can forget about the different number systems that you have to worry about when you program in most other languages.

Perl figures out when you probably want to think in terms of integers instead of real numbers. When you specify a number without a decimal point, Perl knows that it needs to try to operate as if the number were an integer.

You specify integers as numbers without decimal points:

```
$Count = 43; # An integer
```

You specify reals as numbers with a decimal point:

```
$Temperature = 43.955; # A real
```

You can also specify numbers by using scientific notation. In Perl, scientific notation consists of the letter *E* and a number preceding it and following it. (Whether the E is uppercase or lowercase isn't important.) The value on the left is multiplied by 10 raised to the power of the number on the right. For example, the Perl scientific notation for the variable $Temperature is equivalent to the real-world scientific notation of 0.43955×10^2:

```
$Temperature = 0.43955E2 # A real in scientific notation
```

In other words, don't sweat the difference between integers and real numbers (that is, unless you're also absorbing some other programming language, too). In Perl, a number is a number is a number, and they work just fine in all the math that you do.

Using Perl's Basic Math Operators

First things first. Perl has a number of math operators that you use very commonly in your programs. These operators are probably the same as the ones that most of us learned in algebra class (well, those of us who stayed awake in algebra class!). I cover more advanced math later in this chapter.

Using operators for simple calculations

The Perl operators for the simple math operations of addition, subtraction, multiplication, and division are +, -, *, and /, respectively. For example, you may want to get the product of 93 and 46:

```
$BigNum = 93 * 46;
print $BigNum;
```

As you can figure out with your calculator, this code displays

```
4278
```

Utilizing parentheses in algebraic calculations

If you know basic algebraic notation, you know that you can use parentheses to force certain operations to happen first in an equation, as shown in the following example:

```
$a = (5 + 2) - (4 * 9) + (3 / 7); print $a;
```

TECHNICAL STUFF

"True" and "false" are numbers, too

Like most programming languages, Perl lets you use mathematical logic to handle values of "true" and "false." The if statement takes one argument, which is either true or false. If the argument is true, the if statement executes the statements in its block. (I cover logic in Chapter 8, and describe all the statements that use logic, including if statements.)

The main reason that I mention if statements here is to demonstrate one essential part of logic: how Perl handles true/false situations. As you may guess (because numbers are one of the main topics of this chapter), Perl uses

numbers for true and false values. A false value is the same as the number 0 (zero), and a true value is any value other than 0.

Therefore, when a statement checks whether an argument is true, it actually checks whether it equals the number 0 or the string "0". If it equals either of these values, it's false; otherwise, it's true.

Besides the number 0, a null string ("") can stand in as a false value, but Perl programmers rarely do that. Thinking of false as 0 and true as everything else is much simpler.

That's five plus two, minus the product of four times nine, plus the result (quotient) of dividing three by seven, which produces the following result:

```
-28.5714285714286
```

Always use parentheses in your mathematical statements so that you can easily see what kind of math you're doing to the numbers and variables in your statements. Perl maintains a list of operators that take precedence over other operators in case you don't use parentheses, but it's easy to forget which operator does what. For example, the equation 5 + 2 - 4 * 9 + 3 / 7 may mean exactly what you intend it to, but then again, it may not. In your mind, it may mean (((((5 + 2) - 4) * 9) + 3) / 7), which comes out to 4.28571; while in someone else's mind it may mean (5 + 2) - (4 * 9) + (3 / 7), which comes out to –28.57143. Why risk doing it wrong when you can definitely do it right? Perl has a specific precedence for the order of which operators are applied, but parentheses always override that order, so using parentheses prevents you from having to memorize the ordering tables.

Working with the positive and negative value operator

As you're aware, you can use a minus sign (–) to make a positive number negative and a negative number positive. For example, –3 means negative three, and –(–4) means positive four. (Two negatives make a positive.) The same is true in Perl; when you put a minus sign in front of a variable, it inverts the variable's positive or negative value:

```
$Count = -2;
$InverseCount = -$Count;
print $InverseCount;
```

This code generates a value of positive 2 on-screen:

```
2
```

Using the exponential calculations operator

Perl uses the ** operator to raise the number on its left to the power of the number on its right. Therefore, to raise 2 to the power of 10, you enter

```
$b=2**10; print $b;
```

This code gives you the following result:

```
1024
```

Introducing the modulo arithmetic calculator

Modulo arithmetic involves dividing one number by an integer and returning the remaining value. To get the remainder for a division operation in Perl, you use the % operator in place of the division operator (/). For example, the following code generates the remainder of 8 divided by 3:

```
$c=8 % 3; print $c;
```

The result is

```
2
```

If the operation were regular division instead of modulo arithmetic, it would look like this:

```
$c=8 / 3; print $c;
```

And it would display this:

```
2.66666666666667
```

Doing Math and an Assignment at the Same Time

Sometimes you want to change a variable based on that variable's current value. For example, you may want to double the value of $d. In English, you would say, "Take the current value of $d, double it, and then make $d equal to that new value." In this case, you can use the following statement:

```
$d = $d * 2;
```

Perl lets you compress the $d = $d * 2; statement a bit by putting the desired operator before the = and skipping the variable on the right side of the equation. In which case, the statement can be written as

```
$d *= 2;
```

Although it may seem confusing, some programmers prefer the second method because they have less to type, and some think it looks better.

Another example of changing a variable based on that variable's current value is adding 1 to the variable $e, as in

```
$e += 1;
```

Autoincrementing and Autodecrementing

A common numbers-based feature in programming is the *counter*. A counter is a variable that you set to increase a value incrementally with each iteration of a *loop* (a set of instructions that are repeated until a desired action occurs). When you use a counter in this way, you're either *autoincrementing* or *autodecrementing* a value.

Using loops with autoincrementing and autodecrementing is common in Perl programs. In your regular, non-programming life, you often read instructions such as "put four teaspoons of salt into the water" or "take this medicine three times a day." In your head, you keep a counter that you increment each time you do the task, and you check that counter against the instructions that you were given. "Okay, there's one teaspoon; is that four? No. Okay, there's two teaspoons; is that four? No. Okay, . . ."

The following example shows a counter in action:

```
$SuccessCount = $SuccessCount + 1;
```

That's one way to express the statement in Perl. Another way is to use the compressed method that I describe in the preceding section of this chapter:

```
$SuccessCount += 1;
```

Counters are so common in programming, however, that Perl's creators included a special construct that lets you shorten the line even more than by using += . The *autoincrement operator*, ++, adds 1 to the value. You can write the preceding example as

```
$SuccessCount++;
```

You can decrement a number (that is, subtract 1 from it) in the same way by using the *autodecrement operator* (--). For example,

```
$SuccessCount--;
```

The ++ and -- operators only add or subtract 1 to your variable. To add or subtract other numbers, you need to use += and -=.

Perl programmers like to get fancy with these special counting operators, but they sometimes instead get cryptic and therefore make mistakes that are difficult to identify later. You can use the autoincrement and autodecrement operators in the middle of an assignment, and Perl interprets the code that uses ++ and -- differently, depending on whether you place the operator before or after the variable.

If the operator appears before the variable name, Perl increments the variable and returns the incremented value. If the operator appears after the variable name, Perl returns the original value of the variable and increments the variable.

The following shows what happens when you place the operator *after* the variable:

```
$f = 7; $g = $f++;
print "Using \$f++, \$g is $g and \$f is $f\n";
```

The result is

```
Using $f++, $g is 7 and $f is 8
```

Here, Perl assigns the initial value of $f (which is 7) to $g and then increments $f by 1 (which now makes $f 8). The position of the ++ operator determines when the variable increments. When you place the operator after $f, it doesn't increment until the actual occurrence of the ++ operator.

A different example shows what happens when you place the operator *before* the variable:

```
$f = 7; $g = ++$f;
print "Using ++\$f, \$g is $g and \$f is $f\n";
```

The result is

```
Using ++$f, $g is 8 and $f is 8
```

Here, Perl assigns $f a value (7), increments the value $f by 1 (so $f now equals 8) and then assigns the value of $f to $g (making $g 8 as well). The key lies in the position of the operator. You can see why most Perl programmers need to look closely at code that involves the ++ or -- operators to make sure that the statement does what they want it to do.

Truth be told, using += 1 and -= 1 is much clearer than ++ and --, but feel free to use whichever method works best for you.

Employing Simple Numeric Functions

The makers of Perl included several functions for simple math. These functions are as easy to use as operators, even though explaining them involves a world of technical terms. The sqrt function returns the square root of the function's *argument* (the value or statement that's processed by the function), the log function returns the *natural logarithm* (a logarithm with *e* as its base) of its argument, and exp returns *e* raised to the power of its argument. The following statements are examples of all three functions:

```
print "The square root of 121 is " . sqrt(121);
print "The log of 121 is " . log(121);
print "e raised to 121 is " . exp(121);
```

The abs function returns the absolute value of the argument, meaning that it returns a positive value whether the value of the argument is negative or positive. The int function returns the integer portion of the argument. Examples of these two functions are

```
$ThePosValue = abs($SomeValue);
$MyWhole = int($SomeValue);
```

You should know this about the int function: It rounds down for positive numbers but rounds up for negative numbers. The following is an example of what I mean:

```
$h = 3.4; $i = int($h); print "$i\n";
```

```
$h = -3.4; $i = int($h); print "$i\n";
```

These statements display, respectively

```
3
```

```
-3
```

Converting Numbers into Strings

Perl makes converting numbers into strings more convenient than most other programming languages. You don't have to do anything special because Perl "understands" that when you use numbers for string-like purposes, you want it to treat the numbers as a string. For example, you may want to make a variable that consists of a number plus a text label.

Here's an example of converting a number to a string:

```
$Ann = 5; $Ann += 1;
$Ann = $Ann . "bcd";
print $Ann;
```

The result is

```
6bcd
```

In the first line, $Ann is a number (6). In the second line, $Ann is changed from a number to a string (6bcd). From this point on, $Ann is a string, and you shouldn't treat it as a number.

After you convert a number variable into a string, you should treat that variable like a string. Technically, you *can* treat strings like numbers, but predicting the results accurately is next to impossible. For example, you can use the * operator to multiply two strings together. Perl tries hard to find numbers in the strings and do the "right thing" with them, but you can't always guess what that right thing is. Don't risk it: Always use math functions and operators exclusively with numbers.

Working with Really Big Numbers

Perl's normal math capabilities work for almost everyone. Some folks, however, need to be able to use very large numbers, or to use normal-sized numbers but with incredible accuracy. If you are one of those people (at least part of the time), Perl makes this easy.

To load Perl's big number support, include the following statement in your program :

```
use bignum;
```

You are safe to use this any time, but be aware that this causes your Perl programs to run more slowly (depending on how much math you do in your programs).

The following examples shows how Perl gives higher-precision results for both real numbers and integers when using bignum:

```
$a = sqrt(44);
$b = 34 ** 25;
print "Before bignum\n";
print "   sqrt(44) is $a\n";
print "   34 ** 25 is $b\n\n";
use bignum;
$a = sqrt(44);
$b = 34 ** 25;
print "After bignum\n";
print "   sqrt(44) is $a\n";
print "   34 ** 25 is $b\n\n";
```

The output is:

```
Before bignum
   sqrt(44) is 6.6332495807108
   34 ** 25 is 1.9363012510498e+38

After bignum
   sqrt(44) is 6.63324958071079969822986547334137336 7854
   34 ** 25 is 19363012510498042793276603337416271462 4
```

Using bignum also allows Perl to calculate numbers that are normally too big for it. Without bignum, Perl is limited to very large numbers (the exact measure of "too big" depends on the kind of computer that you are using). For example:

```
$b = 34 ** 250;
print "Before bignum\n";
print "   34 ** 250 is $b\n\n";
use bignum;
$b = 34 ** 250;
print "After bignum\n";
print "   34 ** 250 is $b\n\n";
```

This prints out:

```
Before bignum
   34 ** 250 is inf

After bignum
   34 ** 250 is 7408482520763135179705732557785133
```

```
1093184843600594103703072028794552581232110478
4800773084446147766341713371913342220107600272
6188669171040825983828428115563215469457383949
7071217982383686626957378688388814935058550324
2572679947028790740750724263931161454161475055
9656685545605304178804382930192431595406089504
0790688418303908992546915208312272253428210483
214219397671432036208869376
```

When Perl says "inf", it means "infinite", at least as far as Perl can tell. After using bignum, Perl can calculate this very large number.

Counting in Nondecimal Number Systems

If you like to count by using either the *hexadecimal* numbering system (one based on 16 digits) or the *octal* numbering system (one based on 8 digits), you can use them easily in Perl. To specify a number in hexadecimal (sometimes called *hex* for short), you preface it with the characters 0x. To specify a number in octal, you use a leading zero (0). For example,

```
$Mask = 0xFF00;
$SomeOctal = 0177;
```

Perl provides two functions for converting numbers from these two systems to decimal values. The hex and oct functions take strings that represent numbers in their respective formats and return decimal numbers. For example,

```
$Address = 'FFFF';
$Location = hex($Address) + 12;
```

If you use the hexadecimal system, the following program shows how to create a decimal-to-hex conversion chart. It uses some of the math operators shown in this chapter, as well as some of the list processing that I talk about in Chapter 7.

```
# hexchart.pl: Prints a decimal-to-hex conversion chart.
@HexD = ('0', '1', '2', '3', '4', '5', '6', '7', '8',
  '9', 'A', 'B', 'C', 'D', 'E', 'F');
for($i = 0; $i <= 255; $i += 1) {
  printf("%3s=$HexD[int($i / 16)]$HexD[$i % 16] ", $i);
  if(($i % 8) == 7) { print "\n" }
}
```

The output of the chart generated by this program is 32 lines long, so it won't all fit on a standard-size computer screen. Figure 6-1 shows how the output looks under Windows 95 with a larger-sized MS-DOS window.

Figure 6-1: The output from the decimal to hexadecimal conversion program.

Perl versions 5.6 and 5.8 lets you enter numbers as binary. This feature is particularly handy if you know which bits you want to represent, but don't want to convert them to hexadecimal. To enter numbers in binary, you preface it with the characters 0b. For example:

```
$Mask = 0b1101110;
```

Chapter 7

Learning to Love Lists and Hashes

In This Chapter
▷ Constructing lists
▷ Adding and removing list elements
▷ Slicing lists
▷ Splitting strings and returning them into lists
▷ Distinguishing scalar context from list context

*I*n addition to the two basic kinds of data — text and numbers (which I cover in Chapters 5 and 6) — Perl uses a third type of data called *lists*. When a Perl function returns more than one value, it always returns those multiple values as a list. Perl also uses lists to gather its own internal data, which helps you and your programs to work more efficiently. Plus, understanding how to use lists is crucial to your taking full advantage of Perl's most powerful features, such as its ability to organize large chunks of data into a manageable whole.

Listing the Basics

A *list* is an ordered gang of *elements* (or *items*), each of which is usually a number or a string. A list follows a definite order: The first element is always first, the second element is always second, and so on. Note that "ordered" doesn't mean "sorted" as with other programming languages. The order of the items in the list doesn't change unless you tell Perl to change it. A list also has a definite length, so you can always tell how long a list is. The length of a list can change, however, as you add or subtract list items.

Incidentally, Perl programmers also use the term *array* when referring to a list. For all practical purposes, *list* and *array* mean the same thing and can be used interchangeably (which I do in this book to add variety).

Perl programmers use another special term to refer to anything that's a string or a number and nothing else — they're called *scalars*. Keep in mind that a scalar is never a list, and a list is never a scalar. You'll soon see why the term *scalar* came to be: To repeatedly say "strings or numbers" can get really tedious.

Constructing basic lists

A Perl list is constructed somewhat like a grocery list:

```
juice
bread
paper towels
asparagus
```

This list contains individual elements, it follows a particular order, and the list as a whole can be thought of as one item — for example, my shopping list.

If you keep track of your car's gas mileage, you may end up with a list that looks something like this:

```
23.4
23.6
23.4
22.9
```

Both the mileage list and the grocery list are perfectly valid lists for Perl.

The elements in a single list can include both text data and number data. For example, you may have a list that looks similar to this:

```
juice
bread
9
juice
```

Although imagining what kind of logic went into the ordering of this list is difficult, it is nevertheless a valid list as far as Perl is concerned.

Creating literal lists

A *literal list* in Perl is almost always shown as a series of elements with a comma (,) between each element. Typically, literal lists are also enclosed within parentheses. The parentheses are not absolutely required, but you can end up with some difficult-to-diagnose problems if you leave them off, so I recommend always using them so that Perl doesn't misinterpret your intentions. Lists often appear on a single line, but they can span multiple lines. For example, the grocery list from the preceding section of this chapter may look like this:

```
('juice', 'bread', 'paper towels', 'asparagus')
```

This list contains four string *literals*. (See Chapter 5 for a discussion of literals.) You always use quotation marks around a string literal so that Perl knows where the string starts and ends.

Understanding variable names

Many of the variable names that you see in this book start with a dollar sign ($). Perl uses another symbol to begin the variable names of lists: the at sign (@). For example, examine the following assignment in which multiple values are stored in the variable @Shop:

```
@Shop = ('juice', 'bread', 'paper towels', 'asparagus');
```

This statement tells Perl, "The list called Shop is assigned to be four elements long; the first element is 'juice', the second element is 'bread', the third element is 'paper towels', and the fourth element is 'asparagus'."

List variable names start with @, and scalar variable names start with $. When you see a variable name such as @Shop, you know you have a list on your hands; when you see a variable name such as $Shop, you've identified it as a string or a number.

Considering null lists

Not all lists contain elements. A list that consists of no elements is called an *empty list* or *null list*. You can specify a list to have no values with an assignment like the following, in which you make @Shop an empty list:

```
@Shop = ();
```

The () in the previous statement is actually a list: It's a list with no elements between the (and). You can also specify an empty list with one or more spaces between the parentheses because you still have no elements in it:

```
@Shop = ( );
```

Specifying Elements and Slices of Lists

What happens if you want to address just one element of a list, and not the list in its entirety? Because lists are ordered, you can refer to each element by its numbered place in the list. You can then say to Perl, "Set the variable $Dub to the value of the third element of the list @Music." For example:

```
$Dub = @Music[2];
```

If you're thinking that the preceding statement should say @Music[3] and not @Music[2], remember that Perl counts list elements starting at 0, and not at 1. Therefore, the first element of a Perl list is always element number 0, the second element is element number 1, and so on. (If you've used other programming languages, such as C and Pascal, you're probably already familiar with this programming quirk.) If Perl is your first programming language, be sure to drill this into your brain: Perl counts items in lists beginning at 0.

You can refer to a connected range of elements of a list as a *slice*. You specify a slice by putting the element number(s) of the slice in square brackets ([and]). If you're talking about a slice with a single element, that slice is a *scalar slice,* and you must place a $ at the beginning of the list's variable name.

For example, if you want to print the first element of the @Shop list, you enter

```
@Shop = ('juice', 'bread', 'paper towels', 'asparagus');
print $Shop[0];
```

This command displays

```
juice
```

You can assign elements to scalar variables, such as

```
$Third = $Shop[2];
```

This statement assigns the string paper towels (element number 3 in the list designated by [2] in Perl-speak) to the variable $Third.

You may be wondering why you change the symbol for a slice from @ to $ when discussing a slice that's only one element. That's because the values in a list are always scalars and are never lists. For example, the value in Shop[0] is a scalar, and not a list. Thus, its name should start with $, the symbol for a scalar variable.

Slices of lists can contain more than one element. Multi-element slices are themselves lists, and thus their variable names start with @. For example, a slice of the @Shop list that consists of the second and third elements can be assigned with something like this:

```
@TwoEls = @Shop[1,2];
```

You can also place list slices on the left side of assignments. This practice is commonly done to change the value of one element without redefining the whole list. For example,

```
@Shop = ('juice', 'bread', 'paper towels', 'asparagus');
$Shop[1] = 'muffins';
```

turns the list in @Shop into

```
('juice', 'muffins', 'paper towels', 'asparagus')
```

Perl makes it easy to find out how many elements are in a list without having to count each of them. The variable $#listname is the number of the last element in a list. So, for the four-element shopping list I've been using in this chapter, entering

```
print $#Shop;
```

displays the number

```
3
```

This number is not the length of the list; it's the number of the last element. The length of the list is actually that number plus 1.

Using Lists to Simplify Basic Tasks

Perl's list-handling abilities simplify a number of programming tasks. For example, assume that you want to compare a single string against a lengthy set of strings in a dictionary to determine whether the test string matches any in the set. Further assume that your test string is in the variable $Test and consists of the following words:

```
. . .
interest
interested
interesting
interface
interfaith
interfere
interferon
intergenerational
. . .
```

When Perl doesn't know your list

Perl has what I consider to be a nasty feature that supposedly exists for the sake of programming friendliness. You can have a list variable and a scalar variable with the same name that are completely unrelated. For example, you can have a program that has both @Shop and $Shop, and the two variables may have nothing to do with each other.

This feature can create confusion when you're first learning how to use single-element array slices. If you forget to put the square brackets and the element number in the variable name, you can easily miss the fact that you're using a scalar variable that has nothing to do with the list variable.

To keep your sanity, never purposely use a scalar variable with the same name as a list variable. If you have a list called @Shop, do not use a scalar called $Shop; call it something else, such as $ShopNum.

Without using lists, your program would have to look something like the following:

```
. . .
if($Test eq 'interest') { print "A match was found.\n" }
if($Test eq 'interested') { print "A match was found.\n" }
if($Test eq 'interesting') { print "A match was found.\n" }
. . .
```

Creating such a program can be sheer tedium. Furthermore, if you want to perform some different action if the test is successful, then you should remember that updating every line of the program is subject to human error because you have to enter that action into every line by hand.

You can make this task simple if you use a list. First, you create a list whose elements consist of all the words to test against the dictionary, and then you *loop* through the list, as in the following example. (I cover loops in Chapter 8.)

```
. . .
@WordList = (
  'interest', 'interested', 'interesting', 'interface',
  'interfaith', 'interfere', 'interferon',
  'intergenerational'); # Line breaks are ignored
$ListPos = 0; # Start at position 0
# Loop until you go off the end of the list
until($ListPos > $#WordList) {
  if($Test eq $WordList[$ListPos])
    { print "A match was found.\n" }
  $ListPos += 1;
}
. . .
```

You now have just one place where the action is given (the `print` statement), which makes updating the program faster and easier.

Using lists simplifies more than just the process of updating a program. For example, what if you don't know which list you're testing against until you run the program? This situation frequently happens because lists are kept in text files that are updated separately from the Perl program. With lists, getting this information is a cinch. Instead of assigning the list at the beginning of the program, you can write two or three lines of Perl code (which I describe in Chapter 10) that read lines from the text file and add each line to the list. The loop in the program remains identical; only the source of the list changes.

Using the print Statement with Lists

Many functions take lists as *arguments* (values that are entered after the function to modify the operation of the function). The most widely used example of a function that takes a list is the `print` statement. The `print` statement takes one argument — a list. It's common for that list to have a single element. For example,

```
$Color = "mossy teal";
print $Color;
```

displays

```
mossy teal
```

You can also print a list in exactly the same fashion by specifying a list instead of a single value. For example,

```
@Color = ('mossy teal', 'burnt umber', 'bone white');
print @Color;
```

displays

```
mossy tealburnt umberbone white
```

The `print` statement runs the elements together, rather than separating them with a space as it does with the words in each element, because the list is simply a gang of items. You can print the elements individually by entering the following statement

```
print $Color[0] . ' ' . $Color[1] . ' ' . $Color[2];
```

which displays the string

```
mossy teal burnt umber bone white
```

In the preceding example, you print a list that consists of a single string that is formed from five strings — the first slice, the string that is a single space, the second slice, the string that is a single space, and the third slice. You can also print a list of five elements with a statement, such as

```
print ($Color[0], ' ', $Color[1], ' ', $Color[2]);
```

which displays the string

```
mossy teal burnt umber bone white
```

This is a true list with five elements: the first slice, a string, the second slice, another string, and the third slice.

Adding and Removing List Elements

You don't have to construct your lists by using assignments. In fact, building up a list by starting with a null list and adding elements one by one is a common practice.

Adding elements to a list with the push and unshift functions

The two functions that you use to add elements to a list are push and unshift. push adds one or more elements to the end of a list, whereas unshift adds elements to the beginning of a list. Each of these functions takes two arguments: the name of the list to which you want to add elements and the list of elements that you want to add. The following lines show push and unshift in action:

```
@SomeList = (8, 'eight', 9, 'nine');
@TenList = (10, 'ten');
push(@SomeList, @TenList);
unshift(@SomeList, "The Big Seven");
```

Given the previous lines, the list @SomeList becomes

```
('The Big Seven', 8, 'eight', 9, 'nine', 10, 'ten')
```

Removing elements from a list with the shift and pop functions

You can also remove an element from the beginning or end of a list with the shift and pop functions, respectively. These functions take one argument — the name of the list — and return the value that was removed. For example:

```
@SomeList = (8, 'eight', 9, 'nine');
$Removed = shift(@SomeList);
print $Removed;
```

displays

```
8
```

and the list @SomeList now contains only three elements:

```
('eight', 9, 'nine')
```

The functions that I just described enable you to alter the two ends of a list in order to make it expand and shrink as you desire. Table 7-1 shows you these functions at a glance.

Table 7-1	Functions for Adding or Subtracting Elements from the Ends of Lists
Function	*Result*
push	Adds items to right side of list
pop	Removes items from right side of list
unshift	Adds items to left side of list
shift	Removes items from left side of list

Adding and removing elements from a list with the splice function

Perl, being the lenient and flexible language that it is, also has a function that lets you add or remove elements from any part of a list. The splice function removes some elements and adds others in their place. It takes four arguments:

✔ The list to modify

✔ The position (element number) that indicates where to start replacing

✔ The number of elements to remove

✔ The list of elements to insert

The following example illustrates each of the splice arguments:

```
@Nums = (1, 2, 3, 4, 5);
splice(@Nums, 3, 1, ('dog', 'cow'));
```

The result is

```
(1, 2, 3, 'dog', 'cow', 5)
```

You don't have to remove any elements in order to add elements with splice. If you set the third argument (the number of elements to remove) to 0, you're simply adding elements to the list. For example, if you enter the following:

```
@Nums = (1, 2, 3, 4, 5);
splice(@Nums, 3, 0, ('dog', 'cow'));
```

@Nums list equals

```
(1, 2, 3, 'dog', 'cow', 4, 5)
```

When you don't remove any elements, the new elements go *before* the element indicated by the second argument.

You can also use splice to remove elements by using a null list. (See the section "Null lists" earlier in this chapter for more information.) For example, the following entry

```
@Nums = (1, 2, 3, 4, 5);
splice(@Nums, 3, 1, ());
```

results in this:

```
(1, 2, 3, 5)
```

Perl allows you to leave off the fourth argument if it's a null list. The equivalent splice statement without a null list would be

```
splice(@Nums, 3, 1);
```

Two nifty list operators

There's more to lists than functions. Perl also has two useful operators that operate on lists to simplify list creation. In Chapter 5, I describe how the x operator repeats strings. That same operator can also be used to repeat lists. Given the following statement

```
@h = (883, 895) x 3;
```

@h now equals

```
(883, 895, 883, 895, 883, 895)
```

Perl also makes it easy to create lists that consist of sequential integers (and not real numbers, such as 3.45 or 8.76) by using the *range operator,* which consists of two periods ("..")

between the starting and ending values, as in the following code:

```
@n = (3 .. 8);
```

The result is the list

```
(3, 4, 5, 6, 7, 8)
```

You must list the smallest number in the range first when using the range operator; you can't use the range operator, for example, to create the list (8, 7, 6, 5, 4, 3). You can also use the range operator with characters. For example, to create the list ('a', 'b', 'c', 'd', 'e', 'f'), you can enter the following:

```
('a' .. 'f')
```

When you use splice to remove items, Perl returns those items. (I describe returning values from a function in Chapter 3.) For example:

```
@Nums = (1, 2, 3, 4, 5);
$GotOne = splice(@Nums, 3, 1);
print $GotOne;
```

displays

```
4
```

If you're removing more than one item, return the items into a list. For example:

```
@Nums = (1, 2, 3, 4, 5);
@GotSome = splice(@Nums, 3, 2);
```

The @GotSome list now equals

```
(4, 5)
```

The push, unshift, shift, and pop functions pretty much boil down to special cases of splice that you can use interchangeably. Table 7-2 shows the functions and their splice equivalents.

Table 7-2	How splice Relates to push, unshift, shift, and pop
Function	*splice Equivalent*
push(@r, @s)	splice(@r, $#r+1, 0, @s)
pop(@r)	splice(@r, $#r, 1)
unshift(@r, @s)	splice(@r, 0, 0, @s)
shift(@r)	splice(@r, 0, 1)

Splitting Strings with the split Function

As I mention frequently throughout this book, Perl is a superb text-handling language. The split function is one of the greatest text-handling tools in Perl.

After you work with lists, you can see why split is the greatest thing since, um, split bread. split looks at a string and splits it apart, returning a list of strings. For example, you can use split to examine a sentence and return a list of each word in the sentence. Or, if you have a tab-delimited text file that is a database (such as the empdata1.pl program described in Chapter 4), split can split the lines in the file into fields in a single function.

Unless you use the split default arguments in Perl (and I recommend against this practice because it makes your programs difficult to read), split takes two or three arguments. If you want to create a list of all the split-out strings in your program, you use two arguments: the pattern to use as the *delimiter* (the indicator of the end of one thing and the beginning of the next) and the string to search. Later in this section, I tell you how you can use three arguments with split.

String patterns are among the more advanced topics in Perl. I cover them in more depth in Chapter 12, but for now, I show you some very simple patterns. The patterns start and end with a slash (/) character and contain the exact character that you want to split between the slashes.

For example, to split a sentence that is in a string into a list of words (using the space as the delimiter), you would use

```
$Sentence = "It is time for our tea, Sir.";
@Words = split(/ /, $Sentence);
```

The @Words list now looks like this:

```
('It' , 'is' , 'time' , 'for' , 'our' , 'tea,' , 'Sir.')
```

Splitting by tab characters is just as easy. For example, consider the following lines:

```
($LastName, $FirstName, $ID, $Tel) =
    split(/\t/, $TheRec);
```

The first argument in the preceding `split` statement is the pattern for a tab character (`\t`). Because each record has four fields, instead of splitting the `$TheRec` string into a named record, you can split it directly into a list of variables. This process is somewhat akin to (but much simpler than) entering the following:

```
@TempList = split(/\t/, $TheRec);
$LastName = $TempList[0];
$FirstName = $TempList[1];
$ID = $TempList[2];
$Tel = $TempList[3];
```

If you need just the first few items in a string and don't care about the rest, you can use a third argument in `split` to say how many elements should be in the resulting list. Using the preceding example, if the only data that you want to use are the first names and last names, you can enter

```
($LastName, $FirstName, $RestOfLine) =
    split(/\t/, $TheRec, 3);
```

In this case, `$RestOfLine` may or may not have tab characters in it. `split` stops looking for more elements after the second tab character and stuffs whatever remains into the last element of the array onto the left side of the assignment. In the preceding example, the remainder of the record is put into `$RestOfLine`.

You can probably find many uses for `split` as you write your own Perl programs. For example, you may have a text file that contains lines like this:

```
Temperature=28.3
Size=large
Color=crimson
Texture=rough
```

For each line, you want to know what the attribute on the left is, and the value on the right. In a line-by-line loop of the program, you can use

```
($Attribute, $Value) = split(/=/, $TheLine);
```

You can then do some testing based on `$Attribute`.

Using Scalar Variables

The list-creation assignments in previous sections of this chapter all use *literals* for their values. However, you can also use scalar variables in your list assignments just as easily. (See Chapter 3 for definitions of literals and scalars.) For example, examine the following lines:

```
$LakeName = "Mammoth";
$LakeLen = 1291.3;
@Lake[8,9] = ($LakeName, $LakeLen);
```

The previous statements cause $Lake[8] to become the string Mammoth and $Lake[9] to become the number 1291.3.

Employing Existing Lists

You can also use existing lists when defining new lists. When you name a list while assigning a new or existing list, Perl expands the list inside the assignment to all its elements. The following is a quick way to insert the elements from one list into another. For example, if you use the following statements

```
@a = (12, 24, 36);
@b = ('Dozens', @a);
```

@b is set to

```
('Dozens', 12, 24, 36)
```

Perl behaves like this because list elements can't be lists themselves. If you try to make a list an element of another list, Perl politely pulls out all the elements of the inner list and replaces them in the list at the left side of the assignment.

Distinguishing Context Types

Perl operates in two contexts: scalar (anything in the form of strings or numbers) and array. (*Array* and *list* are synonymous.) Perl uses the context of an expression to determine what kind of output a function or operator will produce. You can determine which context you're in by looking at what kind of assignment is being created. Consider the following example:

```
$a = somefunction($b); # scalar context
@c = somefunction($d); # array context
($e, $f) = somefunction($g); # array context
```

The general rule is that if the item on the left of an assignment is a scalar, you're in scalar context; if the item on the left of the assignment is a list, you're in array context. Note that in the third line of the preceding example, even though scalar variables are shown, they are in a list, so the statement is in array context.

Most of the time, you don't have to be bothered with which context a function is in because the function returns the same result in either case. However, some Perl functions give you completely different results depending on the context. A few Perl operators also change their output depending on the context.

In the previous examples shown in this chapter, the split function is in array context — that is, the left side of each assignment is always a list. If the left side of an assignment were a scalar, however, split returns the number of elements that it finds. For example, in the following case

```
$x = "This has exactly five words.";
@y = split(/ /, $x);
$z = split(/ /, $x);
```

@y is set to the list

```
('This', 'has', 'exactly', 'five', 'words.')
```

However, $z is set to

```
5
```

The two varying results I just noted, both of which come from the same function call of split(/ /, $x), are due to the differences in the context.

Now here's a place where Perl can get really confusing: If you use the name of a list in a scalar context, Perl interprets the name as the length of the list. This little bit of shorthand can be confounding to even advanced programmers, unless the statement with that shorthand is carefully examined to see why the particular results were achieved. For example, you can say something like

```
@h = ('A', 'short', 'list', 'of', 'words');
$ListLen = @h;
print $ListLen;
```

and Perl will display

```
5
```

Using $#h+1 to get a list length is always less confusing than using @h.

From time to time, you may want to force Perl to evaluate a function in a scalar context. You can use the `scalar` function to do this. If you must use @ to get a list length, you can use `scalar` to make your program less confusing when reading it later. For example,

```
@h = ('A', 'short', 'list', 'of', 'words');
print scalar(@h);
```

prints

```
5
```

Without the `scalar` function in this case, Perl prints out all the elements of the list.

Using List::Util in Perl 5.8

The `List::Util` module, which is built into Perl 5.8, gives you some handy features that are missing in earlier versions of Perl. To use the module, include the following near the beginning of your program:

```
use List::Util qw(first max maxstr min minstr shuffle sum);
```

You don't have to list all of the names in the parentheses; only include the ones that you intend to use in your program. Table 7-3 shows the subroutines that are added by `List::Util`.

Table 7-3	Subroutines Available in List::Util
Subroutine	*Use*
`first { BLOCK } LIST`	Executes the conditional test in the block on the list, and returns the first value of the list that matches the test.
`max(LIST)`	Returns the largest numeric value in the list
`maxstr(LIST)`	Returns the highest string value in the list
`min(LIST)`	Returns the smallest numeric value in the list
`minstr(LIST)`	Returns the smallest string value in the list
`shuffle(LIST)`	Returns the list in random order
`sum(LIST)`	Returns the sum of the numbers in the list

The following example shows how each of these subroutines works:

```
use List::Util qw(first max maxstr min minstr shuffle sum);

@Nums = (12, 70, 27, 48);
print "\@Nums is ", join(' ', @Nums), "\n";
@Words = ('fluffy', 'shiny', 'juicy', 'nice');
print "\@Words is ", join(' ', @Words), "\n\n";

$Above40 = first { $_ > 40 } @Nums;
    print "The first value in \@Nums over 40 is $Above40\n";
$HighNum = max(@Nums);
    print "The highest number in \@Nums is $HighNum\n";
$LastWord = maxstr(@Words);
    print "The last word alphabetically in \@Words is $LastWord\n";

$LowNum = min(@Nums);
    print "The lowest number in \@Nums is $LowNum\n";
$FirstWord = minstr(@Words);
    print "The first word alphabetically in \@Words is $FirstWord\n";
@MixedUp = shuffle(@Nums, @Words);
    print "The two lists, combined and randomized:\n   ",
        join(' ', @MixedUp), "\n";
$Total = sum(@Nums);
    print "The sum of the numbers in \@Nums is $Total\n";
```

Running this example program displays:

```
@Nums is 12 70 27 48
@Words is fluffy shiny juicy nice

The first value in @Nums over 40 is 70
The highest number in @Nums is 70
The last word alphabetically in @Words is shiny
The lowest number in @Nums is 12
The first word alphabetically in @Words is fluffy
The two lists, combined and randomized:
    48 fluffy 27 shiny nice juicy 70 12
The sum of the numbers in @Nums is 157
```

Of course, as you learn in Chapter 6, the random list that is printed out for the shuffle subroutine will probably be different each time you run the program, so it is unlikely to be the same as what you see here.

Understanding the Basics of Working with Hashes

Items in a list are usually accessed by using the item's numerical position (for example, $Names[4] is the fifth item in the @Names list). Or, for example, suppose that you're searching through a list for an item whose value is 82; that item is actually defined by its position in the list — not its value.

Imagine that you're working with a printout containing two columns of information: employee numbers and names. Exactly one employee exists for each employee number, and the numbers are not sequential. For example:

ID	Name
742	Kathi Stennis
5280	Roberta Wallace
3279	Daniel Exon

You can use this printed list to look up an employee by his or her ID number or to look up an ID number by using an employee's name. To create such a list in Perl, you would write the following statement:

```
(742, 'Kathi Stennis', 5280, 'Roberta Wallace',
   3279, 'Daniel Exon')
```

However, this Perl list isn't as easy to read as a printed list because the even-numbered items are ID numbers, and the odd-numbered elements are names. To search for a particular ID number, you have to look at every other item in the list, instead of every item.

Locating items by their keys

Lists in which the elements have two parts, an index and an associated value, are commonplace in programming. So, Perl offers a second kind of list, called a *hash*. Instead of looking up an item by its position in a list, you look it up by its *key*. A hash is a list of *key-value* pairs, and each key-value pair is called a *record*.

In the employee ID example given earlier, the hash has three records. One record has the key 742 and the value Kathi Stennis; another record has the key 5280 and the value Roberta Wallace; and another record has the key 3279 and the value Daniel Exon. In a hash, the order of the records is unimportant and, in fact, the order is usually randomized by Perl.

You use keys to get to the records instead of using record numbers as you do with normal lists. Therefore, following the previous example, the record associated with key 5280 is the one that has the value Roberta Wallace.

Identifying records solely by their keys leads to an important attribute of hashes: Only one record can be associated with a particular key. You're guaranteed that when you say, "the record with key 5280," either zero or one record will be associated with that key. This also means that hashes aren't good for some tasks. For example, if you have a list of telephone numbers and names, you don't want to use a hash because two people may have the same phone number and one person may have more than one phone number.

A few Perl programmers call hashes _associative arrays_ because technically that's how they're stored in your computer's memory; Perl uses a _hash function_ (a mathematical way of storing and retrieving values quickly) to determine how to best store the keys and values. However, I prefer the term _hash_ because it is shorter.

You don't need to use hashes (except in the few cases when they're handed to you by Perl as the return value of an operation). However, they have a couple of major advantages over simple lists for many applications.

For lists of name-value pairs, hashes are useful because you can take advantage of a handful of built-in Perl functions for them; these save you the trouble of creating your own functions to do certain things, such as finding a value based on a name or deleting a name-value pair from the middle of the list.

Searching through a hash is much faster than searching through a simple list, particularly if the list contains lots of data. Finding a particular record in a hash is much faster than looking through every other item in a list. The average search through a list of key-value pairs requires Perl to look at half the pairs before finding the one that you want. Hashes, on the other hand, require much less processing power to find the same record.

Comparing hashes with standard lists

Hashes use different notations than regular lists:

- You name a hash with a percent sign (%) instead of the @ used in regular lists (for example, %IDList).
- You refer to an element in a hash by its key.
- You put the key in curly braces ({ and }) instead of the parentheses used in regular lists.

Given these notations, the following assigns the value of a record whose key is 5280 to the variable $NextPerson:

```
$NextPerson = $IDList{"5280"};
```

Creating a hash

You assign a record to a hash as a pair of items. For example, to create the hash %IDList, you can use

```
%IDList = (742, 'Kathi Stennis', 5280, 'Roberta Wallace',
    3279, 'Daniel Exon');
```

The preceding statement may be a bit difficult to read, given that you have to view the assignment in pairs. Beginning with Perl 5, you can use the => operator instead of the comma operator to separate the values in a list. Many programmers use the => operator between the key and the value (indicating that this key is associated with this value) and commas between records, as shown in the following statement:

```
%IDList = (742 => 'Kathi Stennis',
    5280 => 'Roberta Wallace',
    3279 => 'Daniel Exon');
```

If the key is more than a single word, it must be in quotation marks. For example, if you have a hash whose keys are street names and whose values are zip codes, you use

```
%Streets = ("Pine" => "92484", "North Elm" => "92481",
    "River" => "92484");
```

If you want to start an empty hash before adding records, you can use the following simple statement:

```
%Streets = ();
```

Adding records to a hash

To add a record to a hash, you must assign a value to a key. For example, to add another record to the array %Streets, you can use

```
$Streets{"South Elm"} = "92481";
```

When Perl sees an assignment statement, such as the one in the previous example, it looks to see whether the key South Elm already exists. If so, Perl replaces the corresponding value with 92481; if not, Perl creates a key and gives it that value. Assigning values in hashes is just like assigning values in regular lists, except that you use keys instead of locations in the list.

Removing records

You can use the `delete` function to remove an existing record. This function takes as its argument the key that you want to remove. For example:

```
delete($Streets{"North Elm"});
```

The `delete` function returns the value of the key that it just deleted.

Examining records with the keys function

In the section "Comparing hashes with standard lists," you see how to examine the value of a record by placing its key within curly braces. The format for this is

```
$ARRAYNAME{"KEY"}
```

You may want a list of all the keys in a hash so that you can look at each record in the array. The (appropriately named) `keys` function accomplishes this task for you. The argument to `keys` is the name of the hash. For example, the following program prints the records from a hash:

```
@AllKeys = keys(%Streets);
foreach $TheKey (@AllKeys)
  { print "$TheKey is the key for $Streets{$TheKey}\n" }
```

The order in which the keys are returned is fairly random. Because `keys` returns a simple list, you can sort the returned list before using it with a statement, such as the following one:

```
@AllKeys = sort(keys(%Streets));
```

Returning values with the values function

The `values` function returns a list of the values in a hash. This feature is useful when you just need to know the values in the array but not which key each value is associated with. When you use the `values` function, remember that you may have duplicate values (but never duplicate keys).

For example, to create an array @AllVals that contains all the values in the hash %Streets, you can use the following:

```
@AllVals = sort(values(%Streets));
print join("\n", @AllVals), "\n";
```

Stepping with the each function

If you have a very large hash, you may not want to create lengthy lists with the keys and values functions. Instead, you can use the each function to step through the records one at a time. The each function returns a two-element list: the key and the value. When you reach the end of the hash, each returns a false value.

For example, the following program prints out the key and the value for every record in %BigList. It does so by using the each function to get each record, one at a time:

```
while(($TheKey, $TheVal) = each(%BigList))
{ print "$TheKey is the key for $TheVal\n" }
```

The counter used by each resets when you use either a keys or values function, so don't use either of those functions in your loop. The each function works correctly if you delete records, but not if you add them.

If you just want to check that a particular key is in a hash, use the exists function:

```
unless(exists($Streets{"Main"}))
   { print "Main Street has disappeared.\n" }
```

Checking for any existing records

You can find out whether any records at all exist in a hash by evaluating the array in a scalar context. This process returns true only if any records exist. For example, the following shows the %IDList hash used as the argument of the unless function, which forces the array into a scalar context:

```
unless(%IDList) { print "The assoc. array is empty.\n" }
```

Writing Hash Data to a File

Rarely do you keep all the data that a Perl program uses. Instead, you probably keep the data in a file on your hard drive and read it into your program. You may also use Perl to change the data in your database and then write the file to disk. You can use files that contain data with hashes pretty much the same way you use files with simple lists. (See Chapter 10 for more information on files.)

For example, you may keep the program data as a tab-delimited text file and read it into the program when the program first starts up. You can write the data to the file by using something like the following program, which writes out each key and value pair. Each pair is separated by a tab character, and each record is written on a separate line.

```
open(STREETOUT, ">streets.txt") or
  die "Couldn't write to streets.txt file.\n";
foreach $Key (sort(keys(%Streets)))
  { print STREETOUT "$Key\t$Streets{$Key}\n" }
close(STREETOUT);
```

You can read the file that the previous program creates with a program like this one:

```
%Streets = ();
open(STREETIN, "streets.txt") or
  die "Couldn't read from streets.txt file.\n";
while(<STREETIN>) {
  $TheRec = $_; chomp($TheRec);
  ($Key, $Val) = split(/\t/, $TheRec, 2);
  $Streets{$Key} = $Val;
}
```

Chapter 17 describes how to use database files with much faster access than the files I just described.

Creating Multidimensional Lists

Until Perl 5 arrived, Perl programmers were limited to creating lists that consisted solely of scalar items (either strings or numbers). For my money, multidimensional lists are among the greatest features ever introduced.

A *multidimensional list* is essentially a list of lists. For example, suppose that you want to create a list of company employees, and within each item you want to list each employee's name, ID number, and telephone number. Or you may want to create an inventory list in which each item consists of a list of the item's inventory location, part number, name, and the quantity in stock. Perl 5 introduced an easy way to handle lists that have items consisting of other lists. You can even have hashes whose values are lists.

In this section, I show you how to use lists of lists, but I don't explain what the individual symbols and operators that are used with multidimensional arrays mean. If you want to find out more about these symbols and operators in the Perl documentation, use the perldoc perlref command at the command line (the perldoc program is described in Chapter 2). Otherwise, you

Don't assume order

Perl stores records in a seemingly random order. "Seemingly random" means that the order makes no sense if you just look at the keys or the values in the list. As soon as you assign a record to an array, Perl determines where in the hash the record should go and puts it there, disregarding the order in which you input the records. However, Perl knows the order based on the hash function that it uses to store the records.

The following program demonstrates that hashes aren't necessarily kept in the order in which you enter them. The result of running the program may surprise you.

```
%IDList = (742 => 'Kathi
    Stennis',
    5280 => 'Roberta Wallace',
    3279 => 'Daniel Exon');
print join("\n", %IDList);
```

When you run this program, Perl displays

```
3279
Daniel Exon
742
Kathi Stennis
5280
Roberta Wallace
```

Note: The records come out in a different order than they went in; Perl outputs them in the order that they are stored internally in Perl.

can still use lists of lists just fine without knowing every detail of how and why they work. (Lists of lists are based on Perl *references* and *pointers* @— which are familiar to most advanced programmers, and included in most modern programming languages.)

Creating two-dimensional lists

In this section, you have an example program to assemble and use a list that has lists as its items (a two-dimensional list). Assume that you have an inventory database, @AllInv, composed of various items. Each item has four parts:

✔ Warehouse location

✔ Part number

✔ Part name

✔ Quantity in stock

An item in the database may be represented by the following Perl statement:

```
('Shelf 17B', '35J912', 'Tool chest, black', 11)
```

Another item may be represented as

```
('Shelf 19A', '20N14', 'Allen wrench set', 47)
```

Lists composed of items like those in the previous examples are called *two-dimensional lists*. In this case, one dimension consists of rows, and the other dimension consists of columns. Each row contains the specific item in stock, and each column is a category, such as the item's location or part number. Suppose that you want to create a list that contains the preceding two lists. You may assume that the following statements can accomplish the task (but you'd be wrong):

```
# WRONG, BUT CLOSE
@AllInv = (
   ('Shelf 17B', '35J912', 'Tool chest, black', 11),
   ('Shelf 19A', '20N14', 'Crescent wrench set', 47)
);
# WRONG, BUT CLOSE
```

In lists of lists, you need to enclose the lists within lists in square brackets ([and]), not parentheses. Therefore, the following is the correct way to enter the previous example:

```
# THE RIGHT WAY
@AllInv = (
   ['Shelf 17B', '35J912', 'Tool chest, black', 11],
   ['Shelf 19A', '20N14', 'Crescent wrench set', 47]
);
# THE RIGHT WAY
```

Always mark the outermost list with parentheses, just as you would with simple lists, and the inner lists with square brackets.

Accessing list elements one piece at a time

In a simple list, you access a list element by using a *subscript* (the value to be offset from the beginning of an array) in square brackets. For example, the sixth element of @MyList is identified with $MyList[5]. (The first element in a list is always at offset 0.)

In two-dimensional lists, you need to use two subscripts to access a list element — first the row, and then the column. For instance, in the example used in the preceding section, the fourth column in the second row of @AllInv is accessed with $AllInv[1][3]. Therefore, the following statement

```
print $AllInv[1][3];
```

displays

```
47
```

You can set values in lists of lists exactly as you do in simple lists. For instance, using the example in the preceding section, if you want to decrease the number of crescent wrenches in stock to 35, you use

```
$AllInv[1][3] = 35;
```

You can also use variables in the subscripts. For instance, to double the number of all the items in this example, you can use the following statements:

```
$NumItems = @AllInv;

for($i = 0; $i < $NumItems; $i += 1)
  { $AllInv[$i][3] *= 2 }
```

You may want to get a whole row as a list instead of each of its pieces. This task seems easy, but the syntax to accomplish it is a tad bizarre-looking due to the way that Perl handles references. The format looks like this:

```
@{@ARRAYNAME[ROW]}
```

For example, you may have something in your program that fills in an array called @TopRow with the first record of your database. It may look like this:

```
@TopRow = @{@AllInv[0]};
```

You have no direct way to refer to an entire column in a similar fashion, so you always have to take multiple steps if you want to fill an array with the values from a column.

Adding rows and columns to two-dimensional lists

You may want to add items to a list one full row at a time (for example, when new items are added to a list of in-stock inventory). You can use the venerable push function for this. For example, if you have a list called @NewItem that you want to add to the end of the list @AllInv, you can use

```
@NewItem = ('Floor 2J', '82B297', 'Keyhole saw', 18);
push(@AllInv, [ @NewItem ]);
```

Beyond two dimensions

In Perl, it's possible to have lists of lists of lists of. . . well, you get the picture. Perl doesn't restrict you to two-dimensional lists. In fact, many programs have multidimensional lists with three or more dimensions. For example, imagine that the parts inventory database @AllInv is meant to inventory *all* the locations in your company — not just one. The location and amount fields would then contain more than one entry.

You can specify lists within lists within lists just as easily as you can specify just lists within lists. For example, a multilocation inventory list may be written in Perl to look like this:

```
@AllInv = (
  [['New York Shelf 17B', 'Ohio
    Slot 135'] ,
```

```
  '35J912', 'Tool chest, black',
    [11, 13]],
  [['New York Shelf 19A', 'Ohio
    Slot 142'],
  '20N14', 'Crescent wrench set',
    [47, 12]]
);
```

This example program indicates that 11 tool chests are in stock at "New York Shelf 17B" and 13 tool chests are in stock at "Ohio Slot 135," and so on. To access this information directly, you need to use a third subscript, such as the following:

```
$OhioQuant = $AllInv[0][3][1];
```

If you don't want to use a temporary variable, such as @NewItem, you can say

```
push(@AllInv, [ 'Floor 2J', '82B297', 'Keyhole saw', 18 ]);
```

Adding a column takes a little more work than adding a row, but the process is still fairly easy. It requires your adding an item to the end of each list in the main list. For example, if you want to add a column at the end of each list that shows the date on which you last examined the item, you can write something like the following:

```
# Start by using today's date
($Second, $Minute, $Hour, $DayOfMonth, $Month, $Year,
  $WeekDay, $DayOfYear, $IsDST) = localtime(time);
$RealMonth = $Month + 1;
$Today = sprintf('%02d/%02d/%02d', $RealMonth,
  $DayOfMonth, $Year);
$NumItems = @AllInv;
for($i = 0; $i < $NumItems; $i += 1)
  { $AllInv[$i][4] = $Today }
```

Perl automatically extends a list as you add columns to the end of it, just as it does for simple lists.

Creating Hashes Consisting of Lists

The more you work with Perl, the more uses you find for hashes that have lists as values. Instead of searching record by record in order to find information on an item in a list, a hash enables you to find the record quickly by using its *key*. (See the section "Locating items by their keys" earlier in this chapter.)

You can create hashes with list values by using statements like these (here, the part numbers `'35J912'` and `'20N14'` are the keys):

```
%AllInvByNum = (
    '35J912' => ['Shelf 17B', 'Tool chest, black', 11],
    '20N14'=> ['Shelf 19A', 'Crescent wrench set', 47]
);
```

You can look at an individual item with the following statement:

```
$WrenchCount = $AllInvByNum{'20N14'}[2];
```

You can add records to a hash with an assignment. For example, you can add a record whose key is `'82B297'` with the following statement:

```
$AllInvByNum{'82B297'} = [ 'Floor 2J', 'Keyhole saw', 18 ];
```

You can find a particular record in a multidimensional hash with a statement like this:

```
@Tools = @{$AllInvByNum{'35J912'}};
```

When using the hash functions (`keys`, `values`, `each`, and `exists`), you have to be careful how you handle anything that's a value. (Remember that the value is a list, and not a scalar.) For example, in order to print a list of inventory locations sorted by part number, you can use

```
foreach $Part (sort(keys(%AllInvByNum))) {
    print "Key $Part is found at location " .
      "$AllInvByNum{$Part}[0]\n";
}
```

If you want to print out the records, you can use

```
foreach $Part (sort(keys(%AllInvByNum))) {
    print "Key $Part: ",
      join("--", @{$AllInvByNum{$Part}}), "\n";
}
```

Writing the Files for Lists within Lists

If you want to keep your data that's handled in lists of lists in a file on disk, be careful how you read and write the data. Actually, the reading part isn't so difficult, but writing data that's in a multidimensional list isn't as straightforward a process as it would be if it were in a simple list.

I generally use tab-delimited files for all my data storage. Each line in the text file is an element of the top-level list. This sort of file structure simplifies reading and writing data, and I can always examine the files with a text editor if I need to troubleshoot any problems with a file.

Text files for two-dimensional lists of lists

For a two-dimensional list, you can use something like the following program to write your data to a text file:

```
# Format is location, part number, description, quantity
open(INVOUT, ">inventory.txt") or
   die "Couldn't write to inventory.txt.\n";
$NumItems = @AllInv;
for($i = 0; $i < $NumItems; $i += 1)
   { print INVOUT "$AllInv[$i][0]\t$AllInv[$i][1]\t" .
     "$AllInv[$i][2]\t$AllInv[$i][3]\n" }
```

To read the preceding database file, you can use something like this:

```
# Format is location, part number, description, quantity
@AllInv = ();
open(INVIN, "inventory.txt") or
   die "Couldn't read from inventory.txt.\n";

while(<INVIN>) {
   $TheRec = $_; chomp($TheRec);
   @NewItem = split(/\t/, $TheRec, 4);
   push(@AllInv, [ @NewItem ]);
}
```

Text files for more complicated lists of lists

If your list of lists has more than two dimensions, you have to be especially careful when you write and read the text file on which your list is based. Otherwise, you may accidentally fail to write out the data, but instead write out a Perl structure that doesn't include the data. When writing to a text file, remember to get the data for every item in the lists within the main list. For example, in the program that I presented in the preceding section, you'd use the following lines because of the additional dimensions in the list:

```
# Format is New York location, Ohio location, part number,
#   description, New York quantity, Ohio quantity
open(INVOUT, ">inventory.txt") or
  die "Couldn't write to inventory.txt.\n";
$NumItems = @AllInv;
for($i = 0; $i < $NumItems; $i += 1) {
  print INVOUT "$AllInv[$i][0][0]\t$AllInv[$i][0][1]\t" .
    "$AllInv[$i][1]\t$AllInv[$i][2]\t" .
    "$AllInv[$i][3][0]\t$AllInv[$i][3][0]\n";
}
```

To read the preceding database file, you can use the following:

```
# Format is New York location, Ohio location, part number,
#   description, New York quantity, Ohio quantity
@AllInv = ();
open(INVIN, "inventory.txt") or
  die "Couldn't read from inventory.txt.\n";
while(<INVIN>) {
  $TheRec = $_; chomp($TheRec);
  @NewItem = split(/\t/, $TheRec, 6);
  push(@AllInv, [ [ $NewItem[0], $NewItem[1] ],
    $NewItem[2], $NewItem[3],
    [ $NewItem[4], $NewItem[5] ] ] );
```

Chapter 8

Creating Cool Conditionals and Lovely Loops

In This Chapter

▶ Using comparison operators

▶ Exploring conditionals

▶ Looking at loops

▶ Stepping through list elements

*A*lmost every Perl program that you write contains an if statement. The if statement offers two simple choices: If such-and-such is true, do A, otherwise, do B. Another common programming instruction says: Loop through this code while such-and-such is true. (Examples of these types of statements include: "As long as there are more lines in this file, do this" or "While elements still exist in this list, do that.") The while statement makes looping easy because your program checks to see whether a loop is done every time it goes through a block of statements.

In this chapter, I explore the means to create highly useful conditional if statements and looping while statements by using the powers of Perl. A *conditional statement* is one that tests a condition (for example, determining whether it's true or not) and then decides what should be done based on the result of the test.

Exploring Basic Logic Statements

Before delving too far into the intricacies of if statements, you need to know a little about Perl logic. The if statement takes one argument: a logical value. Given this, the simple format of the if statement is as follows:

```
if(LOGICAL) { BLOCK }
```

The preceding statement means that if the argument (LOGICAL) is true, execute the block of statements; otherwise, just go on to the next statement after the if statement. The following is a slightly more complex form of this statement:

```
if(LOGICAL) { BLOCK1 } else { BLOCK2 }
```

This line means that, if the argument (LOGICAL) is true, execute BLOCK1; otherwise, execute BLOCK2.

Perl uses 0 (zero) for logical false and every other value for logical true. In order to generate a true or false value, you typically use Perl's comparison operators to compare two items. (Table 8-1 shows the true/false comparison operators that you use in functions.) For example, by using these operators, you can test whether one numeric variable is larger than another, whether a certain variable equals a specific value, or whether a string variable is equal to 'finished', and so forth.

It's a good idea to place comparisons within parentheses so that you can readily see what's going on in a statement.

Table 8-1	True/False Comparison Operators	
Comparison	*Math Operators*	*String Operators*
Equal to	==	eq
Not equal to	!=	ne
Less than	<	lt
Greater than	>	gt
Less than or equal to	<=	le
Greater than or equal to	>=	ge

Using the math operators

When you do a comparison, Perl returns a 0 if the comparison is false or a value other than 0 if the comparison is true.

The following example compares the values 5 and 3 using one of the math operators listed in Table 8-1. When given the following instructions,

```
$T1 = 5;
$T2 = 3;
if($T1 > $T2) { print "$T1 is greater than $T2\n" };
```

Perl displays

```
5 is greater than 3
```

If you change the values for $T1 and $T2 to 4 and 6, respectively, you get different results — namely, Perl doesn't print anything because 4 is not greater than 6 and therefore the block with the print in it is not executed.

A common mistake made with numeric comparison operators is to compare two numbers with the = operator instead of the == operator (two equal signs with no space between them). You must use the == operator in comparisons because = almost always returns true; it's not comparing anything. For example:

```
$a=3;
if($a = 7) { print "It's true!\n" }
else { print "It's false!\n" }
```

always prints

```
It's true!
```

If you replace the if($a = 7) with if($a == 7), the program works as you expect it to.

Using the string operators

To compare strings, you must use the comparison operators listed in the third column of Table 8-1. For example:

```
if($Time eq 'early') { print "It is early!\n" };
```

Most of the time, you use the eq and ne string comparison operators. However, you can also use the other operators to determine which string comes first in a comparison of the character values in two strings. (For example, *a* is less than *b*, *ad* is less than *ae*, and so on.) The ranking of each character is derived from ASCII standards, which I cover in Chapter 5.

Perl compares two strings until it finds a letter in the same position that is not equal in each, and it bases the result on that different letter. For example, in comparing *abcd* to *abxy*, Perl would find that the first two letters were identical and would make the comparison based on comparing *c* (from the first string) to *x* (in the second string).

Working with three-value compare statements

Perl also features a comparison operator that returns three different values. This operator, sometimes called a *three-value compare,* is <=> for numbers and cmp for strings. The operator returns -1, 0, or 1 if the value on the left is less than, equal to, or greater than, respectively, the value on the right. Consider the following mathematical examples:

- If $a is set to 4, 3 <=> $a would return -1.
- If $a is set to 4, 4 <=> $a would return 0.
- If $a is set to 4, 5 <=> $a would return 1.

Consider the following examples involving strings rather than numbers:

- If $b is set to Frank, 'Bob' cmp $b would return -1 because *B* is less than *F*.
- If $b is set to Frank, 'Frank' cmp $b would return 0.
- If $b is set to Frank, 'Fred' cmp $b would return 1 because *e* is greater than *a*. (The first two letters are the same.)

Linking conditional tests

You can link conditional tests together in Perl just as you would in a conventional English sentence. For example, you may say to yourself, "If I am hungry and cashews are in the cupboard; I will have a snack." This means that only if both statements "I am hungry," and "cashews are in the cupboard" are true will you have a snack; if either statement is false, you won't. Another example is "If it is Mickey or Billy on the phone, I'll take the call." In this case, if either of the two statements "Mickey is on the phone" or "Billy is on the phone" is true, then you will take the call.

Perl can handle this kind of multipart logic with ease. The two most common operators you use for if/then statements are and and or, just as you may expect. You place these operators between logical tests, and the result is another logical value.

Again, you should always use parentheses to make your programs easier to read.

The following example uses an and expression:

```
if(($Hunger >= 8) and ($Cupboard[4] eq 'cashews'))
  { print "OK, OK, you can have a small snack.\n" }
```

The following example uses `or`:

```
if(($Caller eq 'Billy') or ($Caller eq 'Mickey'))
  { print "Answer the phone already!\n" }
```

Using the not operator

You can also use the `not` operator to invert the meaning of the comparison tests. That is, the `not` operator changes the result of a test from false to true or from true to false. For example, you may say, "If it's not Saturday night, you can't have a fever." You can write such a statement in Perl like this:

```
if(not($Night eq 'Saturday'))
  { print "No fever tonight!\n" }
```

You can use `&&` instead of `and`, `||` instead of `or`, and `!` instead of `not` if you want. In fact, if you're using Perl 4, you have to use `&&`, `||`, and `!` because the `and`, `or`, and `not` operators were not introduced until the release of Perl 5.

Using the xor operator

If you use Perl 5, you can also use the `xor` operator (although typical programmers rarely use it). This operator returns true if the two items being compared have different truth values, but returns false if they have the same truth value. Another way to think of this is that the operator returns true only if exactly one of the two values is true. (See Table 8-2.)

Table 8-2	The Results of the xor Operator	
If A is	*And B is*	*Then A xor B is*
True	True	False
True	False	True
False	True	True
False	False	False

`xor` isn't that useful in daily life, but some programs have a need for it, so it's nice that Perl 5 provides it.

Working with Conditional Statements

As I mention at the beginning of this chapter, a *conditional statement* is one that tests a condition and then decides what the outcome should be based on the result of the test. In this section, I cover a few conditional tests that get a lot of mileage in Perl.

The else and elsif statements

As I note earlier in this chapter, an if statement can look something like this:

```
if(LOGICAL) { BLOCK }
```

Now, take a look at the following statement:

```
if(LOGICAL) { BLOCK1 } else { BLOCK2 }
```

If you have the second statement and the else block starts with another if, you can use an elsif clause, which means "otherwise, if this is true, execute the next block." The format of elsif may look like this:

```
if(LOGICAL1) { BLOCK1 } elsif(LOGICAL2) { BLOCK2 }
    else { BLOCK3 }
```

In the example I just listed, if the first comparison is true, Perl executes BLOCK1 and ignores the rest. If the first comparison is false but the second one is true, Perl executes BLOCK2 but not BLOCK1 and BLOCK3. If neither of the comparisons is true, Perl executes BLOCK3. In short, regardless of the form of the if statement, Perl executes only one of the blocks.

By the way, you can group a number of elsif clauses:

```
if(LOGICAL1) { BLOCK1 }
    elsif(LOGICAL2) { BLOCK2 }
    elsif(LOGICAL3) { BLOCK3 }
    elsif(LOGICAL4) { BLOCK4 }
    else { BLOCK5 }
```

You don't have to use an else statement if you've used elsif, but ending with an else is always good programming style because you're assured that all possible situations are covered.

elsif is not spelled with a second *e*. Do not use elseif or else if — Perl gives you an error message if you do.

The unless statement

If your conditional test in the `if` statement starts with `not`, you can use `unless` instead of `if`. `unless` is exactly the same as `if not`. For example,

```
if(not($Flavor eq 'banana'))
    { print "Excuse me, but I ordered banana.\n" }
```

is the same as

```
unless($Flavor eq 'banana')
    { print "Excuse me, but I ordered banana.\n" }
```

Using `unless` makes programs clearer, particularly if the logic inside the argument is already convoluted enough without the `not` statement.

Conditional operators

When you have an `if` statement that's used to determine an assignment, you may want to use the `?` operator as shorthand. The `?` operator always has a test preceding it — if the test is true, it returns the result to the right of the `?` expression; if it's false, it returns the result that's to the right of the following `:` operator. That is, the `?` operator returns the value before the `:` operator if the test is true and returns the value after the `:` operator if the test is false.

For example, if you're testing "if the texture is smooth, you should use paint; otherwise, you shouldn't use paint," you can write something like

```
if($Texture eq 'smooth') { $PaintVal = 'yes' }
else { $PaintVal = 'no' }
```

which you can then turn into

```
$PaintVal = ($Texture eq 'smooth') ? 'yes' : 'no';
```

Although the second version is a more compact way to structure this statement, it's difficult to read. Therefore, you may want to avoid using it for general aesthetic principles, because even if it works, you may not be able to remember what it does when you reread the program later.

Going Around in Loops

The `if` statement is useful when you want to conduct a test, execute one block of code if the test is true, and then move on after executing that block. However, the `if` statement can't help much if you want to loop around and keep trying the test. For example, you may want to create a program that does something like the following:

```
Look for any corners that have dirt in them. If you find
one, clean it. Keep looking and cleaning until you don't
find any more dirty corners.
```

The following is a similar example, with more of a computer bent:

```
See if there are any characters left in the string; if so,
cut off a character, do some more processing, and then
go back and see if there is anything left in the string.
```

Looping with the while statement

Perl makes it easy for you to create the kind of loops I describe in the previous section. The format of the while statement looks like this:

```
while(LOGICAL) { BLOCK }
```

The first time Perl comes across a while statement in a program, it looks to see whether the argument of the statement is true. If it's true, Perl executes the statements in the block. When it reaches the end of the block, Perl checks the while argument again; if the argument is true, Perl executes the block once more, and so on.

Avoiding infinite loops

You may be thinking, "Why in the world would I write a program that keeps looping around forever?" Good question. The answer: You wouldn't. Perl terminates while loops whenever one of the following actions occurs:

✔ Something inside the loop causes the logical test to change from true to false.

✔ The last statement in the loop is executed.

Commonly, a conditional statement inside a while loop affects the test on which the while loop is based. For example,

```
$Counter = 3;
while($Counter > 0) {
  print "$Counter ";
      $Counter -= 1;
}
print "\nI made it to zero.\n";
```

displays

```
3 2 1
I made it to zero.
```

In this example, Perl changes the $Counter variable inside the loop and performs the test each time with a new value.

Incidentally, an until statement is exactly like a while statement followed by "not" or a similar negative expression. The relationship of until and while is just like that of unless and if. The preceding program written with an until statement (and with the > operator changed to <=) looks like this:

```
$Counter = 3;
until($Counter <= 0) {
   print "$Counter ";
      $Counter -= 1;
}
print "\nI made it to zero.\n";
```

Navigating with the next and last statements

Another method for getting out of a loop is the last statement. A last statement basically says, "Jump to the end of the loop, to right after the closing brace." You can use a last statement instead of using a logical test in the while statement. For example,

```
$Counter = 3;
while(1) { # This is always true!
   print "$Counter ";
      $Counter -= 1;
   unless($Counter > 0) { last }
}
print "\nI made it to zero.\n";
```

displays

```
3 2 1
I made it to zero.
```

The next statement tells Perl to jump up to the top of the loop and perform the test in the conditional again. You often use next to avoid executing the rest of the lines in a block.

Another similar statement, redo, is rarely used. Like next, it causes Perl to jump to the top of a block but not go through the logical test, whereas next always results in a test. You're better off using last to get out of a loop at the end of a block or next to jump back up to the top.

Yet another form of the while loop exists, but it's rarely used:

```
while(LOGICAL) { BLOCK1 } continue { BLOCK2 }
```

In this case, BLOCK2 is executed after BLOCK1 but before the LOGICAL is tested for a second time. The value of constructing a statement such as this is that BLOCK2 gets executed even if you use next. You can use this treatment if you want some steps that are executed after a next or at the end of BLOCK1, such as some "cleanup" steps or steps that check to see whether any more data is left to process.

Utilizing the for statement

Although while loops are pretty useful, they aren't the end-all-be-all loop mechanism. For example, if you have a counter that increments in your loop and you use that counter for the conditional test, it may be desirable to put the test and the incrementing together in a single statement so that they are easier to see. For that task, Perl offers the foreach and for statements.

At times, you may want to use the data in a list to do some element-by-element processing. For example, if the list is a set of words in a sentence, you may want to look at each word to determine whether it matches some specific value. Or, if the list is a set of numerical measurements, you may want to determine which items in the list exceed a certain test value.

You can use while statements to step through each element in a list, but Perl offers you a simpler way to accomplish the same task — the foreach statement — which looks like this:

```
foreach $VARIABLE (LIST) { BLOCK }
```

This statement says that for each item in the list, Perl sets $VARIABLE to the value of the element and executes the BLOCK. For example:

```
@StartTimes = (25.6, 34.0, 26.7, 30.8, 32.7);
@LowTimes = ();
foreach $i (@StartTimes) {
  if($i < 30 ) {
    print "$i is a low time.\n";
    push(@LowTimes, $i);
  }
}
```

The preceding block results in the following output:

```
25.6 is a low time.
26.7 is a low time.
```

The list @LowTimes ends up with the value (25.6, 26.7).

If necessary, a foreach statement can contain a continue statement, such as the following:

```
foreach $VARIABLE (LIST) { BLOCK1 } continue { BLOCK2 }
```

Perl also offers the for statement, which lets you loop based on a counter that you initialize at the beginning, and then check and change each time through the loop. The format of a for loop looks like the following:

```
for(INIT; LOGICAL; REINIT) { BLOCK }
```

In the preceding line, INIT is a statement that is executed once before the loop begins, LOGICAL is a test just like that in a while loop, and REINIT is a statement that is executed just before LOGICAL is tested after each round through the loop (except the first).

For example, a for loop may say to Perl

```
for($i = 0; $i <10; $i +=1) { print "$i " }
```

This displays

```
0 1 2 3 4 5 6 7 8 9
```

The for loop acts exactly like the while loop but is more compactly built. For example, the format

```
for(INIT; LOGICAL; REINIT) { BLOCK }
```

is identical to

```
INIT;
while(LOGICAL)
   { BLOCK }
continue
   { REINIT }
```

To get a better idea of how the for loop works, examine the following chunk of code:

```
# hexchart.pl: Prints a decimal-to-hex conversion chart.
@HexD = ('0', '1', '2', '3', '4', '5', '6', '7', '8',
   '9', 'A', 'B', 'C', 'D', 'E', 'F');
```

```
for($i = 0; $i <= 255; $i += 1) {
    printf("%3s=$HexD[int($i / 16)]$HexD[$i % 16] ", $i);
    if(($i % 8) == 7) { print "\n" }
}
```

In this block of code, the for loop is used to count from 0 to 255, and the block itself is designed to display data. The printf statement in the block uses the value of the counter $i in its calculations, and the if statement uses $i to decide where to put in line breaks.

Perl's for loops really come in handy when you need to cycle through a limited set of values and execute a block on each. It's an efficient way of defining a loop in a single argument and allowing the associated block to do the basic processing work.

Using the map statement with lists

Another function, map, offers even more convenience than foreach in some cases. The map function returns a list based on executing either a Perl expression or an entire block on each element of a list. Note that map does not change the list in its argument: It returns a different list. (This function is available only with Perl 5 and later versions.)

If you have a single expression that you want to execute on each element of a list, you can use

```
map(EXPRESSION, LIST);
```

For example, if you want the lowercase equivalent of every string in a list, you can use

```
@LCWords = map(lc, @Input);
```

Or if you want a list that is the logarithm of all the numbers in another list, you can use

```
@Logs = map(log, @Measurements);
```

If you have a block that you want to execute on each element of a list, you would use a different format for map:

```
map { BLOCK } LIST;
```

At the beginning of the BLOCK, the Perl special variable $_ is set to the value of the element being examined. (See Chapter 13 for more info about the $_ variable.) For example, if you want to create a list of elements and put them all in lowercase, you can use

```
@AllLC = map { if(lc($_) eq $_) { $_ } } @Input;
```

You can even make this example a bit more interesting by returning the elements that are all lowercase and returning the string error for every element that isn't lowercase. To do that, you use

```
@AllLC = map
   { if(lc($_) eq $_) { $_ } else { 'error' } }
   @Input;
```

Creating switch structures in Perl 5.8

Starting with Perl 5.8, the task of making lists of conditional choices became much easier. The switch statement lets you test a variable for many different values, selecting a different action for each value. Most other programming languages have this feature, and many Perl users wondered why it took so long to appear in Perl.

A typical use of the switch statement is when you have a text variable that can have many different values. Imagine a program in which the user enters a person's name, and the program does something different based on whose name was entered. "If it is Chris, create a new record; if it is Sam, delete the first record; if it is Norm, do nothing." Instead of having to string together a bunch of if statements, the switch statement lets you make a nice, simple structure.

In order to use the switch statement, you must first include the following statement in your program:

```
use Switch;
```

After you have done that, you create a switch structure, with each choice being done with a case statement. The following short example shows how this works:

```
use Switch;

switch($manufacturer) {
   case('ford') { $type = 'car'; $color = 'blue'; }
   case('apple') { $type = 'computer'; $color = 'white'; }
   case('wiley') { $type = 'book'; print "Good choice!\n" }
   case('showtime') { die "Cannot use a cable channel\n"; }
}
```

As you can see, you can put anything inside the actions for each case statement. The variable that you use for the switch statement is usually a string, but it can also be numeric.

Using Expressions as Logical Values

The conditional and loop statements listed to this point in the chapter all use comparison statements in their arguments. Perl does not require that you use comparisons in conditional and loop statements, however. You can put anything in the argument to `if` or `while`, for example. Comparisons make the most sense to beginners because they are simple to construct, but Perl *expressions* can be used as well.

Every Perl expression returns some value. If you use an expression as an argument to a conditional or loop statement and the expression returns a value of 0 or a null string, the expression is treated as false and any returned value other than 0 is treated as true.

Using expressions in the arguments of conditional statements is a good way to make your programs more compact, although doing so sometimes affects the readability of the program. For example, if you have the conditional statement

```
if($Counter != 0) { ... some statements... }
```

you can replace it with

```
if($Counter) { ... some statements... }
```

In this case, `$Counter` being not equal to 0 is the same as `$Counter` being true, and therefore you can simply use its value in the argument to `if`.

Some Perl functions return a true value if they are successful and a false value if they are not. You can use those functions in `if`, `while`, and other statements instead of comparisons. (In Chapter 13, I describe how to write subroutines, which return values, so you can also use subroutines as logical values.)

Opening files with the open function

You use the `open` function to open text files, among other things. Programs return true if they successfully open a file and false if they don't (such as when a file can't be found). Armed with this knowledge, you can write a program like this:

```
$CheckOpen = open(DATA, "datafile.txt");
unless($CheckOpen)
   { die "The file datafile.txt could not be opened." }
```

The unless statement looks to see whether open returned a false value, and if so, unless causes the program to quit with the die statement. You can shorten the preceding three lines to

```
unless(open(DATA, "datafile.txt"))
   { die "The file datafile.txt could not be opened." }
```

You can find more info on open in Chapter 4.

Short-circuiting

In Perl, the or and and operators (and their Perl 4 equivalents of || and &&) "short-circuit" the evaluation of a statement. Perl evaluates only statements that are strung together with or or and if it must in order to determine the result of the logical expression.

The or operator and and operator are not exactly the same as || and &&, but they're close enough. Serious Perl programmers will tell you that or and and take "lower precedence" than || and && and lower precedence than many other operators. *Precedence* refers to the order in which operators are evaluated if they aren't placed within parentheses. Therefore, avoid using or and and in places in which you aren't surrounding your function arguments with parentheses. Always use parentheses to prevent any misunderstanding, regardless of the operators and functions that you use.

The or comparison is true if either the statement to the left of the or operator is true or the statement to the right of the operator is true. Therefore, the statement

```
STATEMENT1 or STATEMENT2
```

means "Evaluate STATEMENT1; if it is true, ignore STATEMENT2."

In the following open statement, Perl first evaluates open(INFILE, $TheFile). If that expression returns true, Perl doesn't even evaluate the expression on the right side of the or operator. So, a true value "short-circuits" Perl's examination of whatever is to the right of the or operator (in this case, the die statement).

```
open(INFILE, $TheFile) or die "The file $TheFile could " .
   "not be found.\n";
```

"Short-circuiting" Perl by using the and operator has similar results. Because an and comparison is true only if both sides of the comparison are true, no reason exists for Perl to look at the right side if the left side is false. Therefore, the statement

```
STATEMENT1 and STATEMENT2
```

means "Evaluate STATEMENT1; if it is false, ignore STATEMENT2." You can use this statement when you are sure you don't want Perl to execute a second statement unless the first one returns a true value.

Caveat Emptor: Jumping around Programs by Using Labels

Like most programming languages, Perl allows you to jump around your programs at will. So far in this chapter, I have shown you how to do that with conditional and loop statements. *Labels,* by comparison, allow you to jump to a named part of your program.

Using labels is generally a bad idea. I'm not saying that you should completely avoid using labels; but in general, you're better off using other Perl mechanisms because labels make your program difficult to read. Nevertheless, you may see them in programs written by people who disagree with me, and you may want to use them, but I find that they're more trouble than they're worth.

In Perl, a label is indicated by a single word followed by a colon. By tradition, labels are shown in all uppercase, but mixed case is also allowable. A label can appear before a loop statement (such as while, until, for, and foreach), or it can appear by itself before a block.

Perl programmers commonly use labels to avoid using a loop. The last or next statements inside a block redirect Perl to the beginning or end of the block, just as they do in loop statements. The last and next statements, when used with labels that tell the program where to jump to, are useful for determining whether a certain value is one of many different values and then doing something different based on each outcome.

For example, suppose that the variable $CheckID holds the ID number of a product. If that ID is one of three special values, then you'll want to print one of three different messages; otherwise, you just want to put that ID into the end of a list for later searching. This sort of program makes use of a last statement, and the program may look like this:

```
ID1CHECK: {
    if($CheckID == 101) {
    print "Supervisor's signature required.\n";
    last ID1CHECK;
    }
    if($CheckID == 121) {
    print "Backordered.\n";
    last ID1CHECK;

    }
    if($CheckID == 131) {
    print "Import duties apply.\n";
    last ID1CHECK;
    }
    # Here if everything is OK
    push(@OnHold, $CheckID);
}
```

You can also use Perl labels with the goto statement. The goto statement causes Perl to jump from wherever the statement is to the label. Some programmers will tell you to never, ever use goto. A decade or so ago, many professional programmers began to claim that unsystematic jumping with goto (or its equivalent in other languages) was inherently evil and counterproductive, and they tried to get everyone to agree. They're probably right to some degree, but I'm not absolutely set against it. Nevertheless, I recommend against using goto statements.

Another bad idea is the reset statement, which you can use in loops to reset the values of variables to their initial state. Because it's so troublesome, I'm not even going to tell you how to use a reset statement. If you see it used in somebody else's Perl program and are curious about what reset does, you can find out in Appendix A. But don't even think about using it yourself. Really.

Chapter 9

Doing Advanced Stuff with Operators and Functions

*I*f you have perused the previous chapters in this part of the book, you should have a pretty solid grounding on Perl's basic string, numeric, and list operators and statements. In this chapter, I delve into intermediate-level Perl features on a wide variety of topics that let you spread your wings a bit and explore additional programming possibilities.

Using Undefined Variables

Here's a basic rule for constructing statements in Perl: You should always define your variables before using them on the right side of an assignment. Doing so prevents Perl from inserting default values for undefined variables.

You may, however, have some good reasons for using undefined variables. For example, the pop function (covered in Chapter 7) returns an undefined value if you try to pop from an empty list. Having pop return an undefined value instead of returning a false value is preferable because false is a perfectly reasonable value for an item in a list.

Because some functions return an undefined value, you want to be able to determine whether an undefined value was, in fact, returned. You can use the defined function to accomplish this task. The defined function takes one argument, an expression, and returns true if the argument is defined and false if that argument is undefined. For example,

```
unless(defined($Yummy = pop(@Bonbons)))
    { print "There are no more bonbons left." }
```

After executing the preceding statements, the variable $Yummy contains the value popped off the @Bonbons list. But, if the list is empty, the defined function will return false, Perl will print the message about the depleted supply of bonbons, and $Yummy will hold the undefined value.

Looking for Strings within Strings

As I note in Chapter 5, strings are groups of characters. At times, you may want to examine a *substring*, which is a string that's part of a larger string.

Using the substr function

The substr function lets you view just a part of a string in many different ways. The substr function returns a string that's a substring of a larger string. Its format is

```
substr(FULLSTRING, POSITION, LENGTH)
```

The first character is at position 0, the second character at position 1, and so on. If you want to count from the right side of the string instead of from the left side, use a negative number for the position. For example:

```
$Small = substr("This is a long string", 5, 4);
print $Small;
```

displays

```
is a
```

because is a are the four letters (a space is also a letter) that start from position 5 from the left side of the string. However,

```
$Small = substr("This is a long string", -5, 4);
print $Small;
```

displays

```
trin
```

because `trin` are the four letters that start from the fifth position from the right side of the string.

You don't have to include a length argument with the `substr` function. If you leave the argument off, Perl returns everything from the position specified in the second argument to the end of the string. For example,

```
print substr("This is a long string", 5);
```

displays

```
is a long string
```

You can also use the `substr` function on the left side of an assignment to add a substring into a string. In that case, the first argument is the name of the string variable that you want to change, and the length is the number of characters that you want to delete from the full string at the position that the substring is being added. You can probably understand this function better by examining a few examples, so here goes.

To add a substring without removing anything that's already there, set the length argument to 0. For example, if you tell Perl

```
$TestStr = "Long string";
substr($TestStr, 4, 0) = "er";
print $TestStr;
```

Perl displays

```
Longer string
```

To delete some characters as you add others, set the length argument to the number of characters that you want to delete:

```
$TestStr = "Long string";
substr($TestStr, -3, 3) = "ange trip";
print $TestStr;
```

displays

```
Long strange trip
```

If you use Perl version 5.005 or later, the `substr` function has a fourth argument that lets you specify a replacement string right in the `substr` function. So, if you're working with Perl 5.005 or a later version, the previous example can be written as

```
# Works in Perl 5.005 or later only
$TestStr = "Long string";
substr($TestStr, -3, 3, "ange trip");
print $TestStr;
```

The result is the same:

```
Long strange trip
```

Using the index function

Instead of looking in a string by location, you may want to look into a string to see whether a particular substring lurks inside of it. The index function works great for this purpose. The format of the function is

```
index(FULLSTRING, SUBSTRING, POSITION)
```

The previous statement tells Perl to look for the substring in the full string, starting at the given position. If you don't specify that position, Perl starts at the left side, position 0.

Perl returns the first position at the point where the beginning of the substring is found. If the string isn't found, Perl returns -1, the position before the first position. For example,

```
print index("Will call", "ll");
```

displays

```
2
```

But note that

```
print index("Will call", "L");
```

displays

```
-1
```

Using the rindex function

The rindex function complements the index function. It returns the position of the last (that is, the rightmost) match for the string:

```
print rindex("Will call", "ll");
```

displays

```
7
```

Applying Some Fancy Formatting to Text and Numbers

The `print` statement (described in Chapter 5) is flexible, but it isn't good at restricting what it prints. For example, you may want to print a column of numbers, some of which are two-digit numbers and some of which are three-digit numbers. The following is an example of that:

```
for($i = 98; $i <= 101; $i += 1) { print "$i\n" }
```

This statement displays

```
98
99
100
101
```

However, you may want the right side of the numbers to all line up nicely, like this:

```
 98
 99
100
101
```

No easy way exists to right-align a column of numbers with the `print` statement. However, `print` has a cousin called `printf` that lets you specify a format for each argument that you print. The function looks like

```
printf(FORMAT, LIST)
```

The format is a string that tells Perl the format of the output, and the list is a list of items that will be formatted by using that string.

An almost-identical function to `printf`, the `sprintf` function, is used for assigning strings. `sprintf` returns what `printf` would have printed so that you can then assign the returned value to a string variable.

TIP

The printf function is powerful and gives you lots of flexibility in how you format your strings and numbers. Unfortunately, the strings used in formatting are not all that easy to remember. To be honest, they're downright complicated, and many Perl programmers have to look in the Perl online manual every time they use format strings. Nevertheless, you should find out how to use strings for formatting because the results are worth it.

Each format string starts with a percent sign (%). The format string consists of four parts, the first three of which are optional:

- A flag to indicate what will come before the output
- The minimum field width
- The precision
- The field type

It makes sense to examine the parts of a format string in reverse order because the last segments are the most important ones. The four parts of the format string, from last to first, are the following:

- **Field type:** Tells Perl the type of format to use. The field type options are listed in Table 9-1.

Table 9-1	Field Type Options
Option	*Description*
s	String
d	Integer
f	Real number
g	Compact real number
u	Unsigned integer
x	Hexadecimal (lowercase)
X	Hexadecimal (uppercase)
o	Octal
b	Binary (Perl version 5.6 and 5.8 only)
e	Scientific notation (lowercase)
E	Scientific notation (uppercase)
c	Single character (by value)

Table 9-1 *(continued)*

Option	Description
ld	Long integer
lu	Long unsigned integer
lx	Long hexadecimal
lo	Long octal

✔ **Precision:** (Optional) Expressed as a period (.) followed by a number. For real numbers and scientific notation, the precision is the number of digits shown after the decimal point in the resulting string. For strings, it consists of the maximum number of characters extracted from the beginning of the string.

✔ **Minimum field width:** (Optional) Tells Perl that it should pad a number or string to a certain width, which is useful for getting columns to align. For example, if you have a column of two-digit and three-digit numbers, you would set the minimum field width to 3 to get the padding on the left of the two-digit numbers. Note that if the number doesn't fit in the minimum field width given, Perl will use additional characters as needed to print the number correctly.

✔ **Flag:** (Optional) Can be one of five values. The flags are used mostly with numbers, rather than strings and characters. Table 9-2 explains the meaning of each flag.

Table 9-2   Flag Values and Their Meaning

Flag	Meaning
+	A + or - should always appear in the output.
-	Left-adjust the output (this also works with strings).
0	Pad the number with zeros instead of spaces, if needed.
#	Use the alternate form. In hexadecimal, this flag causes 0x or 0X to be placed before the number; for octal, this flag causes a 0 to be put before the number.

In addition to the flag values shown in Table 9-2, one more flag can be used. A *blank space* inserts a space before positive numbers so that they line up with negative numbers.

Got all that? Don't worry if you haven't. It becomes clearer when you see some examples. For example, the following shows how to format a real number so that only two decimal places show:

```
$TestNum = 283.357;
printf("%.2f", $TestNum);
```

This code displays

```
283.36
```

Note that Perl correctly rounded the number before truncating the extra digits. The following is a similar example, using scientific notation:

```
$TestNum = 283.357;
printf("%.2E", $TestNum);
```

This segment displays

```
2.83E+02
```

A format string can have text other than the actual format string in it. As long as your other text doesn't have any percent signs (%), Perl interprets the other characters as text to be displayed. For example,

```
$TestNum = 283.357;
printf("The answer is %.2f, give or take.", $TestNum);
```

displays

```
The answer is 283.36, give or take.
```

If you want to display a percent sign, you must use two percent signs together:

```
printf("Two thirds is about %.3f%%.", ((2/3)*100));
```

This statement displays

```
Two thirds is about 66.667%.
```

The examples so far in this section of the chapter have just a single formatted number. However, a format string can specify many values with different formats. The following statements

```
$Str = "Two thirds is about ";
$Num = (2/3)*100;
printf('%s%.3f%s', $Str, $Num, '%.');
```

are another way of displaying the string in the previous example:

```
Two thirds is about 66.667%.
```

The sprintf function works just like printf, except that it returns strings instead of printing them. For example, you may use it in a statement such as the following:

```
$Answer = sprintf("The answer is %.2f.", $TestNum);
```

The program in Listing 9-1 shows you all the different permutations of the various formats. The output of those formats is shown in Listing 9-2. The program shows a way to use printf to get two columns of text to line up when the length of the material in the first column changes. By using printf with a format of %-29s, the program forces the second column to start in position 30, regardless of what was in the first column. The program also uses a *subroutine,* which I cover in Chapter 13.

Some versions of Perl may output slightly different answers than those shown in Listing 9-2.

Listing 9-1: The entire printf.pl program is designed to output the formatting examples shown in Listing 9-2.

```
$Str = 'Dummies';
$Num = 3.141593;
$Int = 4142;
@StrFmts = ('s', '4s', '.4s', '4.4s', '10.4s',
   '10.9s', '-10.9s' );
print "The original string is \"$Str\"\n";
&OutList(@StrFmts, $Str);
@NumFmts = (
   'd', '4d', '.4d', '4.4d', '10.4d', '10.10d',
   '-4.4d', '+4.4d', ' 4.4d', '04.4d',
   'f', '4f', '.4f', '4.4f', '10.4f', '10.10f',
   '-10.4f', '+10.4f', ' 10.4f', '010.4f',
   'e', '4e', '.4e', '4.4e', '10.4e', '10.10e',
   '-10.4e', '+10.4e', ' 10.4e', '010.4e',
   'g', '4g', '.4g', '4.4g', '10.4g', '10.10g',
'-10.4g', '+10.4g', ' 10.4g', '010.4g',
);
print "\nThe original number is $Num\n";
&OutList(@NumFmts, $Num);
@HOFmts = ('x', 'X', '3x', '.3x', '3.3x', '10.3x',
   '10.10x', '#x', 'o', '#o' );
print "\nAnd a few hexa and octal examples on $Int.\n";
&OutList(@HOFmts, $Int);

sub OutList {
   local($TestStr) = pop(@_);
   local(@TestFmts) = @_;
```

```
    local(@OutFmts, $Fmt);
    foreach $Fmt (@TestFmts) {
      unshift(@OutFmts, sprintf("%s%$Fmt%s", ("%$Fmt=|",
        $TestStr, "|")));
    }
    until(@OutFmts == 0) {
      printf('%-29s%-29s%s',
        pop(@OutFmts), pop(@OutFmts), "\n");
    }
}
```

Listing 9-2: The output of the printf.pl program shown in Listing 9-1.

```
The original string is "Dummies"
%s=|Dummies|              %4s=|Dummies|
%.4s=|Dumm|               %4.4s=|Dumm|
%10.4s=|      Dumm|       %10.9s=|  Dummies|
%-10.9s=|Dummies  |

The original number is 3.141593
%d=|3|                    %4d=|   3|
%.4d=|0003|               %4.4d=|0003|
%10.4d=|      0003|       %10.10d=|0000000003|
%-4.4d=|0003|             %+4.4d=|+0003|
% 4.4d=| 0003|            %04.4d=|0003|
%f=|3.141593|             %4f=|3.141593|
%.4f=|3.1416|             %4.4f=|3.1416|
%10.4f=|    3.1416|       %10.10f=|3.1415930000|
%-10.4f=|3.1416    |      %+10.4f=|    +3.1416|
% 10.4f=|    3.1416|      %010.4f=|00003.1416|
%e=|3.141593e+00|         %4e=|3.141593e+00|
%.4e=|3.1416e+00|         %4.4e=|3.1416e+00|
%10.4e=|3.1416e+00|       %10.10e=|3.1415930000e+00|
%-10.4e=|3.1416e+00|      %+10.4e=|+3.1416e+00|
% 10.4e=| 3.1416e+00|     %010.4e=|3.1416e+00|
%g=|3.14159|              %4g=|3.14159|
%.4g=|3.142|              %4.4g=|3.142|
%10.4g=|     3.142|       %10.10g=|  3.141593|
%-10.4g=|3.142     |      %+10.4g=|    +3.142|
% 10.4g=|     3.142|      %010.4g=|000003.142|

And a few hexa and octal examples on 4142.
%x=|102e|                 %X=|102E|
%3x=|102e|                %.3x=|102e|
%3.3x=|102e|              %10.3x=|      102e|
%10.10x=|000000102e|      %#x=|0x102e|
%o=|10056|                %#o=|010056|
```

Tracking Time

All computers are good at keeping time, and Perl gives users easy access to the current time through four functions. You can include these functions in your programs for displaying the current time and date, determining how long something takes to run, displaying the age of a file, and other neat tricks.

The `time` function, which has no arguments, is the number of non-leap year seconds since January 1, 1970. (In MacPerl, it's the number of seconds since January 1, 1904.) You use this function with the `localtime` and `gmtime` functions to find out the month, day, and so on.

By itself, the `time` function isn't all that useful. For example,

```
print time;
```

prints

```
1034805216
```

(Well, that's what it printed at the time I wrote this.)

The `localtime` function takes a time as its argument and returns a list of nine elements:

- ✔ Second
- ✔ Minute
- ✔ Hour
- ✔ Day of month
- ✔ Month (January = 0, February = 1, and so on)
- ✔ Years since 1900
- ✔ Weekday (Sunday = 0, Monday = 1, . . .)
- ✔ Day of the year (January 1 = 0, January 2 = 1, and so on)
- ✔ Whether the local time zone is using daylight saving time (true or false)

The following lines demonstrate one common way to use the `localtime` function to receive information on the current time:

```
($Second, $Minute, $Hour, $DayOfMonth, $Month, $Year,
    $WeekDay, $DayOfYear, $IsDST) = localtime(time);
$RealMonth = $Month + 1;
$FullYear = $Year + 1900;
print "$RealMonth/$DayOfMonth/$FullYear";
```

displays

```
9/13/2002
```

For this program, you have to add 1 to the month before you use it in a date string. If you forget to do that (as many people do), your month will be off by 1.

The `gmtime` function returns the time as Greenwich Mean Time (as in Greenwich, England), which is the basis of standard time throughout the world.

If you want to display the date and time in a standard format (with each number in two digits), you have to use the `printf` function that I cover in the section "Applying Some Fancy Formatting to Text and Numbers" earlier in this chapter. The following statement produces that standard format:

```
printf('%02d:%02d:%02d %02d/%02d/%02d', $Hour, $Minute,
    $Second, $RealMonth, $DayOfMonth, $Year+1900);
```

displays

```
15:40:01 09/13/2002
```

If you want to use *list slices* (covered in Chapter 8) instead of explicit variable names, you can use something like the following:

```
@DayNames = ('Sun', 'Mon', 'Tues', 'Wed', 'Thur',
    'Fri', 'Sat');
@TimeArr = localtime(time);
print $DayNames[$TimeArr[6]];
```

In the chunk of code I just listed, `$TimeArr[6]` is the element that represents the current weekday and is used to pick the element out of `@DayNames` for the current weekday name.

Another time-related function is `sleep`. The argument is the number of seconds that you want Perl to take a nap. For example, if you want your program to do nothing for two seconds, you would enter

```
sleep(2);
```

When you use the `localtime` and `gmtime` functions, the year returned from those functions is the number of years since the year 1900, not the two-digit year number. This has a significant effect on the way that you program for display. Take the example from an earlier edition of this book:

```
($Second, $Minute, $Hour, $DayOfMonth, $Month, $Year,
    $WeekDay, $DayOfYear, $IsDST) = localtime(time);
$RealMonth = $Month + 1;
print "$RealMonth/$DayOfMonth/$Year";
```

Assuming that you ran the program in 1998, this program displayed

```
9/13/98
```

However, if you run the program four years later, it displays:

```
9/13/102
```

which is clearly not what you wanted it to display.

For all your programs that display year values taken from the localtime and gmtime functions, you must take into account the fact that the year returned is the number of years since 1900. You can do that in one of three ways:

- ✔ Display a four-digit year by adding 1900 to the value returned. This method causes your displayed dates to look like 9/13/1998 and 9/13/2002, which assures accuracy.

- ✔ Check whether the value returned is greater than 100, and if so, subtract 100 from the returned value. This method always gives you a one-digit or two-digit number (well, up until the year 2100, at which point you're going to cause the same problems people caused with Y2K!), but you won't know whether the time period being described is 1900–1999 or 2000–2099.

- ✔ Display a one- or two-digit year using the % operator.

I strongly prefer the first solution, because you always know which time period is being displayed. The second solution is difficult to read, so you almost never see it in Perl programs. If you insist on using the third solution, the following is some Perl code that always returns a two-digit year using the third solution:

```
($Second, $Minute, $Hour, $DayOfMonth, $Month, $Year,
    $WeekDay, $DayOfYear, $IsDST) = localtime(time);
$RealMonth = $Month + 1;
$ShortYear = ($Year % 100); # Use modulo arithmetic
printf('%02d/%02d/%02d', $RealMonth, $DayOfMonth,
  $ShortYear);
```

When you run this program now, you get a display that looks like this:

```
09/13/02
```

Picking Random Numbers

A few programming tasks require the use of *random numbers*. For example, if you use Perl to write games, you may want to create a game that involves an element of chance, such as the rolling of dice. You may also want to generate some random numbers by picking random records from a database.

The rand function returns a somewhat random real number between 0 and the argument you give to the function. (I say "somewhat random" because these aren't true random numbers; I explain the difference a little later in this section.) If you don't have an argument, rand returns a random real number between 0 and 1. For example, the following statement produces a random integer between 1 and 10:

```
$PickANumber = int(rand(10)) + 1;
```

Because rand in this example chooses a number between 0 and 10, the int function produces integers between 0 and 9. To increase the range to between 1 and 10, you add 1 to the result.

Perl's rand function doesn't produce truly random numbers. In fact, if you don't tell Perl which seed to use, Perl produces the same series of numbers each time you run Perl. (The *seed* is the first random number in the series of random values that Perl returns.) If you want numbers that look really random, you must set the seed for the random values with Perl's srand function.

The srand function takes a single argument that is used as the seed. If you don't specify an argument for srand, it uses the current value from time. For example, a program that resets the seed to the current time would look like this:

```
srand();
$PickANumber = int(rand(10)) + 1;
```

The rand function is not meant to be used in strong cryptography (that is, codes that can't be broken even with a great deal of concerted effort) or other applications that require truly random numbers. Unless you employ a foolproof method for picking the seed for srand, a clever hacker who knows that you're using Perl can figure out the random-number seed with little effort.

Shifting Bits with Bit-Level Operators

Numbers in the land of Perl are either false (with a value of 0) or true (with any value other than 0). Each bit in a byte has a value of either 1 or 0. For bits, a value of 1 translates to true and 0 translates to false. Therefore, you can think of a byte, which has eight bits, as something that holds eight true-false values. You can operate on the bits in Perl's numbers using logical operators (which I describe in Chapter 8).

The three basic bit-level logical operators for combining two numbers are | (or), & (and), and ^ (exclusive-or). You always want to use these operators on integers. Perl won't let you use them on real numbers because Perl truncates a real number before using the operators (see Chapter 6 for more information on real numbers). Normally, bit-wise logic is used on hexadecimal and octal numbers. However, Perl typically displays all numbers as real numbers, so you have to use the printf function to display your results in hexadecimal. For example, the following printf statement

```
$H1 = 0xfed0; $H2 = 0xedc4;
$Result = $H1 & $H2;
printf("The 'and' of %x and %x is %x", $H1, $H2, $Result);
```

displays

```
The 'and' of fed0 and edc4 is ecc0
```

printf is necessary in order to get Perl to print hexadecimal values. If you instead use

```
print "The 'and' of $H1 and $H2 is $Result";
```

Perl displays

```
The 'and' of 65232 and 60868 is 60608
```

Perl also employs something called a *unary bit-wise negation operator,* ~ (a tilde), which turns all 1 bits into 0, and 0 bits into 1. For example, if you write the following:

```
$H3 = 0xfed0;
$H4 = ~$H3;
printf("The negation of %x (%d) is %x (%d)",
   $H3, $H3, $H4, $H4);
```

Perl prints

```
The negation of fed0 (65232) is ffff012f (-65233)
```

The negation operator (~) and the exclusive-or operator (^) work on values that are 32 bits long. Most systems that run Perl use 32-bit integers, but not all do. This means that bit-moving logic that runs fine on one operating system may not run well on another. Some versions of UNIX, for example, go one way, while other versions of UNIX go the other.

You can shift numbers one bit at a time with the << and >> operators. These operators move a number to the left of an operator by the number of bits to the right of the operator. As you may guess, << shifts bits to the left and >> shifts bits to the right. For example, given the following lines,

```
$H3 = 0x0f30;
$H4 = $H3 << 2;
printf("The left shift of %x (%d) by 2 bits is %x (%d)",
    $H3, $H3, $H4, $H4);
```

Perl displays

```
The left shift of f30 (3888) by 2 bits is 3cc0 (15552)
```

Converting Lists to Strings

In Perl, printing data that consist of numbers and text is relatively easy. Printing lists, however, is another matter. Consider the following:

```
@Nums = (2.7, 80, 46.2);
@Strs = ("Who's", "on", "first?");
print @Nums, "\n";
print @Strs, "\n";
```

The preceding lines of code run the values in the lists together, with somewhat unattractive results:

```
2.78046.2
Who'sonfirst?
```

Because printing lists where the values don't get squished together is desirable, Perl has a nifty way to convert a list into a string with whatever characters you want between each list item. You can accomplish this task with the join function. The join function takes two arguments: the separator (which can be as many characters as you want) and the list. For example:

```
@Nums = (2.7, 80, 46.2);
@Strs = ("Who's", "on", "first?");
print join('--', @Nums), "\n";
print join(' ', @Strs), "\n";
```

gives you the following results, which read much better than the previous example:

```
2.7--80--46.2
Who's on first?
```

The `join` function is also handy for printing list elements on separate lines, as shown in the following example:

```
@Nums = (2.7, 80, 46.2);
print join("\n", @Nums), "\n";
```

The `join` function returns a string, so it's also useful outside of the `print` function. For example, to create a string that is a tab-delimited record, you can use

```
@Nums = (2.7, 80, 46.2);
$TheRecord = join("\t", @Nums);
```

Rearranging Lists

In Chapter 7, I explain how to put lists together, how to look at just parts of lists, how to pull items out of lists, and how to stuff (or splice) items into lists. Here, I describe how to rearrange the order of the elements in lists.

If I say to you, "Name two ways you may want to change the order of some of your lists," you may reply, "Reverse the order," and "Sort the items." Perl, being the versatile language that it is, has simple functions to accomplish both of these tasks.

The `reverse` function reverses the items in its argument. For example:

```
@Strs = ("Who's", "on", "first?");
print join(' ', reverse(@Strs));
```

displays

```
first? on Who's
```

As you may have guessed, you use the `sort` function to sort lists. The `sort` function returns the original list in sorted order. Perl also lets you define how `sort` will sort.

If you want to sort your list in alphabetical order, use the `sort` function with a single argument, namely, the list. For example, the following statement

```
@Strs = ('cognition', 'attune', 'bell');
print join(' ', sort @Strs);
```

displays

```
attune bell cognition
```

Another, more complicated form of the sort function lets you define the method that Perl uses to sort. This form has two arguments: a block or sub-routine that tells Perl how you want to sort, and the list itself (Chapter 13 offers more information on subroutines). In the following example, the block compares two values, $a and $b, and returns a -1, 0, or 1 depending on how $a compares with $b. The cmp and <=> operators really come in handy here. (I cover those operators in Chapter 8.)

For example, suppose that you want to sort a list of strings by their length and ignore their alphabetical order. You can use

```
@Strs = ('cognition', 'attune', 'bell');
print join(' ', sort { length($a) <=> length($b) } @Strs);
```

which displays

```
bell attune cognition
```

If you were using sort with subroutines, the previous example would look something like the following:

```
sub lensort { length($a) <=> length($b) }
@Strs = ('cognition', 'attune', 'bell');
print join(' ', sort lensort @Strs);
```

Part III

The Nuts and Bolts of Perl

"We're here to clean the code."

In this part. . .

The chapters in this part describe some of the intermediate techniques that you need to know in order to put together even more useful and versatile Perl programs. You can find out about reading and writing files and directories, searching strings in incredibly interesting ways, and using subroutines to make your programs more modular.

Chapter 10

The Files Go In, The Files Go Out

*W*hen you use a computer, it's easy to take seemingly simple things for granted. For example, consider your electronic files. You probably think of them as merely "those things on my disk." They have names, they have stuff in them, and that's about it. But, as you may suspect, the whole business of managing files is complex — complex enough that I devote an entire chapter of this book to it.

In the following pages, I tell you how Perl handles files and how file handling is related to lots of other areas of Perl programming. After you read this chapter, you'll be able to write programs that read text files for information and write text files that contain your program results. For example, you may want to write a program that reads a text file and writes out the same file in a different format. With Perl, you can accomplish this task by typing just a few lines.

Understanding Perl File Types

In general computer terms, a *file* is an ordered set of bytes stored on disk and given a filename. The bytes in a file are ordered so that you know where the beginning and end of the file are; the file is stored on disk so that you can retrieve it later and it's given a filename so that you can access the exact file you want.

For most computer users, this definition covers it. However, Perl's roots in UNIX complicate matters a bit. UNIX files don't have to reside on a disk; they can consist of any stream of ordered bytes that a program can access. You can view program output or a stream of data coming in from a network as a file in Perl. (To see some pretty snazzy things that you can do with special files that don't reside on disk, check out the section "Moving File Streams in UNIX: Standard In, Standard Out, and Standard Error," but for now, just think of files as disk files.)

As for what's inside a file, the bytes in a file can have any value. The contents of a file are relevant only to the programs that read that file. That is, you may not care about the contents of a file that you don't read, but that file may be valuable to other programs that run on your computer.

You can divide files into two broad categories based on their contents: *text files* and *binary files.* No hard-and-fast rules exist for separating the two kinds of files. Text files contain values that you can see on-screen, such as letters, digits, and punctuation, as well as the special characters for spaces, carriage returns, line feeds, and tabs. Text files are typically human-readable, although many text files are meant to be read by programs. Binary files are not human-readable because they contain nonprinting characters; they almost always are meant to be read solely by programs.

You should know the difference between text and binary files because Perl has some handy features that apply only to text files. Because so many of the files that Perl programmers need to read are text files, Perl makes text file handling as easy as possible. This isn't to say that handling binary files is difficult, but if you know that a file is a text file, your program for reading from and writing to that file will be shorter and easier to read than a program meant to handle binary files.

Opening and Closing Files

Whether you want to read from or write to a file, you must first open it. Every operating system has a different way of opening files, but Perl takes care of the differences among Windows, Mac, and UNIX systems without the user needing to worry about the technical differences. Regardless of your operating system, you can use Perl's open statement in the same way. The format of open in Perl version 4 and version 5 is

```
open(HANDLE, FILENAME);
```

Giving a file a handle

The *handle* is a name that you use in a program to talk about a file. File handles are shown in Perl programs without any special characters in front of them. The naming rules for file handle names are the same as the rules for variable names (see Chapter 3).

It has become a Perl convention to use all uppercase letters for file handle names.

For example, the following is a typical `open` statement:

```
open(INFILE, 'sample.txt');
```

It's also common to use a variable to hold the filename, and to use that variable as the second argument to `open`:

```
$TheFile = 'sample.txt';
open(INFILE, $TheFile);
```

In both these cases, the file handle is `INFILE`. This is an arbitrary choice; you can name your file handles whatever you want, as long as you follow the rules for variable names that I cover in Chapter 3.

Reading, writing, or appending: Choosing a file opening mode

When you open a file, Perl needs to know what you want to do with it: You can open a file for reading, writing, or appending. If you want to program with files, you must understand the differences among the following three tasks:

- ✔ **Opening a file for reading:** You read a file to look through it and not change its contents in any way. You can read a file in any order, but people usually read from beginning to end. Of course, you can only read from a file that already exists.

- ✔ **Opening a file for writing:** You open a file for writing when you want to enter new information into a file. You can write to a new file, which is how you create a file, or you can write to an existing file, in which case you immediately delete everything that's already in the file. Opening a file for writing is like starting fresh, whether anything exists in that file or not.

✔ **Opening a file for appending:** You open a file for appending when you want to write into a file, but only at the end of it. This process differs from opening a file for writing in that appending doesn't wipe out the current contents; it only amends it. You can open a new file for appending, which is the same as opening it for writing because you're adding to the "end" of this new file in both cases.

You *cannot* read and write to a file at the same time. At first, you may be frustrated by this fact, but a good reason exists why you can't do both simultaneously. If you write into some part of the file and then attempt to read it near the place where you wrote, Perl isn't sure whether it should read strictly what is on disk (that is, before you just wrote to the file) or whether it should read what is on disk plus what you just wrote. Perl is absolutely sure of what you want to read only if you write out what you want to disk.

You have to tell Perl in the open statement which of the three modes (reading, writing, or appending) you want to open the file in.

In Perl version 4 and version 5, Perl looks at the first character or two of the filename you give it and determines the open mode from that. For example:

✔ **To read a file:** Precede the name with < (because reading a file is the default mode when opening a file in Perl, you can also safely leave off the < character, if you prefer).

✔ **To write a file:** Precede the name with >.

✔ **To append to a file:** Precede the name with >>.

Here are some examples of filenames that determine how a file is opened:

```
open(INFILE, '<sample.txt'); # For reading
open(INFILE, 'sample.txt'); # Also for reading
open(INFILE, '>sample.txt'); # For writing
open(INFILE, '>>sample.txt'); # For appending
$TheFile = '>sample.txt'; # Prepare for writing
open(INFILE, $TheFile); # This will open for writing
```

In Perl version 5.6 and 5.8, a new method for using the open statement uses three arguments instead of two. The syntax for the statement is

```
open(HANDLE, MODE, FILENAME);
```

The MODE argument is the prefix that you added to the filename, as described in the preceding section. So, instead of using the following code:

```
open(INFILE, '>sample.txt'); # For writing
```

you could use this code:

```
open(INFILE, '>', 'sample.txt'); # For writing
```

The two forms are equivalent, and I expect that almost all the Perl programs you see for a very long time will use the first form (the one with two arguments).

Determining whether a file really opened

The open statement returns a value of true if Perl successfully opens the file. For reading a file, open returns true if the file exists and is readable. For writing or appending a file, open returns true if the file can be written to. If the file exists and you're attempting to open it for writing, it must not be set to "read only" in the operating system; otherwise, the open statement returns a value of false.

A file doesn't have to exist to be written to, but you can't always create a file that you can write to; for example, you may not have permission to write to the directory in which the file is located.

If an open statement doesn't work, it returns a false value. This is the catalyst for the "open or die" statements contained in the sample programs in Chapters 3 and 4. This type of statement translates to "quit the program immediately if the open statement fails."

Using files after they're opened

After you open a file, all the other Perl statements that you use on that file have the file handle as an argument. Specifically, you use the file handle and not the filename in an open statement because not every Perl file has a name. Also, file handles are usually much shorter than filenames:

```
open(THEDATA, "C:\EMPLOYEE\DATA\NAMES.DB");
```

You can have multiple files open in a single program. In fact, it's quite common to have two or more files open if your program converts a file into a new file. In that case, your program would have open statements near the beginning of the program that look like this:

```
open(ORIG, 'original.txt') or die "Can't open input.\n";
open(NEW, '>new.txt') or die "Can't open output.\n";
```

In the previous example, the rest of the statements in the program would then use the `ORIG` file handle when reading from the file being converted and the `NEW` file handle when writing into the new file.

Closing files

After you finish processing a file, you can close it with Perl's `close` statement. If you forget to close a file, it's no big deal: Perl closes all open files when a program ends. The `close` statement takes one argument, the file handle of the file that you want to close:

```
close(ORIG);
```

Close a file that you opened for writing or appending as soon as you're done with it because Perl won't necessarily write out the last part of the file to disk until the file is closed. If another program opens the file for reading before you've closed the file, that program may think the file is shorter than you intend it to be because Perl hasn't written out the last part. Always use an explicit `close` for any file that you are writing or appending, just in case your computer crashes before the program finishes.

Specifying Filenames and DirectoryPaths for Various Operating Systems

Most of the filenames in this book are generic enough to work on every operating system (the various versions of Windows, Mac OS, and UNIX). Perl allows you to use any name that's valid in the operating system you use. However, each operating system has different rules for naming files. For example, the following `open` statement works on a Mac under Mac OS 8 and 9, but not on Windows because Windows filenames can't have a slash (/) character:

```
open(EITHER, "This/that");
```

Chapter 13 explains how Perl searches in different directories for files that you include with the `require` statement. The `open` statement doesn't search for files, however. You must give an explicit path to the file in the filename; otherwise, Perl looks only in the current directory for that file. For example, if you want to read a file by using the statement

```
open(IN, 'jan97.dat');
```

that file must be in the directory from which you started Perl, or Perl won't be able to find the file.

Fun with Mac's Open command

Now it's time for Mac lovers to gloat a bit. You probably know how to specify a file by its name. MacPerl also lets you specify a file's name with the standard file interfaces that you use with the Open and Save commands in every Mac program. (ActivePerl should have features for this, but doesn't yet.)

To create a filename string using the Mac interface, you must include the library called StandardFile.pl. Therefore, the following statement must appear near the beginning of your program:

```
require 'StandardFile.pl';
```

The StandardFile.pl library contains subroutines called `GetFile` and `PutFile`. You use `GetFile` for the same reason you use the Open command in programs: to select a file. You use `PutFile`, on the other hand, like you would the Save command in programs: to choose a folder and to enter a name for the file that you want to save.

The arguments for the `GetFile` and `PutFile` subroutines are a bit confusing, but luckily you can safely use these subroutines with no arguments. For example, to get the full filename for a file that already exists, you can use something like the following statements (which have no arguments):

```
$InFile =
    StandardFile::GetFile();
open(INPUT, $InFile);
```

In order to get the name of a file that the user wants to create from that user, you can write something like this:

```
$NewText =
    StandardFile::PutFile();
open(TEXTOUT, ">$NewText");
```

To explicitly state the default directory that you want to be in, use Perl's `chdir` function. The `chdir` function takes one argument — a string with the name of the directory that you want. For example, on Mac OS X and UNIX, you may use

```
chdir('/usr/bin/accounting/data');
```

The `chdir` function returns false if Perl can't change to a specified directory, so you should always check the value returned. For example, the following statement checks to see whether the `chdir` was successful:

```
chdir('/usr/bin/accounting/data') or die "Could not " .
   "change to the accounting data directory.\n";
```

If you use the `open` statement to open a file for writing or appending and don't specify the directory into which you want to write the file, you should make a note of which directory you're in before opening the file. If you're in a directory other than the one you want, you may unintentionally wipe out or alter a file that you didn't mean to touch. At a minimum, you may have a hard time later finding a file that you created if you're not sure what directory you were in.

The way that you specify directories in the various operating systems differs. Under Windows, you must use the drive letter followed by a colon, and then the directory names separated by a backslash character (\):

```
open(IN, "D:\ORDERS\DATA\JAN97.DAT");
```

On Mac OS 9, you must use the disk name and folder names separated by colons:

```
open(IN, "Main:Order entry:Data files:January 1997 data");
```

On UNIX, you must use the standard path name to a file, with the directory names separated by a slash character (/):

```
open(IN, "/usr/home/orders/data/jan97.dat");
```

You can use *relative references* rather than absolute filenames. A relative reference refers to a directory relative to the current directory. For example, under Windows and UNIX, the directory named . . indicates the directory above the current directory. On a Mac, you specify the folder above the current folder with two colons (: :). For example, you can specify that you want to open for writing the process.log file in the directory above the current directory with the following code:

```
open(PLOG, '>..\process.log'); # for Windows
open(PLOG, '>::process.log');  # for the Mac
open(PLOG, '>../process.log'); # for UNIX
```

Reading from a Text File the Easy Way

Perl offers you an economical way to read text files. The *file input operator* returns a line from a named text file. By "a line," I mean all the text up to and including the next line separator. The first time that you use the file input operator on a file handle, Perl returns the first line of text. The next time you use the file input operator on the same file handle, you get the next line, and so on until there is no more text to be read from the file.

The file input operator consists of angle brackets around the name of a file handle. For example, in the following statement, the file handle INFILE is surrounded by the file input operator:

```
while(<INFILE>) {
    . . .
}
```

Imagine that you have a text file that contains the following information:

```
What I Did Over Summer Vacation
I wanted to go to the park and play ball a lot, but my
mother made me read a bunch of boring books instead.
The first one I read was about a dumb programming language
. . .
```

If this file has the handle IN, the first thing returned by <IN> is the string
What I Did Over Summer Vacation\n (that's a single linefeed character at
the end of the string). The next item returned by <IN> is the single character
\n, then I wanted to go to the park and play ball a lot, but
my\n, and so on.

Every string returned by the file input operator ends in a line terminator.

You have two ways to get the result of the file input operator. One is to assign
a string to the input, such as in the following statement:

```
$ThisLine = <INPUT>;
```

The other is to use Perl's $_ special variable, which gets assigned by the file
input operator.

You typically see the file input operator in Perl programs as part of while
loops. For example, here is a little Perl program that prints a file:

```
open(A, "somefile.txt");
while(<A>) { print $_ }
```

Many programmers also assign $_ to a variable in the first statement inside
the while loop:

```
while(<INPUT>) {
   $ThisLine = $_;
   chomp($ThisLine);
   . . .
}
```

If you intend to use the line you got from the file input operator in more than
one statement, you should immediately assign $_ to a variable and use that
variable instead of $_ because another statement may wipe out $_ and put in
its own results.

The while(<HANDLE>) syntax is very handy because it accomplishes a few
things at once. The file input operator always returns a true value as long as
text is left in the file. As such, the while statement gets a true value when
text is in the file and a false value as soon as no additional text remains to be
read in the file.

For some programs, you want to use both a variable assignment and a loop with the file input operator. For example, if you're not sure that the file you're opening is the right one, check the first line before processing the file by using something like this:

```
open(THEFILE, $FileName);
$FirstLine = <THEFILE>;
unless($FirstLine eq "What I Did Over Summer Vacation\n")
  { die "This is not the right file.\n"}
while(<THEFILE>) {
  $Line = $_;
  . . .
}
```

In scalar context (see Chapter 7), Perl reads one line and puts it into the variable. In list context, Perl reads the *entire* file into a list in one step. Therefore, you should avoid using the file input operator in list context in a loop because everything happens in one call (instead of needing the loop).

A simple file printing program, using the list context, would look something like this:

```
open(A, "somefile.txt");
@B = <A>; # reads the whole file
print @B;
```

You can also use a `while` loop to read each element of the list:

```
open(A, "somefile.txt");
@B = <A>; # reads the whole file
while($Line = shift(@B)) { print $Line }
```

The previous two programs accomplish the same thing — @B is filled with the lines of the file, one line per element. However, you can't use the following statement to fill @B because the `shift` function doesn't put the value it received into `$_;`:

```
while(shift(@B)) { print $_ } # This is WRONG
```

The file input operator is intended for use with text files only — and not binary files. The operator actually works just fine with binary files, but the file input operator is slower than the binary file statements described in Chapter 11.

Writing Text to a File the Easy Way

After you know how to read text from a file, you'll probably want to learn how to write it to a file. The `print` and `printf` statements have a format that enables you to put strings into a file instead of on-screen:

```
print HANDLE LIST;
printf HANDLE FORMAT LIST;
```

You do *not* put a comma after the file handle.

For example, the following program creates a file with ten lines in it:

```
open(OUT, '>lineout.txt') or die "Couldn't open the " .
   "lineout.txt file for writing.\n";
for($i = 1; $i <= 10; $i += 1)
   { print OUT "This is line $i\n" }
```

The previous program doesn't display anything. Instead, it creates a file called `lineout.txt` whose contents are simply

```
This is line 1
This is line 2
```

and so on through `This is line 10`.

The `printf` statement produced similar results in the same context. For example, the following program

```
open(OUT, '>lineout.txt') or die "Couldn't open the " .
   "lineout.txt file for writing.\n";
for($i = 1; $i <= 10; $i += 1)
   { printf OUT "This is line %.2d\n", $i }
```

creates a file with these lines:

```
This is line 01
This is line 02
```

and so on through `This is line 10`.

As a special bonus, you discover in Chapter 11 that you can use `print` and `printf` to write to binary files as well. Not bad, huh?

When used without file handles, the `print` and `printf` statements print to the screen. (Actually, they print to the *standard output*, which is described at the end of this chapter in "Moving File Streams in UNIX: Standard In, Standard Out, and Standard Error.") When you want to print to a file, normally you use that file's handle in the print and printf statements. However, Perl lets you change where Perl will print when you don't use the file handle.

The select statement, which you can see in the following sample program, tells Perl to cause print and printf to start printing to the specified file handle (but not to the screen):

```
open(OUT, '>lineout.txt') or die "Couldn't open the " .
  "lineout.txt file for writing.\n";
select(OUT);
for($i = 1; $i <= 10; $i += 1)
  { printf "This is line %.2d\n", $i }
```

The printf statement writes to the lineout.txt file because of the select statement.

The select statement returns the file handle that it's replacing. Using the select statement makes it easy to use one file handle temporarily and then switch to using a different one. The following statements show switching between two file handles, FH1 and FH2:

```
select(FH1);
print "This will go to the file with FH1.\n";
$TempHandle = select(FH2);
print "This will go to the file with FH2.\n";
select($TempHandle);
print "This will go to the file with FH1.\n";
```

You should try to avoid using select for the following reason: If you use it and later in the program forget that you did, you may wonder why a print statement doesn't result in anything being shown on-screen. (Of course, that's true for what happens when you forget almost anything in a Perl program!) The only advantage that select gives you is that the print and printf statements are a bit shorter, but that isn't worth the confusion that it may cause.

Running Tests to Get Information on a File

In addition to reading and writing text files, you may also want to get some information on a file before you open it. Perl has a number of test functions that enable you to determine whether a file exists, how long it's been since the file was created or last updated, the file's size, and other characteristics of the file. The file tests are written in this form:

```
-X FILENAME
```

Here, X represents the specific test, and FILENAME is, as you may guess, represents the name of the file. (All the file test names are a hyphen followed by a single letter.)

The file tests take filenames, and *not* file handles. There's a good reason for this: You may want to test a file before opening it. Or, you may want to test a whole slew of files because it takes less time to run simple file tests than to open and close several files.

For example, the -w test is used to find out whether you can write to a file. When used in a program, it appears like this:

```
if(-w 'somefile.txt') { open(CLIST, '>somefile.txt') }
```

The most widely used file tests also happen to be common to all operating systems. Table 10-1 lists the file tests that return true or false. By the way, the stat function (covered in Chapter 11) returns values for many of the file characteristics that are tested.

Table 10-1	Common File Tests
Test	*What It Tells You*
-e	File exists.
-r	File can be read.
-w	File can be written to.
-z	File is exactly 0 bytes long.
-d	Named item is a directory, and not a file.
-T	File is a text file. (A portion of file is examined, and if fewer than approximately 30 percent of the charac ters are nonprintable, it's a text file. In Perl version 5.6 and 5.8, this test checks for UTF-8 text, as described in Chapter 5.)
-B	File is a binary file. (A portion of file is examined and if fewer than approximately 30 percent of the charac ters are printable, it's a binary file.)

Some file tests make sense only on UNIX and Mac OS X because they address aspects of UNIX that have no equivalent on Windows or the Mac. Table 10-2 lists the UNIX-specific tests; they all return true or false values. (Some of these make sense on Windows NT, but they aren't yet implemented in ActivePerl.)

Table 10-2	UNIX-Specific File Tests
Test	*What It Tells You*
-x	File can be executed.
-o	File is owned by the effective user of the running program.
-R	File is readable by the real user of the running program.
-W	File is writeable by the real user of the running program.
-X	File is executable by the real user of the running program.
-O	File is owned by the real user of the running program.
-u	File has its setuid bit set.
-g	File has its setgid bit set.
-k	File has its sticky bit set.

Some file tests return numbers. For example, the -s test tells you the size of a file. -C, -A, and -M tell how long it's been (in days) since the file was created, accessed, or updated. The values returned by these three tests are measured from when the program started (see Table 10-3).

Table 10-3	File Tests That Return Numbers
Test	*What It Tells You*
-s	Size of the file in bytes
-C	Creation age of file
-A	Access age of file
-M	Modification age of file

The tests listed in Table 10-3 are useful for programs that are supposed to execute on files that are older than a certain age. For example, if you write a backup program that checks whether a file has been modified in the past 12 hours, you can write something like the following:

```
if((-C $TheFile) < 0.5) { &BackupThis($TheFile) }
```

File tests used for more advanced levels of programming are listed in Table 10-4, but are rarely used, even by high-powered Perl programmers. I list them here just in case you run across them in Perl programs that other programmers have created.

Table 10-4	Advanced Programming File Tests
Test	*What It Tells You*
-f	Named item is a plain file (not a special file or directory).
-l	Named item is a symbolic link.
-p	Named item is a pipe.
-S	Named item is a socket.
-b	Named item is a block special file.
-c	Named item is a character special file.
-t	Named item is a file handle that is opened to a terminal.

Moving File Streams in UNIX: Standard In, Standard Out, and Standard Error

Perl's roots in UNIX show up at times I wish they wouldn't. A case in point is the UNIX *standard file* descriptors, which are methods for displaying and receiving data. Although most experienced UNIX jockeys are able to use these descriptors effortlessly, lots of other folks have trouble making heads or tails of them.

The concept of *standard file input/output (I/O)* runs throughout file handling with Perl. Understanding standard file input and output is useful for getting ahead in Perl. UNIX, and Perl by extension, defines a *file* as an ordered stream of bytes that can be identified by the operating system. The stream can be from any input process (such as keyboard entry or reading from a disk file) to any output process (such as an on-screen display or writing to a disk file).

Distinguishing the big three file streams

Three file streams have special properties in Perl — *standard file in, standardfile out,* and *standard file error* (you can also drop the "file" part and call them *standard in, standard out,* and *standard error*). They're also often referred to by the abbreviations STDIN, STDOUT, and STDERR. These streams constitute a system's standard file I/O because they are universal to all UNIX implementations.

✔ STDIN: The byte stream associated with a keyboard, which means that when you type something while a Perl program is running, what you type becomes the contents of STDIN.

✔ STDOUT: The byte stream that is sent to your computer screen. When you write to STDOUT, it's like saying, "Instead of writing to a file, write to the screen."

✔ STDERR: A bit more complicated than the other two properties, it's a defined file stream, but different operating systems handle it differently. For example, most versions of UNIX display characters sent to STDERR on-screen, just as STDOUT does. However, you can also tell UNIX to send error messages to a file instead of to the screen. This technique comes in handy when you want to keep a log of error messages, but not one for the regular text displayed on-screen.

Perl lets you use STDIN, STDOUT, and STDERR as predefined file handles. This means that you don't have to use open to name these file handles. For example, you can say

```
$GetALine = <STDIN>;
```

The previous statement causes Perl to wait for you to type something followed by an end-of-line character on the keyboard; it then assigns what you entered to the $GetALine string.

If you want to print to STDERR instead of STDOUT, you can use something like the following statement:

```
print STDERR "Bad user input.\n";
```

Perl allows you to use the empty file input operator, <>, instead of <STDIN>, if you don't give arguments on the program's command line. In this case, <> means "all the files listed on the command line." This can be pretty darn confusing, and you may want to avoid using <> because of it.

Piping data in and out of a program

UNIX allows you to use something called *pipes* to give a stream of bytes (that is, a file) to a program, or take a stream of bytes from a program, through the standard file input and output. You can use pipes in Perl's open statement.

A program that uses STDIN to take in data can also take in data through a pipe. A program that puts out its data on STDOUT can output its data through a pipe. The pipe acts as a conduit for data going from one source to another.

For example, UNIX's `uptime` program displays how long a system has been up and its load averages. The `uptime` program displays these statistics by sending them to `STDOUT`, so you can capture this information with a Perl `open` statement that has a pipe from `uptime` to a file handle:

```
open(UPIN, 'uptime |');
```

This `open` statement tells Perl to run the `uptime` command and take its `STDOUT` output and feed it into the `UPIN` file handle. `uptime` outputs only a single line, and you can read it with something like this:

```
$UptimeInput = <UPIN>;
```

For UNIX programs that output many lines, you can use a `while` loop just as you would for reading from actual files. For instance, the following example program can be used to find out which directories exist under the `/tmp` directory on your system:

```
open(LSIN, 'ls -l /tmp | ');
while(<LSIN>) {
   $TheLine = $_;
   chomp($TheLine);
   if(substr($TheLine, 0, 1) eq 'd') {
     $LastSpace = rindex($TheLine, ' ');
     $DirName = (substr($TheLine, $LastSpace +1));
     print "$DirName is a directory\n";
   }
}
```

(You will see in Chapter 11 another way to process directories.)

You can also use pipes to write to other programs, although this is done infrequently. A few UNIX programs can take input from `STDIN`; for example, the `mail` program allows you to send mail with the message coming from `STDIN`. You can create a program like the following, which sends mail that's created in a Perl program:

```
$MTo = 'someone@someplace.com';
$MSubject = 'Data from the accounting program';
open(DOMAIL, "| mail -s $MailSubject $MTo");
print DOMAIL <<"EndOfMessage";
Your department has a balance of $DeptBal.
If you have questions about this, please send mail
to accounting@someplace.com.
EndOfMessage
```

The rule for using pipes in `open` statements is this: When piping *from* a `print` statement, put the pipe to the left of the UNIX command; when piping *to* a file handle, put the pipe to the right of the UNIX command.

Chapter 11

Beyond File and Directory Basics

· ·

· ·

*T*his chapter covers a zillion (give or take a few million) things about files — such as what to do if you want to read or write to a nontext file, how to change file characteristics and statistics, and how to deal with directories. (For more basic information about dealing with files, see Chapter 10.)

Reading from and Writing to Binary Files

As I note in Chapter 10, to read a text file line by line, you can use the *file input operator* (the name of the file handle enclosed in angle brackets), as shown in the following statement:

```
$TheLine = <ACCTFILE>;
```

In some cases, the file that you want to read from may not be a text file: It may be a binary file. In this case, you must use a set of functions that enables you to read from any part of any file so that you can access just the part of the file that you want. (Incidentally, you can also use these functions on text files.)

To read from a binary file, open it by using the open statement just as you would with a text file, and then use the read function to read from the file. The format of the read statement is

```
read(HANDLE, VARIABLE, LENGTH, POSITION);
```

The first argument, HANDLE, is the handle name (handles are covered in Chapter 10) from which you want to read; the second argument, VARIABLE, is the place that you want to read into; LENGTH is the number of bytes to read; and POSITION is the byte in the file from which you start reading. Perl uses 0 as the position for the first byte in a file.

For example, to read the first seven bytes from a file that has the handle ACCTDATA, you use the following statement:

```
read(ACCTDATA, $Start, 7, 0);
```

The read statement returns the number of bytes actually read. That number comes in handy when you don't know the length of a file, but you want to know whether you've accidentally read beyond the end of the file. For example, if you tell Perl to read 7 characters with the read function and Perl tells you that it has read only 5 characters, you know that you haven't read off the end of the file. For example, you can detect whether you've read to the end of a file by using something like this:

```
$NumGot = read(ACCTDATA, $Start, 7, 0);
if($NumGot < 7)
  { print "You read off the end of the file.\n" }
```

Keeping track of your position in a file

Perl keeps track of where you read in a file compared to the beginning of the file. For instance, after the read function in the example in the previous section, Perl sets the file position keeper for the ACCTDATA file handle to 6, which is the position in the file that was last read. You can use the eof function to test whether the next read starts at the end of the file. The eof function returns true if the pointer is at the end of the file. (By the way, *eof* is dweeb-speak for *end of file*.)

The following example demonstrates the use of the eof function in an until loop that is reading data:

```
unless(eof(ACCTDATA)) {
  $NumGot = read(ACCTDATA, $Start, 7, 0);
  if($NumGot < 7)
    { print "You read off the end of the file.\n" }
}
else { print "Already at end of the file.\n" }
```

eof won't tell you if you're near the end of a file, only if you're *at* the end of a file. That's why you need to check how many characters you receive with each read to be sure that you don't receive fewer characters than you expected.

The seek statement enables you to place the file position keeper anywhere you want. Its format is

```
seek(HANDLE, RELATIVEPOSITION, FROMWHERE);
```

The third argument in the previous seek statement determines the starting point of the relative position of the second argument: a FROMWHERE of 0 means that the second argument is relative to the beginning of the file; 1 means that the second argument is relative to the current file position; and 2 means that the second argument is relative to the end of the file. So, to move the position keeper forward 12 positions, you would use

```
seek(ACCTDATA, 12, 1);
```

Or, to move the position keeper to the second byte in the file, you would use

```
seek(ACCTDATA, 1, 0);
```

The file position keeper is useful because you don't always have to remember how far you've progressed if you're reading through a file from start to finish. You can leave the last argument off the read function, and Perl uses the file position keeper instead. For example, to read a file ten bytes at a time until the end of the file, you can use the following code:

```
seek(ACCTDATA, 0, 0); # If it wasn't at the beginning
while(read(ACCTDATA, $Start, 10)) {
  # $Start is now the next ten bytes of the file
  # If this is the last chunk of the file, it might
  # be less than ten bytes long, however.
}
```

If you want to know the current location of the file position keeper, use the tell function. For example:

```
$FilePos = tell(ACCTDATA);
```

Writing to a binary file

So, you use read to read from a binary file: What do you use to *write* to a binary file? If you said write, you're wrong. Perl's write function has nothing to do with writing to a binary file. Instead, you use print with a file handle, as described in Chapter 10.

To write nontext data to a file by using the `print` function, you can employ functions such as `chr` and certain special characters (see Chapter 5). For example, to write the five characters whose values are 23, 97, 192, 12, and 0, you can use something like the following:

```
@PrintThese = (23, 97, 192, 12, 0);
foreach $Item (@PrintThese) { print ACCTDATA chr($Item) }
```

Forcing binary reads

The Windows operating system treats binary files differently from text files. If you're running Perl on Windows and you use the `read` function, you must first use the `binmode` function so that Perl can tell the operating system to do binary reads (yes, this is incredibly annoying, but unfortunately a necessity in some cases). You call the function in this way:

```
binmode(FILEHANDLE);
```

Using `binmode` in the programs in which you employ the `read` function won't cause errors, even on operating systems other than Windows. If you later copy a Perl program to a less-intelligent operating system (that is, a Windows-based system), you don't have to remember to search through your programs for `read` functions because you've already covered yourself by including the `binmode` function.

Reading one character at a time

Another method exists for reading characters from a file, but I have to warn you, it's very slow. The `getc` function returns the next character from a named file; if you're at the end of the file, `getc` returns the null character. For example, the following program reads a character and checks whether you're at the end of the file:

```
$TheChar = getc(ACCTDATA);
if($TheChar eq '') { print "At the end of the file.\n" }
```

Changing File Characteristics

Perl gives you complete access to doing anything with your files within your programs. For example, you can rename or delete a file from a Perl program while you work in the program or run a program. Not all programming languages give you this luxury.

Hacking off the ends of files

In a slash-and-burn mood? The `truncate` function tells Perl to whack off the end of a file. The `truncate` function takes two arguments: the name or file handle of the file and the abbreviated length of the file. For example, to make the `nowshort.txt` file exactly 100 characters long, and to tell Perl to discard whatever is in the file beyond that point, you can use this:

```
truncate('nowshort.txt', 100);
```

Renaming files

The `rename` function takes two arguments: the old name and the new name. It returns true if successful at renaming the file. The following example program renames a file and checks to see whether the rename worked:

```
unless(rename('somedata.txt', 'somedata.old'))
  { print "The rename failed.\n" }
```

The `rename` function comes in handy for changing file extensions. (In Windows, file extensions are significant in defining a file. For example, double-clicking a file that has a `.txt` extension causes Windows to do something completely different than double-clicking a file that has the `.exe` extension.) Suppose that you want to change the current extension of a file to `.old`. If the filename is kept in `$FileName`, you can use the following program to accomplish that:

```
$PeriodPos = index($FileName, '.');
if($PeriodPos == -1) { $BareName = $FileName }
else { $BareName = substr($FileName, 0, $PeriodPos) }
$NewName = "$BareName.old";
rename($FileName, $NewName);
```

Changing file access and modification times

To change the times that your computer thinks that a file has been accessed or modified, you can use the `utime` function. The function takes as its argument a list in the following format:

```
(ACCESSTIME, MODIFICATIONTIME, FILE1, FILE2, ...)
```

For example, if you want to change the access and modification time of a file to the current time, you can use

```
$Now = time();
utime($Now, $Now, 'somedata.txt');
```

Deleting files

You can use the unlink function to delete a file. This peculiar function name comes from the way that UNIX deletes files from a directory — by unlinking them from the directory structure. The unlink function takes a list of the names of the files that you want to delete and returns the number of files deleted. For example, the following statement attempts to delete two files, a.dat and b.dat, and prints a message if either or both files aren't deleted:

```
unless(unlink('a.dat', 'b.dat') == 2)
    { print "One of the files didn't get deleted.\n" }
```

UNIX users beware: The unlink function doesn't delete a file if it has multiple links to it. The function simply removes the single link for that file in the named directory or in the current directory. A file isn't really deleted from the system until you remove all links to the file.

Grouping Filenames by Matching Characters

Perl 5 introduced a humorously named feature called *file globbing*. It enables you to create a list of files easily, based on matching characters in filenames. With the glob function, you can use an asterisk (*) as a wildcard character just as you can in Windows or UNIX file commands.

For you Mac OS users who haven't had the pleasure of working with Windows or UNIX, the asterisk wildcard character is used to match one or more other characters in filenames. When you search for files in a directory, you can match one or more files by using the asterisk in your test filename to indicate that you want to find any file that has one or more other characters in that place.

For example, imagine that you have a directory with five files whose names are

- ✔ chartab1.pl
- ✔ counter1.pl
- ✔ edata.txt

✔ empdata1.pl

✔ hexchart.pl

Searching for the file c* matches `chartab1.pl` and `counter.pl` because both filenames start with the letter *c* and have one or more characters after the c in the filename. Similarly, searching for *pl matches `chartab1.pl`, `counter.pl`, `empdata1.pl`, and `hexchart.pl` because all these files have one or more characters followed by the letters *pl*.

In a similar fashion, the `glob` function returns a list of files in the current directory that matches the text argument. For example, to get a list of all the files that start with the letter *m*, you can use

```
@XFiles = glob('m*');
```

The results of the `glob` function can be used to process groups of files that you know have similar names. For example, suppose that you want to delete all the files in a directory that have `.tmp` at the ends of their names. The following statement accomplishes that:

```
unlink(glob('*.tmp'));
```

Suppose that you want to create one big file that contains the contents of every file that starts with the letters *flow*. You'd enter something like this:

```
open(BIG, ">bigflow");
@AllFlow = glob('flow*');
foreach $FileName (@AllFlow) {
  open(IN, $FileName);
  print "Inserting the file $FileName\n";
  print BIG <IN>;
  close(IN);
}
close(BIG);
```

File Features Strictly for UNIX Users

Perl was originally created for UNIX system administrators, and many aspects of the UNIX system are meaningful to only those folks. Nevertheless, some of Perl's file features are useful to UNIX users who at least know how to navigate the UNIX file system and use UNIX file commands. (If you want to find out more about UNIX, I recommend *UNIX For Dummies,* 3rd Edition, by John R. Levine and Margaret Levine Young, published by Wiley Publishing, Inc.)

Working with Perl's version of chown and chmod

You UNIX folks may be familiar with the chmod and chown commands in UNIX; they change file access privileges and the owner of a file, respectively. Perl has its own chmod and chown functions that act like the UNIX commands.

The chmod function takes a list as its argument. The first item of the list is the numerical permission that you want on the files, and the rest of the list is the files that you want changed. For example, to make a file readable and write-able by a file owner and group, with no permission granted to others, you can use the following statement:

```
chmod(0660, 'somefile', 'someotherfile');
```

If you're not familiar with numerical permissions under UNIX, avoid using the chmod function, because changing the permissions can make a file unavail-able to you unless you change the permissions again with chmod.

Most UNIX systems display the numeric file permissions in octal, and you can use these permissions directly in chmod. The octal value 0660 in the previous example looks pretty cryptic, just the way UNIX systems folks like it. Unfortunately, Perl's chmod function doesn't enable you to use the alphabetic file permissions such as "rw-rw——". Alphabetic file permissions are more readable than the octal values because you don't have to do an octal conver-sion in your head.

The chown function also takes a list as its argument. The first item in the list is the numeric user ID, the second item is the numeric group ID, and the rest consists of the files that you want to change:

```
chown(100, 12, 'somefile', 'someotherfile');
```

Creating links with functions

The UNIX file system enables you to create filenames that are nothing more than links to other files on a computer. If you're a UNIX user and familiar with symbolic links, you can use Perl to create both hard links and symbolic links. The link and symlink functions take two arguments: the existing file and the link that you want to create.

The link function is similar to the UNIX command ln with no arguments, and symlink is like the UNIX command ln -s. For example, to create a new file in the current directory, TheLog, that is a symbolic link to the /var/log/mail-log file, you can use

```
symlink('/var/log/maillog', './TheLog');
```

The `readlink` function, whose argument is a filename, returns the value of a symbolic link. The value of the link is the name of the file to which the symbolic link connects. For example, to see the name of the file to which the symbolic link TheLog is linked, you can use

```
print readlink('./TheLog');
```

Getting the Nitty-Gritty Stats on Files

You can find information on file tests that return a true or false value on a number of file characteristics in Chapter 10. Perl also makes it possible to get the information that you'd obtain through individual file tests all at once in a list.

The `stat` function takes either a file handle or a filename as its argument, and returns a wealth of information about a file. The `stat` function returns a list whose elements are shown in Table 11-1. Most of the returned elements have no meaning except on UNIX, as you can see.

Table 11-1	Information Returned by the stat Function
Element	*Information Returned*
0	Device number (UNIX only)
1	Inode number (UNIX only)
2	Inode protection mode (UNIX only)
3	Number of links to the file (UNIX only)
4	User ID of owner
5	Group ID of owner
6	Device type (UNIX only)
7	File size (in bytes)
8	Time of last access (seconds from OS base time)
9	Time of last modification (seconds from OS base time)
10	Time of last file status change (seconds from OS base time)
11	Optimal block size (UNIX only)
12	Number of blocks allocated for the file (UNIX only)

If you're on UNIX and examining a file that's a symbolic link, the lstat function returns the information on the file to which the function's argument is linked, and not the link itself. This is useful if you want the real file information, and not just the information about the link (which itself is a file).

The following is an example of how to use the stat function to determine the size of a file.

```
@FileStuff = stat(MYFILE);
$TheSize = $FileStuff[7];
```

Working with Directories of Files

At times, you may want to process an entire directory at once, instead of dealing with individual files. Perl offers a set of functions that handles directories similar to the way that files are handled. Instead of examining characters in a file, however, they examine the files in a directory.

The directory functions use directory handles as arguments. *Directory handles* are similar to file handles except that you use them for directories (see Chapter 10). Directory handle names must adhere to the same rules as file handle names and are used in generally the same way.

Opening directories

You tell Perl to start processing a directory by using the opendir statement, which functions like the open command for files. (Perl also has an equivalent closedir function.) An opendir statement takes two arguments: the name of the directory handle that you want to use and the name of the directory that you want to open. For example:

```
opendir(DOCS, 'C:\TREES\DOCS');
```

You can also open directories relative to the current directory. In that case, you use just the directory name, and not the full path to the directory. For example, to open the directory called Nancy relative to the current directory, you can use

```
opendir(TEMP, 'Nancy');
```

To open the current directory, you can use the special directory name "." on UNIX and Windows and ":" on Mac OS. To open the directory above the current one, you can use the special directory name ".." (or "::" on a Mac). For example, to open the current directory in UNIX or Windows, you can enter

```
opendir(TEMP, '.');
```

Returning filenames in a directory

The readdir function, when used in a scalar context (with strings or numbers), returns the next filename or subdirectory name in the directory. For example:

```
$ThisName = readdir(DOCS);
```

When used in a list context, readdir returns all the filenames and subdirectory names at once in a list. For example:

```
@AllNames = readdir(DOCS);
```

The telldir function returns the value of the directory position keeper. The seekdir changes the position of the directory position keeper.

The three directory functions readdir, telldir, and seekdir are similar to read, tell, and seek for files (see Chapter 10), except that readdir can return only one filename, whereas read can read one or more characters.

The rewinddir function sets the directory position keeper to the beginning of the directory list.

One catch in using the directory functions is that you can't tell when you get to the end of a directory except by checking to see if readdir returns a null string. Unfortunately, no directory equivalent of the eof (end of file) function exists. Therefore, using readdir in a list context causes readdir to return all the filenames at once into your list.

Walking through directories

The readdir function returns the names of files or subdirectories in a seemingly random order. The order in which files and subdirectories are returned is the order assigned by the operating system, which is usually neither alphabetical nor related to size.

The readdir function returns both filenames and subdirectory names. On UNIX and Windows systems, it also returns the special directory entries "." and ".." (Mac OS users don't have to concern themselves with this). So, when you look through the results of a readdir statement, don't automatically assume that what you have is a filename.

Suppose that you want to find out the total size of every file in the current directory. You can use something like the following program:

```
opendir(HERE, '.'); # Mac OS users would use ':' instead
@AllFiles = readdir(HERE);
$TotSize = 0;
foreach $Name (@AllFiles) {
  if(-d $Name) { next } # It's a directory: skip it
  $TotSize += (-s $Name); # Add its size to the total
}
```

Or, you may want to know the names of the subdirectories of a directory. In which case, you can use a program like this one:

```
opendir(HERE, '.'); # Mac OS users would use ':' instead
@AllFiles = readdir(HERE);
foreach $Name (@AllFiles) {
  if(-d $Name) { print "$Name\n" }
}
```

Creating and destroying directories

Two directory functions, mkdir and rmdir, are used, respectively, to make or delete a directory. Neither function uses directory handles; instead, they use directory names. Both functions return true if they're successful, and false if they aren't.

The mkdir function takes two arguments: the name of the directory that you want to create and a mode. The mode is relevant only on UNIX systems and is ignored on Windows and Mac OS. On UNIX, the mode consists of the read and write permissions for the directory (the settings that say whether you can read from or write to that directory). You can see mkdir at work in the following statement:

```
mkdir('subdir', 0770);
```

To delete a directory, use rmdir, which takes one argument: the name of the directory to delete. For example:

```
rmdir('subdir');
```

Chapter 12

Stringing Along: Pattern Matching and Regular Expressions

. . . .

In This Chapter

▶ Examining regular expressions

▶ Searching for strings within strings

▶ Changing text selectively

▶ Modifying matches

▶ Determining the results of the matches

▶ Translating strings into other strings

. . . .

*P*erl uses a *regular expression* as a consistent means of finding specified text in a program. You can use a regular expression in many ways. For example, you can search through strings for tab characters and turn them into line breaks, or change every instance of two spaces into one, or make sure that every period has a space after it. You can even quickly determine whether a string contains a particular letter.

With all these tasks, Perl first searches for text in a string and then does something with the text (such as copy it to a variable). This kind of searching is called *pattern matching* because you give Perl the pattern of characters that you're looking for, and it finds all the text that matches that pattern.

Different programming languages and operating systems have their own methods for enabling you to say, "I want to specify some text that I'm looking for." Perl uses UNIX's regular expressions for this kind of searching. (You UNIX users may already know how to specify searches, or at least you have been exposed to it.) Because regular expressions come from the murky world of UNIX, many people find them difficult to understand, but this chapter helps you grasp how they're used to simplify text handling in your programs.

In this chapter, I first describe the simple (yet powerful) regular expressions that you can use in your everyday Perl programming. Later on, I describe other regular expression features that you can use in your more advanced programming efforts.

Working with Regular Expressions

Regular expressions turn up in a number of Perl programming applications. For example, consider the split function (which you can read about in Chapter 7 and later in this chapter in "Using the split Function with More-Advanced Regular Expressions"). The split function takes a regular expression as its first argument. The function searches through a string for a particular substring and then splits the string into smaller strings anywhere that the substring is found. You express split arguments with a slash (/), followed by the specific text to be found, and another slash, as shown in the following statement:

```
@TheFields = split(/\t/, $TheRecord);
```

In the preceding example, the regular expression is \t. This line of code returns a list of strings that are found in the $TheRecord variable, where each string is the text between tab characters (\t indicates a tab). Therefore, if $TheRecord contains the word "Speakers", followed by a tab character, the numeral 2, another tab character, and the word "High", the split function in this example returns a list with three values: "Speakers", "2", and "High".

The simplest kind of regular expression consists of the exact character or characters that you want to search for, such as the single tab character in the previous example. You can also place more than one character between the slashes in the argument. For example, suppose that you have a database in a text file in which you use three pound signs (###) between fields instead of a tab character. In which case, you would change the split statement to the following:

```
@TheFields = split(/###/, $TheRecord);
```

Conducting true-false searches with the m// operator

When you get the hang of using regular expressions, the m// operator comes in handy because it enables you to write small programs to test strings. The m// operator returns true or false, depending on whether the operator finds what is being tested for. (Because most programmers use a slash [/] character at the beginning and end of their regular expressions, the m operator is written as the m// operator instead.)

The m// operator is followed by the regular expression that you want to test and preceded by the =~ operator (called the *binding* operator). The binding operator tests the expression against something that is entered to its left. For example, to test whether the string *abc#def* contains the string #, you can use the following:

```
if("abc#def" =~ m/#/)
   { print "True\n" } else { print "False\n" }
```

Running this statement prints True on your screen.

You can also place variables on the left side of the =~ operator. For example,

```
if($Test =~ m/#/)
   { print "True\n" } else { print "False\n" }
```

results in True being printed if the $Test string contains one or more # characters.

You may also want to generate a true value if the pattern that you're searching for is not found. To get a positive result if the searched-for pattern is not found, use the !~ operator instead of the =~ operator. For example, to determine whether no # character exists in a string, you can use something like the following:

```
if($Test !~ m/#/) # If there is no hash character...
   { print "True\n" } else { print "False\n" }
```

You can use variables in your search. In the following line of code, if $Find contains the string that you want to search for, and $Test is the string that you want to search within, you can enter

```
if($Test =~ m/$Find/)
```

Watch out for patterns that are equivalent to the *null string* (that is, a string of zero length) in the patterns that you search for. If the pattern that you give is the null string, Perl uses the value in the special variable $_ as the search pattern, and you may have no idea what's in $_ at the time (see Chapter 10 for more on the special variable $_). If you use a variable as the search pattern, make sure you know what's in that variable first.

Tightening up your statements

Perl has to know where your regular expressions begin and end. More programmers use a slash (/) than any other character to signal the beginning and end of expressions, also known as *delimiting*. (Because almost every Perl program I've seen uses the slash character, that's my choice, too.) However, you can delimit your regular expression with any character, such as a vertical bar (|) for example:

```
if($Test =~ m|#|) . . .
```

Although you can use any character for delimiting, you may want to stick with the slash character because it enables you to use the short form of the m// operator (which most Perl programmers do). If you use the slash character, you don't have to include the m:

```
if($Test =~ /#/) . . .
```

To make your statements even more compact, if you're searching in Perl's special variable $_, you don't need the =~ operator at all. The file input operator <> puts the next line of the file into $_ (see Chapter 10 for more on file input operators). So, you may use something like this:

```
while(<INFILE>) {
   if(/Proprietary/) { # The line has the keyword
   . . .
```

Accounting for those special metacharacters

Regular expressions frequently use special characters that you may also want to search for. For example, the vertical bar (|) has a special meaning in a regular expression. If you want to search for a vertical bar and ignore its special meaning, you have to precede the vertical bar with a backslash (\). So to search for a vertical bar character, you have to construct something like this:

```
if($Test =~ /\|/) . . .
```

Sure, this statement looks kind of goofy, but it's the only way to tell Perl not to treat the vertical bar as anything special. Now you may be asking, "How do I search for a backslash?" Good question, same answer: Precede it with a backslash:

```
if($Test =~ /\\/) . . .
```

Characters that have special meaning to Perl are called *metacharacters*. The following metacharacters require the backslash treatment that I just described when you want Perl to disregard their special significance:

```
^ $ + * ? . | ( ) { } \ [ ]
```

Add slash (/) to this group of metacharacters if you use it as a delimiter for your regular expressions.

How about some cruel and unusual punishment? Determine whether a string has the pattern "slash, backslash, vertical bar, slash, vertical bar, backslash, caret" in it. Give up? Try this:

```
if($Test =~ /\/\\\|\/\|\\\^/) . . .
```

If you're not sure whether a string has metacharacters in it, you can use the *quotemeta* function available in Perl 5 and later versions. The quotemeta function takes a string and returns a string with backslashes in front of its metacharacters. For example,

```
print quotemeta('ab/cd|ef');
```

displays

```
ab\/cd\|ef
```

Making Inexact Matches in Regular Expressions

At times, you may not know the exact characters that you're searching for when you're writing your program. For example, you may be searching for "the letter *x* or the letter *X*," or "one or more hash characters," or even "a hash character followed by any other character followed by a hash character." Regular expressions make these imprecise character matches fairly easy to do.

Alternating matches

To indicate that you want to match either one character or another, insert a vertical bar (|) between the characters that you want to match. This technique is called *alternating* because you give Perl a list of alternate choices to look for. For example, to search for either *x* or *X*, you use the following statement

```
if($Test =~ /(x|X)/) . . .
```

which matches exactly one *x* or *X* in the $Test variable.

Enclosing similar items in parentheses

Just as you would with a numeric equation (which I cover in Chapter 6), you can enclose a group of related items in your regular expression with parentheses in order to group them together. You can have more than one kind of item in a regular expression, such as a fixed expression and an alternating list. For example, to search for the words *candle, candy,* and *candid,* you use

```
if($Test =~ /can(dle|dy|did)/) . . .
```

Matching characters by using a wildcard

If you don't know which character that you want to match, you can use a period (.) as a wildcard character. For example, if you want to match the letter *N* followed by any character followed by the letter *T,* you can use the following statement:

```
if($Test =~ /N.T/) . . .
```

In this example, the statement returns true for NET and N3T and N+T, but returns false for NEST (because NEST has two characters between the *N* and the *T*). This statement returns false for *net* because regular expressions are case-sensitive and therefore distinguish between uppercase and lowercase characters.

The period wildcard matches any character, printable or not, other than \n. Therefore, the wildcard won't match across a line break but does match anywhere else.

Matching character classes

Regular expressions can also match *character classes,* which are lists of individual characters to be matched. To specify a character class, you enclose the characters in square brackets (instead of parentheses) and list the characters. For example, to match *x* or *X* with a character class, you can use this statement:

```
if($Test =~ /[xX]/) . . .
```

To indicate that you want to match any character *not* in a particular range, insert a caret character (^) in front of a list of characters in that range. For example, to match any character that's not one of the first five capital letters, you can use

```
if($Test =~ /[^ABCDE]/) . . .
```

Character classes are structured more compactly and are easier to read than an alternating list when you're searching for many single characters, such as "any digit." For example, the following statement is the *alternation* version (that is, the list of alternates) of a search for the numerals 0 through 9:

```
if($Test =~ /(0|1|2|3|4|5|6|7|8|9)/) . . .
```

Using a character class, the previous statement looks like this:

```
if($Test =~ /[0123456789]/) . . .
```

Character classes can be specified as ranges by using a hyphen (-). So, the "any digit" example that I just provided can be simplified even more:

```
if($Test =~ /[0-9]/) . . .
```

If you want to test for "any uppercase or lowercase letter," you use the following:

```
if($Test =~ /[A-Za-z]/) . . .
```

Note that a range indicated with a hyphen is different than a range indicated with the *range operator* (..) described in Chapter 7, which is used to create a list of numbers.

Because ranges are frequently used in Perl, you should make use of a couple of shortcuts so that you don't have to specify the actual range. These shortcuts (see Table 12-1) are somewhat like the backslash codes used for special characters (such as \t for the tab character) that I describe in Chapter 5, except that they indicate a range to be matched.

Table 12-1	Shortcuts for Character Ranges	
Code	*Replaces*	*Description*
\d	[0 – 9]	Any digit
\w	[a – zA – Z_0- –]	Any alphanumeric character
\s	[\t\n\r\f]	A whitespace character
\D	[^0 – 9]	Any nondigit
\W	[^a – zA – Z_0 – 9]	Any nonalphanumeric character
\S	[^\t\n\r\f]	A nonwhitespace character

Given the shortcuts listed in Table 12-1, you can reduce your "any digit" search statement to the following:

```
if($Test =~ /\d/) . . .
```

You can test for "A capital letter followed by two digits" by using this:

```
if($Test =~ /[A-Z]\d\d/) . . .
```

Note that this test will return true for any string that contains a capital letter followed by two digits, and not just a string that has only those three characters. Thus, "B56" and "AB56" and "aB56" will all return true.

To find a word that has three letters (meaning three alphanumeric characters that are preceded by and followed by a whitespace character), you use the following:

```
if($Test =~ /\s\w\w\w\s/) . . .
```

Searching the Beginning or End of a String

At times, what you want to match in a string is at the very beginning or end of a string. In this case, you use a caret (^) to indicate the beginning of the string and a dollar sign ($) to indicate the end. For example, to see whether a string starts with Beg, use the following statement:

```
if($Test =~ /^Beg/) . . .
```

This statement wouldn't find the string "I Beg Your Pardon" because it doesn't start with Beg.

To match in a string that ends with don, for example, use

```
if($Test =~ /don$/) . . .
```

Using the $ character to indicate the end of a string may result in a big surprise if you don't know about newline characters. If the last character in the string is the newline character, $ forces the search to occur only at the end of the line. Therefore, if the variable $Test is either "I Beg Your Pardon" or "I Beg Your Pardon\n" (without or with a newline character), searching for don$ returns true.

Perl enables you to specify that a search should start at a *word boundary* (the point between an alphanumeric and a non-alphanumeric character, for example) by using the \b character combination. The \b code is useful for finding text at the beginning of a word. For example, to determine whether a word in a string starts with the letter *Y,* you can use

```
if($Test =~ /\bY/) . . .
```

Or, to find the letter *J* at the end of a word, you can use

```
if($Test =~ /J\b/) . . .
```

The \B code indicates the opposite of the \b code: a location that's not within a word boundary (that is, in the middle of a word).

Using Quantifiers for Numerical Matches

What happens when you want to match an unknown number of repetitions of a string? For example, suppose that you want to find one or more hash characters (pound signs) in the string abc#def. You can use the following statement:

```
if("abc#def" =~ /#|##|###|####/) . . .
```

Using exact strings like the one in the previous example isn't a general enough usage for many applications that you want to write. Instead, you can use other special characters outside of the slashes to indicate how many copies of what's inside the slashes to match on. Characters used for this sort of counting are called *quantifiers* because they enable you to tell Perl the number of times that a string can exist before it is matched. (See Table 12-2 for a list of the quantifiers.)

For example, to search for one or more hash characters, you use

```
if($Test =~ /#+/) . . .
```

Or, to search for exactly three digits, you use

```
if($Test =~ /\d{3}/) . . .
```

Table 12-2	Pattern-Matching Quantifiers
Symbol	*Meaning*
+	Match 1 or more times
*	Match 0 or more times
?	Match 0 or 1 time
{n}	Match exactly n times
{n,}	Match at least n times
{n,m}	Match at least *n* but not more than *m* times (these values must be less than 65,536)

You can combine quantifiers with character classes to do some pretty fancy stuff (see "Matching character classes" earlier in this chapter for information on character classes). For example, to search for a word that ends in a digit, you can use

```
if($Test =~ /\w+\d/) . . .
```

This statement translates to "search for one or more alphanumeric characters followed by one digit."

The most frequently used quantifier in regular expressions is the + quantifier. You can also put the * quantifier to good use. Consider the following line of code:

```
if($Test =~ /N.T/) . . .
```

The previous line matches NET but doesn't match NEST because NEST contains one too many characters. This line doesn't match NT either because NT has one too few characters. (The single . character must match a single character.)

If you want to match *N* followed by *one or more* arbitrary characters, followed by *T*, you can use

```
if($Test =~ /N.+T/) . . .
```

The previous line matches NET and NEST and NEATEST, but not NT.

If you want to match *N* followed by *zero or more* arbitrary characters, followed by *T*, you would instead use

```
if($Test =~ /N.*T/) . . .
```

This line matches NT, NET, NEST, and so on.

Getting the Match Results

With open-ended matches, it's nice to find out precisely what is in fact matched. For example, if the following statement

```
if($Test =~ /N.*T/) . . .
```

returned true, it may be useful to know which string or strings actually matched.

To get the results of a test, use *grouping parentheses* in the regular expression and then check Perl's special variables $1, $2, $3, and so on. Grouping parentheses indicate the exact point in a regular expression where the matching should be done. Consider the following program:

```
$Test = 'NESTING';
if($Test =~ /(N.*T)/)
  { print "True\n" } else { print "False\n" }
print "$1\n";
```

When you run this program, Perl displays

```
True
NEST
```

$1 matches the result of the first set of parentheses, $2 matches the result of the second set, and so on. For example, when you run the following program

```
$Test = 'NESTING';
if($Test =~ /(N.)S(.I)/)
  { print "True\n" } else { print "False\n" }
print "$1\n$2\n";
```

Perl displays

```
True
NE
TI
```

Perl's greedy matching

Some of you are probably asking, What's in the string that Perl returns when you have more than one match? For example, what can you expect Perl to print when you run the following program?

```
$Test = 'NITWITS';
if($Test =~ /(N.*T)/)
   { print "True\n" } else {
   print "False\n" }
print "$1\n";
```

The answer is this:

```
True
NITWIT
```

By default, Perl always uses a method that is affectionately called *greedy matching*. It's greedy because it matches as much as possible on the

first try. Perl sees quantifiers as an open invitation to get greedy.

You can suppress Perl's greedy ways by following a quantifier with a question mark (?). Perl then matches the shortest possible string instead of the longest string. For example, note the following small change to the second line of the previous program:

```
$Test = 'NITWITS';
if($Test =~ /(N.*?T)/)
   { print "True\n" } else {
   print "False\n" }
print "$1\n";
```

The slight change results in different output:

```
True
NIT
```

If, for some odd reason, you want to suppress $1 or $2 to prevent them from getting assigned, add a ?: after the left parenthesis (this method only works with Perl 5 and later versions):

```
$Test = 'NESTING';
if($Test =~ /(?:N.)S(.I)/)
   { print "True\n" } else { print "False\n" }
print "$1\n";
```

When you run this program, Perl displays

```
True
TI
```

More Programming Magic with the m// Operator

Many functions and operators, including the m// operator (which returns true or false depending on whether the operator finds what it's looking for) work hand-in-hand with regular expressions. In the following sections, I show you how the m// operator can be employed with regular expressions.

The m// operator when used in a *scalar context* returns true or false depending on whether a string is matched. In *list context,* however, the m// operator returns a list of the strings matched in the parentheses. Using m// in list context is essentially like creating a list that contains the special variables $1, $2, and so on. For example, the following program demonstrates how to create the list @Birds as a result of m// search:

```
$Test = 'NESTING';
@Birds = ($Test =~ /(N.)S(.I)/);
print join("\n", @Birds);
```

When you run this program, Perl displays

```
NE
TI
```

If no grouping parentheses are used in the regular expression, Perl returns the list (1) — a list with a single true value in it.

Using m// operator modifiers

The m// operator uses modifiers that change the way m// searches in some respects (see Table 12-3). The modifiers follow the closing slash character, such as the i modifier that follows the / in the following:

```
if($Test =~ /(N.*T)/i) . . .
```

Table 12-3	Modifiers for m//
Modifier	*Description*
g	Returns each occurrence (global search)
i	Ignores case
m	Allows multiple lines in the string
o	Compiles the pattern once
s	Treats the pattern as a single line
x	Allows whitespace for comments

The m, s, and x modifiers are available in Perl 5 or later versions.

The i modifier forces Perl to ignore case when searching. For example, if $Test is "nest", the statement

```
if($Test =~ /(N.*T)/i) . . .
```

would be true.

The o modifier prevents Perl from using variable substitution in the pattern that you're searching when the value of the variable changes. Using the o modifier allows your program to run slightly faster, but prevents you from using variable substitution in the pattern. Generally, the speed increase gained by using the o modifier is slight, relative to the speed of the whole program.

The x modifier enables you to add spaces, line breaks, and text comments in your regular expressions as a way of making them more readable. You usually need to add spaces and breaks to complex regular expressions only. For example, instead of saying

```
if($Test =~ /(N.)S(.I)/) . . .
```

you can write the following, which is clearer:

```
if($Test =~ /
    (N.) (?# Start with N and any letter)
    S (?# ...followed by the letter S)
    (.I) (?# ...followed by another letter, then I)
    /x) . . .
```

On the other hand, I don't think that these kind of comments make most regular expressions more readable than a regular Perl comment on the line before them. So, it's up to you whether you want comments to precede the regular expression or whether you want to place your comments in the regular expression.

Doing global searches in the m// operator

The g modifier causes Perl to do a global search on a string. This may sound odd because Perl is supposedly already searching the whole string. The term *global* as it's used here, however, refers to the way that Perl returns different results based on the g modifier.

In a list context, Perl returns a list of the strings matched using parentheses. But, if the regular expression (which is N in the following example) contains no parentheses, Perl creates a list of each matched item as shown here:

```
$Test = 'NESTING';
@Birds = ($Test =~ /N./g);
print join("\n", @Birds);
```

When you run this program, Perl displays

```
NE
NG
```

Getting a list is a handy way to find all the matching strings if you don't know how many you'll have.

In scalar context, Perl returns true and false for each match in the string. Perl remembers where in the string it found the last match and starts from there for the next search. Performing m// searches in a scalar context is a good method for determining how many matches exist without looking at the matches. The following example shows how you can examine the number of matches without looking at the matches themselves:

```
$Test = 'NESTING';
$i = 0;
while($Test =~ /N./g) { $i += 1 }
print "There were $i matches.\n";
```

You can use the pos function to determine where Perl is going to start the next global search in scalar context. The argument to pos is the string that you're searching in. For example,

```
$Test = 'NESTING';
$i = 0;
while($Test =~ /N./g) {
   $i += 1;
   print "Now at " . pos($Test) . ".\n";
}
print "There were $i matches.\n";
```

When you run this program, Perl displays

```
Now at 2.
Now at 7.
There were 2 matches.
```

If you want to change the point at which Perl starts searching the string, you can set the starting position in the string to any number that you want. For example, to start searching two characters farther ahead than the current position, you can say

```
pos($Test) += 2;
```

Searching for multiple lines in a string

The ^ and $ characters match the beginning and end of a string. But, you may want ^ to match the beginning of lines and $ to match the end of lines in a string that has more than one line in it.

In Perl 4, to get ^ and $ to match the beginning and end of each line in a string, set the $* special variable to 1 before the test. By default, $* is set to 0, so ^ and $ match the beginning and end of the string, and not lines in the string.

In Perl 5 and later versions, you can use the m modifier in a regular expression in order to get ^ and $ to match the beginning and end of each line in a string. For example, this statement finds a tab character at the beginning of any line in the string.

```
if($Test =~ /^\t/m) . . .
```

You can use the special characters \A and \Z in a regular expression to indicate the beginning and end of a string and whether or not the m modifier is used. That is, these characters always mean "the string" and not "the line."

Using the grep Function

If you want to do a search for the same regular expression within every element in a list, the grep function is what you need. This function takes two arguments: a regular expression or a block, and a list. It then evaluates the regular expression or block on each element of the list and looks for true and false results.

The name of the grep function comes from a handy UNIX utility of the same name. The UNIX command's name was derived from the acronym for *global regular expression and print*. Perl's grep function doesn't print, but because it checks the regular expression globally on each item in the list, it's good enough to be called grep.

In a list context, grep returns the elements from the list for which the regular expression or block returns true; in scalar context, it returns the number of elements that return true. For example, suppose that you want to look through the list @LastNames for every name that starts with the letter *S*. To get the actual names, you can use the following statement:

```
@JustSNames = grep(/^S/, @LastNames);
```

To merely find out how many names start with *S*, you can use

```
$TotSNames = grep(/^S/, @LastNames);
```

The `grep` function also enables you to use a block instead of a regular expression as the first argument to the function. In this case, the special variable `$_` is set to the value of the list element being tested. (This is similar to the `map` function described in Chapter 8.) For example:

```
$TotSNames = grep({/^S/}, @LastNames);
```

As you become more comfortable with regular expressions, you can find many uses for `grep`. For example, if you've read all the lines of a file into a list by using a statement such as the following,

```
@TheFile = <INFILE>;
```

you can then create other lists that contain certain kinds of lines. With the following statement, you can create a list of all the lines that have a whitespace character at the end of the line:

```
@RealLines = grep(/\s$/, @TheFile);
```

Doing Simple Substitutions with the s/// Operator

The `s///` operator acts much like the `m//` operator, except that you specify the replacement for the found string. You put the replacement between the second and third slashes. The `s///` operator returns the number of times that it substituted the second string for the first string. It takes the same modifiers as the `m//` operator.

Suppose that you want to change all the lowercase *e* characters in a string to uppercase *E:*

```
$Count = ($Test =~ s/e/E/g);
```

A slightly more complex exercise involves changing all the vowels in a string to the letter *V:*

```
$Count = ($Test =~ s/[aeiouAEIOU]/V/g);
```

As with the `m//` operator, if you don't use the `=~` operator before the `s///` operator, Perl assumes that it's working on the special variable `$_`. The following is an example of using `$_` as input to the `s///` test:

```
while(<INFILE>) {
  s/\t/|/g; # Change the tabs to vertical bars
  . . .
}
```

You can use variables in either part of the s/// operator. For example, you can search for a group of digits at the beginning of a string and change it to the value of $NewLabel by using the following statement:

```
s/^\d+/$NewLabel/;
```

Using match results in your substitutions

In the section "Getting the Match Results" earlier in this chapter, I show you how to use the $1 and $2 special variables in your Perl programs to find out what was matched by the m// operator. With the s/// operator, these variables prove useful because you may want to replace what you found with something else related to it.

For example, if you want to find all the lines in a program that begin with a number and substitute each number with the word *Line* followed by that number, you can use the following statement:

```
$Test =~ s/^(\d+)/Line $1/;
```

The more complex example that follows changes strings that are formatted as Lastname, Firstname to Firstname Lastname:

```
$Test =~ s/([^,]+), (.+)/$2 $1/;
```

This test statement first finds all the characters up to the comma and puts those characters into $1. (The regular expression [^,]+ means "find all characters other than a comma.") The expression matches the comma and the space, and then it matches the rest of the characters and puts them into $2. The substituted text is $2, followed by a space, followed by $1.

Using expressions in the replacement text of s///

The s/// operator has one modifier that the m// operator doesn't: the e modifier. The e modifier causes Perl to evaluate the second part of the s///; that is, the string that is the replacement, as an expression rather than a string.

Using an expression for what is replaced can be useful if you want to base the replacement on $1, $2, and so on, but need to change the results. For example, suppose that you have a string that begins with a number, and you want to find the first number in the string and increase the number by one. You can use the following statement to do that:

```
$Test =~ s/(\d+)/$1 + 1/e;
```

In this case, if `Test` is `Line 23: go`, it's changed to `Line 24: go`.

Using the split Function with More-Advanced Regular Expressions

The first argument in the `split` function is a regular expression, and not just a string (see Chapter 7 for more info on `split`). You can use the `split` function with simple regular expressions, but it also has some other advanced and complex uses.

For example, suppose that someone at your firm is using a text editor to create a database for you. You told him to insert a tab character and nothing else between fields, but you suspect that he may have accidentally entered one or more spaces before or after the tab in some records. Instead of the following simple `split` statement

```
@TheFields = split(/\t/, $TheRecord);
```

you may use

```
@TheFields = split(/ *\t */, $TheRecord);
```

The previous regular expression says to look for zero or more spaces, followed by exactly one tab, followed by zero or more spaces.

You can get around the text entry problem noted in the previous example in another way — you can preprocess the record with an `s///` operator to get rid of the typos before using the `split` function. In the following example, the first statement substitutes a single tab for any tabs that were entered incorrectly (that is, with spaces before or after the tab), and the second statement then splits the result:

```
$TheRecord =~ s/ *\t */\t/g;
@TheFields = split(/\t/, $TheRecord);
```

Quoting words

If you use the split function to split on whitespace (as described earlier in the chapter in the section "Matching character classes"), Perl 5 and later versions feature a quoting function, qw, that makes statements easier to read. For example, instead of the following statement

```
@TheFields = split(/\s+/, $TheRecord);
```

you can use the qw function:

```
@TheFields = qw($TheRecord);
```

The characters qw stand for *quote words,* which is exactly what this function does. (I describe quoting in more detail in Chapter 5.)

Returning delimiters in split

The split function does not normally return the delimiters in list items. You can, nevertheless, use parentheses in your regular expression and split returns whatever is in the parentheses as items in the list. For example, when you run the following program

```
$TheRecord = "Serling|Rod|Twilight Zone|";
@TheFields = split(/\|/, $TheRecord);
```

Perl returns

```
('Serling', 'Rod', 'Twilight Zone')
```

By comparison, when you run the following program, in which the | delimiter is enclosed in parentheses,

```
$TheRecord = "Serling|Rod|Twilight Zone|";
@TheFields = split(/(\|)/, $TheRecord);
```

Perl returns

```
('Serling', '|', 'Rod', '|', 'Twilight Zone','|')
```

You can suppress your desire to have the delimiters returned by using the (?: extension to regular expressions. For example, given the following statements

```
$TheRecord = "Serling|Rod|Twilight Zone|";
@TheFields = split(/(?:\|)/, $TheRecord);
```

Perl returns

```
('Serling', 'Rod', 'Twilight Zone')
```

Using the tr/// Operator

Although the s/// operator works fine for simple one-on-one changes, such as changing one word to another, at times you may want to change multiple elements simultaneously, such as translating uppercase letters to lowercase letters. For this sort of task, you need the tr/// operator.

The tr/// operator enables you to specify individual letters, or ranges of letters, with a hyphen (-). For example, you can use the following to change the case of the uppercase letters to lowercase in $Test:

```
$Test =~ tr/A-Z/a-z/;
```

For historical reasons, the y/// operator exists, even though it does exactly the same thing as the tr/// operator. The y/// operator is rarely used because most people switched when the tr/// operator was introduced.

The tr/// operator returns the number of changes that it makes. It also has some modifiers that are different from those for the m// and s/// operators (see Table 12-4).

The tr/// operator does *not* use regular expressions for its pattern matching; it uses only actual characters and character ranges.

Table 12-4	Modifiers for tr///
Modifier	*Description*
c	Uses all characters other than what are listed in the first part of the operator
d	Deletes matching characters that are not replaced
s	Removes duplicates in the characters that are replaced

The c modifier is useful for shortening the list of characters between the first and second slash. For example, if you want to change all characters other than digits into linefeed characters, you can use

```
$Test =~ tr/0-9/\n/c; # Note that "c" to invert range
```

The d modifier enables you to delete, rather than replace, certain characters. For example, if you want to delete all nondigits in a program, you can use

```
$Test =~ tr/0-9//cd; # Change non-digits into nothing
```

The s modifier is useful for collapsing duplicate characters into a single character. This modifier causes Perl to treat all the found characters as one before doing the translation. For example, you may want to change every instance of two or more adjacent commas into just one comma. To accomplish that, you can enter

```
$Test =~ tr/,,/,/s;
```

Chapter 13

Looking Like a Pro: Subroutines, Imported Code, and Graceful Exits

▶ Creating subroutines to save time

▶ Using parts from other programs

▶ Leaving your programs with `die` or `exit` statements

*P*erl is a great language for creating useful programs quite simply. In fact, a surprising number of widely used Perl programs running on the Internet are fewer than five lines long. And, unlike other languages, you don't have to bang out lengthy instructions at the beginning of your Perl programs in order to set up the language before you can use it.

Perl also has plenty of features that can make the average program run faster and more efficiently. This chapter covers a number of those structural techniques that you can employ in order to save yourself some time and create a smoother-running program.

Saving Steps with Subroutines

By and large, *subroutines* consolidate repeated sets of statements into a single block. For example, suppose that you're writing a program that uses the same set of statements in several different places. Instead of repeating the lines every place they're needed, you can use a *subroutine* to define the set of lines and have *calls* (that is, functions that execute) to that subroutine. This method offers a number of advantages:

▶ If you need to make changes to a set of lines, you can enter those changes just once in the block instead of having to search the program for every instance of those lines.

✔ Your program runs faster because it's shorter.

✔ In lengthy programs, subroutines can act like named subprograms in order to help you organize the program.

Having everything in a single place so that updates are easier to enter is essential to efficient programming. I can't tell you how many times I've gotten lazy when writing a program and didn't use subroutines, only to be bitten later when I wanted to change numerous repeated lines.

Structuring a subroutine

Creating a subroutine by using the sub statement is a fairly easy task. The statement has the following format:

```
sub NAME { BLOCK }
```

The rules for creating subroutine names are the same as those for variable names: Don't use spaces, the only punctuation that you can use is the underscore (_), and subroutine names are case-sensitive.

To call a subroutine, you use the ampersand (&) character followed by the subroutine name. If the subroutine takes arguments, you include the arguments in parentheses just as you do for Perl's built-in functions. (In Perl 5, you don't have to use the & character if an argument is in parentheses. But doing so lets everyone reading your program know that you're referring to a subroutine, and not one of Perl's built-in functions, such as if or print.)

Inside the block, you can do whatever you please, just as you can in any other Perl block.

Because most subroutines contain arguments, you need a way to use those arguments in the block of code that you're writing in the subroutine. Perl makes the argument available in the special list @_, which is a variable built into Perl. In the preceding example, the argument was a list, so @_ is the entire list.

Subroutines that contain one or two arguments that are *scalars* (that is, either strings or numbers) are common. If you have scalar arguments, you can use the shift function to get the arguments out of the @_ list in the same order in which they went in. For example:

```
sub JustAdd {
    $First = shift(@_);
    $Second = shift(@_);
    return($First + $Second);
}
```

Perl creates the variable $First to hold the first argument and $Second to hold the second argument. You can then treat these variables as you would treat any other variable in your Perl program.

Most subroutines return a value, just as most Perl functions do. The return function, which I describe later in this chapter, is the most common method used to return a value. Some subroutines also change the values of variables in the main program, but most subroutines don't. Instead, most subroutines allow the program to make the changes to the variables by using the value that the subroutine returns.

Incidentally, if you want a smaller, cleaner program, you can replace the first two lines of the preceding subroutine (called JustAdd) with

```
($First, $Second) = @_;
```

You don't have to create new variables in your subroutines. You can just use slices of @_, although that can get cumbersome if you have numerous arguments or if your subroutine is lengthy. For example, the JustAdd subroutine that appears in the four-line block of code earlier in this section can be written more compactly (although the longer form may be easier to read):

```
sub ShorterJustAdd { return(@_[0] + @_[1]) }
```

Saving on labor and avoiding errors with subroutines

Imagine a program that contains a dozen or so lists, and at different points in the program, you want to print just the last item in each list and put a copy of that item into a list variable called @Big. Without subroutines, this program would look like this:

```
. . .
printf("Price: \$%.2f\n", $ListPrice[$#ListPrice]);
push(@Big, $ListPrice[$#ListPrice]);
. . .
printf("Price: \$%.2f\n", $CustPrice[$#CustPrice]);
push(@Big, $CustPrice[$#CustPrice]);
. . .
printf("Price: \$%.2f\n", $NewPrice[$#NewPrice]);
push(@Big, $NewPrice[$#NewPrice]);
. . .
```

Now imagine that you want to change the way that @Big is constructed and push the last two items, instead of just the last item, in each list onto the end of @Big. You have to search for each push function, make sure that the function you find is one that is pushing onto @Big, and change the item that's currently in that function to a *slice* (a portion of a list):

```
push(@Big, @ListPrice[$#ListPrice-1..$#ListPrice]);
```

As you can imagine, the task I just described can be really tedious. In addition, you're also prone to error because of the number of replacements that you have to do by hand. Subroutines can eliminate this problem.

By adding a subroutine and changing the pairs of printf and push statements to a single subroutine call in the six-line program that appears earlier in this section, that program now looks like this:

```
# Print the price and push it on @Big
sub PrintPushBig {
  @TheList = @_;
  printf("Price: \$%.2f\n", $TheList[$#TheList]);
  push(@Big, $TheList[$#TheList]);
}

. . .
&PrintPushBig(@ListPrice);

. . .
&PrintPushBig(@CustPrice);

. . .
&PrintPushBig(@NewPrice);
. . .
```

Instead of repeating the lines that have the push function, they're contained in the subroutine. To make the previously described change (to push a slice instead of a single item) to the subroutine, you simply change the push statement to

```
push(@Big, @TheList[$#TheList-1..$TheList]);
```

After you change this statement, the change is reflected each time the subroutine is called.

My, what a local variable you have: Using the my and local functions

You're not going to like hearing this, but the subroutines I show in the previous sections of this chapter have a major flaw in them. The examples work, but they may cause harm to other variables in the program that calls them. In order to make these first examples easier to read, I didn't do one thing that's very important.

In those subroutines, the first assignments assign values from @_ to variables. But what if those variables are already being used in the program? For example, in the JustAdd subroutine shown in the section "Structuring a subroutine," you may already have a variable called $First that you're using to keep track of who's on first. (I hear an Abbott and Costello routine coming on. . . .) In this case, when you call JustAdd, that subroutine wipes out the previous value of $First, which is probably not what you want to do.

You may ask, "Why not just use variables in your subroutine that aren't used in the main program?" That would certainly avoid the problem, if you're sure to do that every time. Without carefully reading each line in the program, you won't know which variable names are safe for you to use in your subroutine. For example, you may think that the variable $First hasn't been used in the program yet, but you may have simply missed it. Fear not: Perl has a simple solution to this problem.

The my and local functions cause Perl to create a local copy of the variable for the block that comprises the function. A *local copy* is a variable that can only be seen inside that block, so the outer program that called the function won't be affected by changes made to the local variables. Generally, the my and local functions accomplish the same thing, but my runs faster. The my function was introduced in Perl 5, so Perl 4 users must use local instead.

You should use my and local when you first use a variable (using a variable the first time is called *declaring* the variable). You can declare a variable at any time in a block. However, most programmers prefer to declare a variable at the very beginning of a block so that they know where to look for their variable declarations. This programming convention is probably a holdover from other programming languages that require you to declare all your variables before you use them. Perl is accommodating enough not to require predeclaration. You just create a new variable when you feel like it. Nevertheless, if you're going to use my or local to safely declare a variable, you have to do so before using that variable.

You can use the my and local functions as statements by themselves or place them to the left of an assignment. For example, if you just want to declare that a particular variable is a local one, you can simply say

```
my($AirCondNum);
```

In this example, if you want to also set the variable's value when you first declare it, you can say

```
my($AirCondNum) = 3;
```

Given the JustAdd subroutine presented in the "Structuring a subroutine" section earlier in this chapter, if the subroutines declare their variables as local, the JustAdd subroutine would then look like this:

```
sub JustAdd {
  my($First) = shift(@_);
  my($Second) = shift(@_);
  return($First + $Second);
}
```

The first two lines cause Perl to create new copies of the variables $First and $Second that are used only inside the subroutine. If $First and $Second exist somewhere else in the program, they're unaffected by a call to the subroutine.

Essentially, the my and local functions enable Perl to remember other variables that have the same name and store them off to the side. After a subroutine finishes, Perl throws away any new instances of variables and restores the old variables that it momentarily stashed off to the side. That's why these functions are said to create "local" variables: The variables exist only when the subroutine is being run.

You can declare variables with my and local in any block, and not just the block of a subroutine, although those functions are found mostly in subroutines. Perl acts the same way given any kind of block: It preserves any variable with the same name as the argument to my and local, creates a local version of the variable with the desired name, and then destroys the local version at the end of the block.

You can declare as many variables as you desire in my or local. For example, if you know that you're going to use $i, $j, and $k as loop variables in a block, you can define them all at once with a statement such as the following:

```
my($i, $j, $k);
```

Getting into the habit of using the my function when you write subroutines is good. Even if you're certain that you haven't repeated any variable name in a program when you create a subroutine, you may forget and end up using that name later on. Furthermore, a handy way of creating subroutines that you can use in other programs is to include code from other existing Perl programs. In that case, you definitely want to use my for every variable in those pre-existing subroutines.

At times, you may want a subroutine to modify something outside of the subroutine. For example, take a look at the following PrintPushBig subroutine:

```
sub PrintPushBig {
  my($TheList) = @_;
  printf("Price: \$%.2f\n", $TheList[$#TheList]);
  push(@Big, $TheList[$#TheList]);
}
```

The purpose of the previous subroutine is to both print something and to change the value of a list (@Big) that's in the main program. Therefore, this subroutine produces a change outside the subroutine, namely the addition of an element to @Big.

TIP

If you write subroutines that will change the variables in your program, remember to insert an explanatory comment at the top of those subroutines. Then later on, you won't be puzzled as to why the variables in your program keep changing.

Some programmers are adamant about subroutines never changing anything in a program. They believe that making such changes leads to mysterious results in the future after you've forgotten what was changed and why. If you subscribe to this theory, you can return one or more values and force the calling program to change values based on the returned values. (I describe return values in the next section.)

The my function essentially "hides" a variable from all other blocks in a program — both the blocks that call the block with my and subroutines called from the subroutine with my. local, on the other hand, hides the variable only from the enclosing block, thus leaving the variable visible to subroutines that are called from the block with local in it. The following example points out some differences between the local and my functions in action:

```
# Simple subroutine to print the value of $J at the moment
sub PrintJ { print "The value of \$J is $J\n" }
# Simple subroutine to print the value of $K at the moment
sub PrintK { print "The value of \$K is $K\n" }
# Here's the test
my($J) = 5;
local($K) = 10;
&PrintJ;
&PrintK;
```

Because $J is undefined in the PrintJ subroutine and $K is passed through to the PrintJ, you get the following result:

```
The value of $J is
The value of $K is 10
```

Returning a value from a subroutine

Every Perl function returns a value to the program that called the function. At times, you don't need to bother with what's returned, such as when you call a function solely for another aspect of the function. For example, the chomp function described in Chapter 5 returns a value (the character or characters it chomped), but most of the time, you just want to use the function to hack off characters at the end of strings. (Subroutines also return values, which you can pay attention to or ignore.)

The most efficient way to return a value is with the return statement. This statement causes the subroutine to end and returns the list that you give as its argument. Thus, in the JustAdd subroutine that follows, the return statement is used to return the value of the two arguments that are added together:

```
sub JustAdd {
    my($First) = shift(@_);
    my($Second) = shift(@_);
    return($First + $Second);
}
```

You can also use return with no argument, in which case Perl returns the value 0.

You don't have to use a return statement in your subroutines, although it does make subroutines easier to read. If you don't have a return statement waiting when Perl hits the end of a subroutine's block, the subroutine ends and Perl returns the value of the last statement. Therefore, you can write a subroutine like the following one:

```
sub JustAdd {
    my($First) = shift(@_);
    my($Second) = shift(@_);
    $First + $Second;
}
```

Using return makes things a little clearer because the last line of the previous subroutine doesn't look like it's *doing* anything, even though it is returning the value of the expression. My preference is to show functions that suggest action, such as return, rather than just having a plain value dangling at the end.

Who's calling?

If you're in a subroutine and want to know the name of the program that called you, you can use the caller function to find out. This function may not be all that important, but it can provide you with a nice little diversion. In a list context, the caller function format looks like this:

```
($PackageName, $FileName,
    $LineNum) = caller;
```

In a scalar context, caller simply returns true if it is called in a subroutine, or inside an eval function (described in Chapter 18) or require function (see the section "Importing Prewritten Perl Code into Your Programs").

The `return` function also comes in handy if you want to stop a subroutine before you get to the end. You can use `return` somewhat like the `last` statement (covered in Chapter 8) in loops, and your subroutine can have many `return` functions in it. Here is an example of a subroutine with more than one `return` statement:

```
# Subroutine that returns the string "long" if the
#  argument is longer than 10 characters
sub IsLong {
   my($TheStr) = pop(@_);
   if(length($TheStr) > 10) { return('long') }
   else { return('short') }
}
```

The `return` function can return either a scalar or a list. For example, you can write a subroutine that returns a number raised to the second, third, and fourth power that looks like the following:

```
# Returns the argument raised to 2, 3, and 4
sub Raised {
   my($Sq, $Cub, $Quad);
   my($Val) = pop(@_);
   $Sq = $Val ** 2; $Cub = $Val ** 3; $Quad = $Val ** 4;
   return($Sq, $Cub, $Quad);
}
```

You may call this subroutine by using a statement such as

```
@Powers = &Raised(12.3);
```

or

```
($TheSq, $TheCube, $TheFourth) = &Raised(12.3);
```

Importing Prewritten Perl Code into Your Programs

After you write a number of Perl programs, you may to want to reuse some old Perl programs in order to save yourself some time when writing new ones. For example, suppose that you wrote a really handy subroutine that reads a file and creates a list of all the capitalized words in the file. You wrote this subroutine in a program six months ago. Now you find yourself wanting that same subroutine in a program that you're writing today.

Using your text editor, you can simply copy the subroutine from the old program to the new one. Keep in mind, though, if you want to use 10 or 20 old subroutines, your new program can get pretty hefty before you have even begun writing the new code. Instead, you can put the subroutines in one or more separate files and simply call those files into your new program.

Each time you create a new, useful subroutine, you can put it in a file. You can put many subroutines in a single file, or put each one in its own file. Then you can draw upon your library of subroutines whenever you need it.

You can also include existing programs in your new programs by employing the require function that you use for including your own collection of subroutines.

The require function takes one argument — the name of the file that you want to include in your program. For example, if a subroutine that you want to use resides in the numsubs.pl file, you can include that subroutine (and all the other subroutines in the file) in your current program by using this simple statement:

```
require('numsubs.pl');
```

It's not unusual to see the require function without parentheses around the argument:

```
require 'numsubs.pl';
```

Adding a required statement for included files

Stashing away your subroutines in files has one little complication: The require function demands that whatever it reads in a file must return a true value. As it turns out, simply having a subroutine in a file doesn't cause Perl to return a true value. So, you must have at least one statement in the subroutine file apart from a subroutine, and that statement must return true. A common trick is to insert this little statement:

```
1;
```

You insert 1; somewhere in the file, usually at the end. This statement returns the value 1 (a value for true). For this reason, you usually see such a line, or a line with just a string, at the end of every file that is intended to be included with require.

Requiring a particular version of Perl

You can use the `require` function to specify which version of Perl is needed in order to run a particular program. When you use a number as the argument to `require` (instead of a filename), Perl stops the program if the version of Perl isn't that number or higher.

For example, the statement `require 5.6;` indicates that Perl must be version 5.6 or higher.

If it isn't, Perl stops and you get an error message that tells you what version is required and which is running. For example, versions of Perl from a few years ago are only 5.001, so this `require` function would cause the program to stop.

Helping Perl search your libraries for included files

The `require` statement (covered earlier in this chapter) needs a filename in order to know which file to open. The trick is that a file can reside in any one of countless places on your computer. To solve this problem, your `require` statement can specify exactly where a file should be, or you can put the file in one of the directories in Perl's search path.

You want to provide a complete description of where a particular file is located, but that can involve a fair amount of key stroking. For example, the following three `require` statements may appear in Perl programs under Windows, Mac OS 9, or UNIX:

```
require('C:\LANGS\PERL5\LIBS\NUMSUBS.PL');
require('Felicity:Perl 5:My Libraries:numsubs.pl');
require('/usr/home/phoffman/libraries/numsubs.pl');
```

When you use full path names to your libraries, you have an added disadvantage of not being able to move your libraries without rewriting all your Perl programs to point to each new library location. A much better method involves storing your libraries somewhere that Perl would look for libraries and then letting Perl search through those places.

The `@INC` special variable holds the list of directories that Perl searches in order to find your library files. For example, `@INC` in Perl for Windows may contain the following path names:

```
('C:\PERL\lib', 'C:\PERL\site\lib')
```

Running programs in eval

Yet another way exists for you to run imported programs in Perl: the `eval` function. As its name implies, `eval` causes Perl to evaluate its argument. After Perl evaluates the argument, Perl runs it. You use `eval` to include parts of a program when you don't know what they'll be until the program runs. For example, you may want to enable the user to see the value of any desired variable while the Perl program is running. In which case, you can fashion something like the following statements:

```
print "Name of the variable do
    you want to see: ";
$Resp = <STDIN>;
print eval($Resp);
```

If you find that a particular task in your program can't be performed without some information that you won't have until the program is running, you can use `eval` to create a miniprogram to use that run-time information. Advanced programmers typically use `eval`, so you don't need to worry about it too much for now.

In MacPerl, the default value of `@INC` is a single value of the `lib` folder where MacPerl was installed; for example

```
('Felicity:Perl 5:lib')
```

On UNIX, `@INC` usually lists a few different places for the lib folder, such as

```
('/usr/local/lib/perl5/i386-bsdos',
    '/usr/local/lib/perl5',
    '/usr/local/lib/perl5/site')
```

If you stash your libraries in one of the directories listed in `@INC`, you need to use just the specific filename in the `require` function:

```
require('numsubs.pl');
```

Every implementation of Perl I've ever seen has a sensible definition for `@INC`, but even if it doesn't, you can change this variable yourself. For example, suppose that you're a Windows user and you want to store all your libraries in the `C:\PROGR\PERL5\MYSUBS` directory. You can add this directory to the `@INC` list before you make use of any `require` statements by using the following `push` statement:

```
push(@INC, "C:\PROGR\PERL5\MYSUBS");
```

You can use a similar `push` statement for other operating systems.

Wrapping your programs in packages

One method that Perl employs in order to keep variables local to a set of subroutines involves the use of packages. A *package* is a set of things for which you need a set of local variables. An included file is one example of something that may have its own set of variables (see the previous section in this chapter for more on included files).

The `package` declaration tells Perl to start a new package. Until you use `package` for the first time, Perl keeps all your variables in a default package called `main`. To name a package, simply use the declaration followed by the package name:

```
package NetworkStuff;
```

If you use `include` to pull in files that have different packages, when you go to use the subroutines, you must refer to the subroutines in those packages by their package names. You can have two subroutines with the same names in different packages and you must be able to differentiate them. (Because the subroutines in the programs shown earlier in this chapter are all in the same package [`main`], you wouldn't have to specify a package name.)

When you want to call a subroutine that's in a different package than the one you're programming in, you must list that package name, followed by a double colon (`::`). (In Perl 4, use a single quotation mark [`'`] instead of the double colon.) For example, if you have a package called NetworkStuff and a package called MySubs, you can invoke your subroutines with the following statements:

```
&MySubs::Router;      # Perl 5
&NetworkStuff::Router; # Perl 5
&MySubs'Router;       # Perl 4
&NetworkStuff'Router;  # Perl 4
```

You can also refer to variables in other packages by using the double colon. For example, to refer to the variable `$i` in the package called MySubs, you use `$MySubs::i`.

Including code other than subroutines

A file that you include by using the `require` function may contain any sort of Perl code. For example, you can include statements that set variables or print text. However, this inclusion can be a bad idea because you may not always remember what every included file does when you use `require`.

Limiting the files that you use with `require` solely to subroutines is always a good idea. The programs in the subroutines should also be designed to change any variable carefully and should declare every variable that they use (other than Perl's special variables) with `my` and `local`.

Ending Perl Programs Gracefully

You may notice that the Perl programs that you see in this book don't end with a statement that says something to the effect of "Hey, this is the end of the program." That's because Perl programs end when Perl runs out of statements to execute. When Perl gets to the last line of the program, it's smart enough to know that you intended that line to be the end.

You also have the option of actually telling Perl that you want to end a program. I tell you about those options in the next sections.

Using the die function

The `die` function causes Perl to print a message and then stop the program immediately. The `die` function is somewhat like the `print` function. It displays its argument (which can be a list), so you're not restricted to displaying a single string. If the last value in the list doesn't end with a *newline character* (which is usually entered in strings as `"\n"`), Perl also prints the name of the program and the line number, followed by a newline character. If you're in an *input loop* (in which you are awaiting input from the keyboard), Perl also prints the number of times that you've gone through the loop.

Warning without exiting

Perl's `warn` function acts like the `die` function except that `warn` doesn't cause the program to quit. Instead, it just prints out a warning string that you supply, but the program continues. For most people, this process means that `warn` does just the same thing as `print`. The difference between `warn` and `print` is that `warn` displays its message on the *output stream* called STDERR instead of in the STDOUT output stream (see Chapter 10 for info on output streams). Because most operating systems make whatever appears on STDERR also appear on the standard output stream, `warn` and `print` are indistinguishable for most people. Like `warn`, `die` actually puts its argument on STDERR.

Using the exit function

The exit function is a more conventional way to end a Perl program than the die function. Instead of displaying a list, exit takes a numeric argument and returns that argument to the program from which you ran your Perl program. However, the exit function doesn't allow you to create a message for the end user. You can run a Perl program from your operating system (such as from the command line in Windows); in this case, Perl returns the value in exit to the operating system.

Most operating systems ignore the number returned from the Perl program (called the *return code*), or at least don't do anything interesting with it. However, if your operating system does do something significant with this number, such as display the return code of programs when they exit, you may find the exit function useful. If you don't supply an argument to exit, Perl uses 0 for the return code.

Structuring die and exit statements

The die and exit functions typically appear to the right of the or operator in logical expressions (more on or can be found in Chapter 8). If a conditional test in your program absolutely has to result in a true value, you can then exit the program immediately if it's false. Many programmers use the die and exit functions with if and unless statements to end a program if a test doesn't return a true value. For instance, the following two examples both check to see whether $Now is greater than $StartTime+3, and if so, exit the program with a message to the user.

```
unless($Now > ($StartTime + 3)) { die "It's too soon.\n" }

($Now > ($StartTime + 3)) or die "It's too soon.\n";
```

Include the \n string at the end of the final string that you use in a die statement; otherwise, Perl adds the program name and the line number to the end of whatever it prints. If you don't include /n at the end of the string, such as in the following statement

```
($Now > ($StartTime + 3)) or die "It's too soon.";
```

Perl displays the following:

```
It's too soon. at LabMonitor.pl line 12.
```

As you can see from the examples in this book, I prefer `die` to `exit`. It's always courteous to give users an explanatory message when a program ends so they aren't left staring at the screen and wondering what happened. You can create plenty of useful messages with `die`, such as

```
Program ended because the file 'input.txt' was not found.

All done. Thank you!

Finished at 08:27:52 in .03 seconds.

Unable to find the specified file; exiting.
```

Try to provide the kind of error messages that you'd need to see if you were running a program for the first time. Make your end-user messages friendly, or even humorous if you have the knack for it. We've all been stymied by incomprehensible error messages, and the best way to remind others to write understandable error messages is by doing so yourself.

Part IV

Advanced Perl
Demystified

Part IV

Advanced Perl

Demystified

In this part...

Although this book is largely designed for novices and intermediate users, I also recognize the irresistible allure of some really heady stuff, such as using Perl with CGI scripts and other parts of the Internet, XML, databases, and object-oriented programming. The chapters in this part cover subjects that are useful for more advanced programmers, yet are still accessible to most beginners.

Chapter 14

Perl and CGI: Web Server Programs Demystified

*U*nless you've spent the past eight years in a cave without a battery pack and a phone hook-up, you probably have heard lots of talk (maybe too much) about the World Wide Web and the wonders that it brings to all of us. Chalk up another plus for the Web: It has done more than anything else for promoting the widespread use of Perl.

The Web has had an enormous impact on the popularity of the Perl programming language. That's because Perl can be used in tandem with Web servers to make your Web pages more interactive and informative. A large measure of the work that you do using Perl and the Web involves the creation of on-screen forms designed to get information from users and then return it to you. The information generated by these forms is handled by *Common Gateway Interface (CGI)* programs, a topic that also gets a fair amount of coverage in this chapter.

The most interesting aspect of HTML as it relates to Perl is HTML forms. How to process a form after a user has completed it is a topic that I cover in this chapter. If you need some brushing up on HTML, which you need to know before you do much with a Web server, check out *HTML 4 For Dummies*, 4th Edition, by Ed Tittel (Wiley Publishing, Inc.).

Writing CGI Programs in Perl

From the Web's earliest days, Web servers have needed a way to interact with programming languages. The early programmers who created Web servers decided to use a single, standard method for connecting programs to their servers, instead of having to use a different method for each server and each language. Using a standard method simplifies the process of running programs from a Web server. That method is called *Common Gateway Interface (CGI)*.

How CGI works can be stated in simple terms: CGI passes a user's request to a program by using some special variables or standard file input; the program, in turn, passes information to the user by using standard file output (see Chapter 10). Incidentally, CGI programs are often called *scripts*.

Your Perl program works with the Web server software — not around it. Web users coming to your Web site don't run your programs directly. Instead, they access the Web server, and the Web server software launches your programs. Therefore, your CGI programs need to be able to talk to a Web server.

The various Web servers out there have different requirements and perform different actions when you run a CGI program. For example, some Web servers require that all your CGI programs be in one directory on the server and the programs must follow certain naming rules; other servers enable you to put your programs wherever you want and give them whatever names you please.

Beyond CGI

In olden times (before 1994), CGI was the only game in town for interfacing Web servers and programming languages. Every Web server still supports CGI, but now the most popular servers also support their own programming interfaces, and usually in their own programming languages. For example, Microsoft has a system called Active Server Pages (ASP), which interfaces to a server through a different interface than CGI. Another example is Macromedia's ColdFusion environment.

All in all, CGI is pretty limited, even if the programming languages to which it attaches aren't. The custom *application programming interfaces*, or APIs, that are used by newer Web servers give you many more capabilities than plain old CGI. If you get serious about creating programs that work with your Web server and your server has its own API, consider finding out how to use the server's API. (Of course, the API may not be nearly as easy to use as Perl, but few languages are.)

If your Web server runs on a version of Windows, it may use an extended version of CGI, called Windows CGI, that most Windows Web servers use. Although this version is much more complicated than standard CGI, it has a few features not available in standard CGI.

In order to write Web server programs with Perl, you need to know two things:

- ✓ **Input:** Determining what the user requested
- ✓ **Output:** Deciding how to tell the user what you want to say

Collecting the input is more difficult than displaying the output because you have to plan for more variables when accepting input. You can create your output by using a `print` statement. (See Chapters 4 and 5 for the particulars of the `print` function.)

This is not to say that you can just output whatever you want as a result of the input to CGI. Web users have particular expectations about the content and format of the output that they receive. This chapter explains how to use the CGI module both to take in a user's request and to output HTML.

For now, all you need to know is the format of the input and the kind of information in the special variables. The output that you create is the same output that's normally sent by your Web server, such as HTML or, in rare cases, plain text. In the following sections, I show you the format of the file input and the kind of information contained in the special variables used to process user input. I also provide examples of Web server file output created in HTML, the most commonly used file format on the Web.

Read the instructions that come with your Web server software before writing any CGI programs in Perl. Most Web servers are designed to simplify the process of using CGI programs; nevertheless, many programming hopefuls are unsuccessful on their first few attempts at programming CGI scripts because they don't follow the rules of the road for the Web server they're using.

Using Environment Variables

You can obtain information from a Web server in one of two ways: through special variables called *environment variables* or through standard file input (described in Chapter 10). For many requests that come to your program from the Web server, you use environment variables, but for most HTML forms, you use standard file input.

The term *environment* comes from UNIX, although it also applies to Windows. Environment variables are set in the operating system and they're similar to Perl text variables. Perl can read operating system environment variables and use them just like other Perl variables. (Attention Macintosh users: The Mac doesn't really have environment variables, but MacPerl pretends to have them for use in CGI programs.)

UNIX has dozens of environment variables, but this chapter covers only those specific to running CGI programs. They're set by the Web server software as a way to communicate information to programming languages like Perl. The CGI standard defines many of these variables, but only a few of them are truly useful to most Perl programmers.

Getting at variables

Perl variables, like environment variables, have names. (I describe the methods that you use to view and set the values of environment variables in Chapter 18.) The environment variable names in CGI are in all capital letters. For example, to get the value of an environment variable with the name VARNAME, you can use the following statement:

```
$ENV{"VARNAME"}
```

For example, suppose that a variable called REMOTE_HOST has the domain name of the computer making the request. You can set a variable $TheUserHost in your Perl program with the following statement:

```
$TheUserHost = $ENV{"REMOTE_HOST"};
```

Just to give you a feel for the variables' names and the typical values that you may see, the following is a list of the CGI variables that you may see after a Web server request:

```
GATEWAY_INTERFACE -- CGI/1.1
            HOME -- /
     HTTP_ACCEPT -- image/gif, image/jpeg, */*
       HTTP_HOST -- www.mycompany.com
 HTTP_USER_AGENT -- Mozilla/3.01b1 (Macintosh; I; PPC)
 PATH_TRANSLATED -- /usr/local/wn/scripts
    QUERY_STRING -- eastern
     REMOTE_ADDR -- 169.207.113.247
     REMOTE_HOST -- j112.cs.cmu.edu
  REQUEST_METHOD -- GET
     SCRIPT_NAME -- /telltime.cgi
     SERVER_NAME -- www.mycompany.com
     SERVER_PORT -- 80
 SERVER_PROTOCOL -- HTTP/1.0
 SERVER_SOFTWARE -- WN/1.14.2
    WN_DIR_PATH -- /usr/local/wn/scripts
        WN_ROOT -- /usr/local/wn/scripts
```

You need to use only a few environment variables to get information from a user, and you will rarely need to use the others. In the following sections, I describe the most important variables. In the section "A Few Other Environment Variables," I describe some lesser-used variables also worth knowing about.

Posing a query

After a user clicks a link to your program, the Web server launches the program. Your program may need to know certain things about the user's request, so the Web server sets a few variables with this information.

The QUERY_STRING variable contains all the text after the ? in the user's request. For example, suppose that your home page includes the following statement:

```
<p>
To see the current time in the central time zone, choose
<a href="/amy/telltime.cgi?central">this link</a>.
To see what time it is in the eastern time zone, choose
<a href="/amy/telltime.cgi?eastern">this link</a>.
```

When the user selects the time zone link, the value of QUERY_STRING is either central or eastern. Therefore, your Perl program may have something in it similar to this:

```
$TheTime = time();
$DesiredTimeZone = $ENV{"QUERY_STRING"};
if($DesiredTimeZone eq 'central')
   { $TheTime += 3600 } # Add one hour
elsif($DesiredTimeZone eq 'eastern')
   { $TheTime += 7200 } # Add two hours
```

The query string is assigned by you in your HTML pages. To enable the user to make choices on an HTML page, you need to use HTML forms, which I describe in the section "Gathering Information from HTML Forms" later in this chapter.

QUERY_STRING is the one variable that you really need for most kinds of form processing. A raft of other environment variables are available, but they don't help much with what you really want to do, which is to figure out what the user wants so that you can supply it.

Determining the source of a request

You can use two environment variables to log accesses to your Web site. (This process is called *tracking hits*.) These variables, REMOTE_HOST and REMOTE_ADDR, tell you which computer made a request to your Web server.

These variables identify the computer — not the user.

REMOTE_HOST is the *domain name* of the computer making the request (if the Web server is able to determine the domain name), whereas REMOTE_ADDR is the *IP address* of that computer. If you're unfamiliar with domain names and IP addresses, you can find out plenty about them in *The Internet For Dummies,* 5th Edition, by John Levine, Carol Baroudi, and Margaret Levine Young (Wiley Publishing, Inc.).

You may want to use the values of REMOTE_HOST and REMOTE_ADDR to determine what information is given in the Web page that is displayed to the user. For example, you may want to give more detailed information to someone on a computer who you recognize than someone who's a stranger. However, this practice is incredibly unsafe. It's possible for a user to pretend to be on a certain computer by changing an address on the Internet. Just ignoring the values in REMOTE_HOST and REMOTE_ADDR is best.

REMOTE_HOST may be a null string (a string with zero characters) if your Web server can't translate the IP address that it receives with a request into a domain name. Most Web server administrators prefer to see domain names in the logs for their Web servers rather than IP addresses, so your program should check whether REMOTE_HOST has a value, and if not, use REMOTE_ADDR instead. The following is an example of this kind of check:

```
# Get the host name or IP address for the log
unless($ENV{REMOTE_HOST} eq '')
   { $TheWhere = $ENV{REMOTE_HOST} }
else { $TheWhere = $ENV{REMOTE_ADDR} }
```

Gathering Information from HTML Forms

Using a *query string* (the text after the ? in a URL) is a simple, direct way to get a single piece of information from a user (see "Posing a query" earlier in this chapter). However, you usually need more than just one piece of information. For example, you may want to find out a user's name and address or the answers to some yes-or-no questions. If you want this sort of information, the user must fill out a *form*.

An HTML form has two components that are relevant to CGI programs: the *HTTP method* (the syntax) used in the form, and the names of the elements in the form (such as the names of the buttons). Beyond that, the rest of the form consists mostly of formatting designed to make text entry more user-friendly.

The method for submitting forms can be either GET or POST. The GET method puts any responses to a form in a query string, whereas the POST method puts the responses into the body of the HTTP reply that you can read from the standard file input (see Chapter 10 for more on file input). You can use either GET or POST, depending on which one suits your fancy.

For example, the following is the HTML code that displays a short and simple form, the results of which are shown in Figure 14-1:

```
<hr><form method=POST
   action="http://www.bigstate.edu/accts/namecolor.pl">
First name: <input name=FirstName size=30><br>
Last name: <input name=LastName size=30><br>
Favorite color: <select name=FavColor>
<option>crimson<option>apricot<option>saffron
<option>emerald<option>sapphire<option>magenta
<option>pearl<option>coal<option>chestnut
</select>
<br><input type="submit" value="Send">
</form><hr>
```

The form in Figure 14-1 returns values for three named elements: FirstName, LastName, and FavColor. CGI returns values in a very compact yet difficult-to-decipher fashion — as a single string with each element listed as element-name=elementvalue, spaces in the values turned into plus-sign (+) characters, and an ampersand (&) character inserted between each element. For example, if a person named Sharon Fulton who really likes purple fills in the form, the returned string will look like this:

```
FirstName=Sharon&LastName=Fulton&FavColor=magenta
```

Figure 14-1:
A small form designed to return values for three named elements.

Determining what is in the response gets a bit more complicated than what I just described. Many special characters are encoded as a percent sign (%) followed by the hexadecimal value of the character. For example, if Sharon enters Sharon & Pete instead of Sharon, the returned string becomes:

```
FirstName=Sharon+%26+Pete&LastName=Fulton&FavColor=magenta
```

Using GET and POST to Collect Form Data

As I note in the previous section, you can use either GET or POST as the HTTP method for submitting a form to your Perl program. Where you read the form data that's submitted depends on which method you use:

- ✔ **GET:** With GET, the response comes back in the QUERY_STRING environment variable, which you can read with $ENV{"QUERY_STRING"}.

- ✔ **POST:** With POST, the response comes in the content of the reply, which you can read from the standard file input.

The environment variable REQUEST_METHOD tells you whether the GET or POST method was used. To read the correct number of characters, you need to know how long the content of the request is, and then read that many characters by using Perl's read function (I describe the read function in Chapter 11). The environment variable CONTENT_LENGTH tells you how long the request is. Then, you can put the text into the variable $TheReq by using the following statement:

```
read(STDIN, $TheReq, $ENV{"CONTENT_LENGTH"});
```

If you want your Perl program to be robust, check whether the request has either the GET or POST methods:

```
if($ENV{"REQUEST_METHOD"} eq 'GET')
    { $TheReq = $ENV{"QUERY_STRING"} }
else
    { read(STDIN, $TheReq, $ENV{"CONTENT_LENGTH"}) }
```

Splitting apart a strung-together response

If you read the previous sections, you know how to get a response from a user, but that response ends up being a smashed-together string of characters that looks something like the following:

```
FirstName=Sharon&LastName=Fulton&FavColor=magenta
```

Perl is great at handling data like this string. You can write a program that will split this string into pairs of items, such as FirstName and Sharon, LastName and Fulton, and so on, but hey, why bother? Programs that read HTML forms are so common that a module (with the simple name "CGI") has already been written for you. The CGI module is the easiest of the programs used to get the request string because it requires just one or two statements. (It employs some of the object-oriented features covered in Chapter 19.)

To use the CGI module, you have to make it available to Perl. If you are using Perl 5.6 or 5.8, the CGI module comes with the Perl package so you don't have to do anything else; otherwise, you need your system administrator to install it for you. After you have the CGI module installed, start your Perl program by entering something like the following statements:

```
use CGI;
$q = new CGI();
```

In the first line of this code, the use statement tells Perl to read the CGI module into the program that you are writing. For now, assume that use is a way to get a Perl object-oriented module into your program. (I describe modules in Chapter 19.) The second line causes Perl to create an object described in CGI.

Picking values to use as Perl variables

Suppose that someone named Sharon Fulton with a preference for shades of purple fills in the form shown in Figure 14-1.

You want to do something with the values from the form — namely, you want to put them in Perl variables that you can use in your program. You can do this quickly for form elements that have names(not all of them do) with the param function. For example, the following program looks for the name FirstName and then sets $FormFirst to the element after that.

```
# Fill in $FormFirst with the name given
$FormFirst = $q->param('FirstName');
```

If for some reason you don't know the names that your form is using, that's okay; you can determine them easily with the param function. In this case, you call the function with no arguments:

```
@MyNames = $q->param;
```

Displaying Output to the User

The interesting part of using CGI is that it enables you to feed information to end users. After you find out a few rules for how to supply information, you can create your own programs to tell users whatever you desire.

Every message sent from a Web server to a Web client consists of two parts: *header information* and the *main message.* The header information may be very short, but it's essential because it contains format information that the user's Web browser must have. If it isn't included, most Web browsers assume that the main message is a plain text file.

A few servers pass their own header information to the top of the response, in which case, your Perl program isn't supposed to pass any headers. Most servers pass some header information, but not the most important piece: the MIME content type. *MIME* stands for *Multipurpose Internet Mail Extension,* and it's used on the Web and in Internet mail. MIME types are more properly called *Internet media types,* but the name MIME has caught on and stuck.

A MIME type tells a Web client what kind of information is in the response from the server. The Web client then uses this MIME information to decide how to show that information. For example, a Web client reacts differently when you say, "This is an HTML document," than if you say, "This is a GIF image," or "This is a compressed program file."

The header that you send to the client before you start sending your own information starts with the string `Content-type:` followed by a space and then the MIME type. For example, if you're going to send back an HTML document to a user, your Perl program prints the following statement before it does anything else:

```
Content-type: text/html
```

Hundreds of different MIME types exist, most of which you probably won't ever use. Table 14-1 shows some of the MIME types that you're most likely to send over the Internet.

Table 14-1	MIME Types for Common File Formats
MIME Type	*Description*
text/html	A regular HTML document
text/plain	A plain text file that appears exactly as you send it
application/binary	A binary file that's saved to disk
image/gif	A picture in GIF format

MIME Type	Description
image/jpeg	A picture in JPEG format
audio/mpeg	A sound file in MP3 format

The header information is separated from the body of the message by a blank line. Therefore, you have to insert \n\n at the end of your Content-type line.

A few servers send out the Content-type line to the client for you, which means that you shouldn't send it out yourself. (See your server's documentation for instructions on what sort of data you should be sending out in your CGI programs.)

Displaying information directly using print statements

For an example of how to send information back to the user, take a look at the following short Perl CGI program that ignores any client input and returns a brief message formatted as HTML. This program lacks the HTML header information, but it does work:

```
print "Content-type: text/html\n\n";
print "<b>Thank you</b> for running my Perl program.";
```

By comparison, the following is a longer and more complex example program called thetime.cgi. The program displays the time to the user. Note the amount of HTML that the program puts out.

```
# CGI program to tell the user what time it is.
#   The user either got here with a URL of
#   "central" or "eastern" or nothing.
$TheZone = "Pacific";
if ($DesiredTimeZone eq 'central') {
  @TimeArr = localtime(time + 3600);
  $TheZone = "Central";
}
elsif($DesiredTimeZone eq 'eastern') {
  @TimeArr = localtime(time + 7200);
  $TheZone = "Eastern";
}
$Hour = $TimeArr[2];
$Minute = $TimeArr[1];
$TimeString = "$Hour:$Minute";
print <<"EndOfStuff"
```

```
ContentType: text/html

<html><head><title>At the tone...</title></head><body>
<h1>The time<h1>
In the <b>$TheZone</b> time zone, it is now $TimeString.
</body></html>
EndOfStuff
```

The HTML document that relates to the previous program would look something like this:

```
Which time zone do you want to see the time for?
<br>
<a href="/cgi-bin/thetime.cgi?pacific">Pacific</a>?
<br>
<a href="/cgi-bin/thetime.cgi?central">Central</a>
<br>
<a href="/cgi-bin/thetime.cgi?eastern">Eastern</a
```

Using the CGI module to display to the user

The CGI module that you use to read information in forms can also be used to print information. This is useful if you are creating a lot of complex HTML, but is probably overkill if you want to do something as simple as what was output in the program in the previous section. Don't assume that just because you are doing simple things now that you will always be doing simple things. As you have seen throughout this book, it is usually a good idea to have a few extra tools in your Perl toolbox.

If you are familiar with HTML, you are likely to be familiar with the display functions in the CGI module. For example, you start your output with the header function, such as:

```
print $q->header('text/html');
```

You surround your text with the start_html and end_html functions. The start_html function takes pairs of arguments that indicate parts of the HTML header. The first argument starts with a dash (-), as in this example:

```
print $q->start_html(-title => 'At the tone...');
```

Other functions have the same name as their HTML counterparts. For example, the h1 function creates an HTML element for level-1 headers, and the p function creates an HTML element (for paragraphs). Thus, your output may look like this:

```
print $q->header('text/html'),
  $q->start_html(-title => 'At the tone...'),
  $q->h1('The time'),
  $q->p("In the <b>$TheZone</b> time zone, it " .
    "is now $TimeString."),
  $q->end_html;
```

Many of the functions take arguments that match the arguments that are used in HTML tags. For example, in HTML, a level-1 header is indicated by surrounding text with `<h1>` and `</h1>`. However, you can center the heading by changing the opening HTML tag to `<h1 align="center">`. To do this in the CGI module, you simply add the arguments to the h1 function, as in the following:

```
$q->h1({-align => center}, 'The time')
```

Creating an HTML Form

You can use CGI programs to take requests from users and combine them into a single response. This process is useful when the information that you're sending is brief and the user wants to see many different items on a single page.

For example, suppose that you have a Web page designed to sell musical instruments. You can have a master page with links to descriptions of each instrument, but that means your users who are interested in comparing several instruments have to go back and forth from the main page to each of the other pages featuring the instrument descriptions. Instead, you want them to be able to compare all the instruments that they're interested in simultaneously.

To enable your users to compare many items at once, you can create an HTML form by using the following code:

```
<form method=POST action="/cgi-bin/dispguit.cgi">
Please pick the instruments from the following list. You
may choose as many as you want.
<br><input type=checkbox name=GoyaStandard>
Goya standard guitar
<br><input type=checkbox name=GoyaConcert>
Goya concert guitar
<br><input type=checkbox name=VegaArtistGrand>
Vega Artist Grand guitar
<br><input type=checkbox name=HarmonySteel>
Harmony steel guitar
<br><input type="submit" value="Show me">
</form>
```

Part of the program used to process the form looks like what you see in Listing 14-1.

Listing 14-1: **A program for displaying information based on user requests.use CGI;**

```
$q = new CGI();

print <<EndOfTop;
Content-type: text/html

<html><head><title>Guitar Information</title></head><body>
<p>Thank you for considering our guitars. Here is the
information you requested.
EndOfTop

@TheTypes = qw(GoyaStandard GoyaConcert VegaArtistGrand
  HarmonySteel);
foreach $ThisType (@TheTypes) {
  if($q->param($ThisType)) {
    $DisplayThis = &GetData($ThisType);
    print "<hr><p>$DisplayThis\n";
  }
}
print "</body></html>\n";
```

Listing 14-2 shows the same program as Listing 14-1, but uses the CGI module to display the output.

Listing 14-2: **A program for displaying information based on user requests.**

```
use CGI;
$q = new CGI();

print $q->header('text/html'),
  $q->start_html(-title => 'Guitar Information'),
  $q->p('Thank you for considering our guitars. Here is' .
    ' the information you requested.');

@TheTypes = qw(GoyaStandard GoyaConcert VegaArtisGrand
  HarmonySteel);
foreach $ThisType (@TheTypes) {
  if($q->param($ThisType)) {
    $DisplayThis = &GetData($ThisType);
    print $q->hr, $q->p($DisplayThis);
  }
}
print $q->end_html;
```

You can see that the programs in Listing 14-1 and Listing 14-2 read approximately the same but use very different methods for putting out the HTML.

Using Redirection to Link to Other Sites

Links on one Web page that point to a different Web server are common, and most Web administrators want to keep track of who follows their links to other servers. For example, if you list a dozen different sites on your server, you may want to tell the administrators of a site, "I sent 100 people in your direction last week."

The typical way to send someone to another Web site is simply to provide a link to that site, but you won't know when or if a user accesses one of those links. A less common method to link to other sites is *redirection,* which employs a CGI program that sends an HTTP message to the user's browser, which then links the user to the other site. By using redirection, you can also log how many times you send users to each site.

Listing 14-3 displays a program called `ad-url.cgi` that tracks redirections. Long ago, I wrote the program for a newspaper called *MicroTimes.* The newspaper's editor wanted the *MicroTimes* Web page to list the newspaper's advertisers who had their own Web sites and also link the newspaper's site to the advertisers' sites. The first section of the program in Listing 14-3 sets up a variable, `$WebPerson`, that's used in many places within the program. The program then fills in the `$TheSearch` variable with the user's request.

The program in Listing 14-3 then checks to see whether `$TheSearch` is blank (it shouldn't be). If it isn't blank, the program opens the `AdURLs` file and reads through it one line at a time (see Chapter 10 for a description of reading from files). Each line is split into two variables, `$TheName` and `$TheURL`, and the program compares `$TheName` to `$TheSearch`. If they match, the program sets some variables and jumps out of the loop.

After the loop, the program looks to see whether an entry in the database matched the search. If it does, the `PrintFound` subroutine prints the appropriate HTTP redirection headers; if not, the `PrintNotFound` subroutine prints an error message. The HTTP headers put out by the `PrintFound` subroutine cause most Web clients to automatically go to the specified URL; but if they don't, the text in the message enables the user to go to that URL manually.

The sections in the middle of the program in Listing 14-3 create log entries in an external log file using the `sprintf` function (described in Chapter 9). The log is opened, a line is written to it, and then closed (see Chapter 10 for more on this process).

Listing 14-3: A program for redirecting Web clients.

```perl
$WebPerson = 'webmaster@yourcompany.com';

# Look at the string they handed to us in the URL
$TheSearch = $ENV{QUERY_STRING};

# Look in the search string
unless($TheSearch eq '') {
  $RefURL = ''; # The URL we will send them to
  # Open the database
  open(IN, 'AdURLs') or die "Could not open the URL " .
    "database. Please send mail to $WebPerson so " .
    "we can fix this.\n";
  # Read the database line-by-line
  while (<IN>) {
    $TheString = $_; chomp($TheString);
    # Split the line into two parts, based on
    #  whitespace between them
    ($TheName, $TheURL) = split(/\s+/,$TheString, 2);
    # Check if the part we just got is the same as
    #  the part in the search string
    if ($TheName eq $TheSearch) {
      # If so, set some variables and leave
$RefName = $TheName;
      $RefURL = $TheURL;
      last;
    }
}
  close(IN);
  unless ($RefURL eq '') {  # We found a match
    &PrintFound;
  }
  else {  # We didn't find a match
    &PrintNotFound;
    # Change the $RefName for the log
    $RefName = "ErrorNotInDatabase:$TheSearch";
  }
}
else { #The search string was empty
  print "HTTP/1.0 400 Bad Request\n";
  print "Content-Type: text/html\n\n";
  print "<head><title>Incorrect Request</title>" .
    "</head><body>\n";
  print "There was no query.\n";
  print "</body>\n";
  $RefName = 'ErrorNoRequest'; # This is for the log
}

# We displayed what we wanted to, now make a log entry

# Get the time right now into a bunch of variables
```

```perl
  ($Second, $Minute, $Hour, $DayOfMonth, $Month, $Year,
   $WeekDay, $DayOfYear, $IsDST) = localtime(time);
$RealMonth = $Month + 1; # Since $Month starts at 0
# Format the variables to be two digits long
$DateAndTime = sprintf("%02d/%02d/%02d\t%02d:%02d:%02d",
   $RealMonth, $DayOfMonth, $Year, $Hour, $Minute,
   $Second);

# Get the host name or IP address for the log
unless($ENV{REMOTE_HOST} eq '')
   { $TheWhere = $ENV{REMOTE_HOST} }
else { $TheWhere = $ENV{REMOTE_ADDR} }
# Open the log and write the line
open(ADLOG, '>>AdLog') or die "Could not append to the " .
   "URL log. Please send mail to $WebPerson so we can " .
   "fix this.\n";
print ADLOG "$DateAndTime\t$TheWhere\t$RefName\n";
close(ADLOG);

sub PrintFound {
    print <<"EndFound";
HTTP/1.0 302 Found
Location: $RefURL
Content-Type: text/html

<head><title>Redirection Information</title></head><body>
If you are reading this, your Web browser does not support
redirection. That's OK: simply select <a href=\"$RefURL\">
this</a> and you will be taken to the advertiser you
selected.
</body>
EndFound
}
sub PrintNotFound {
    print <<"EndNotFound";
HTTP/1.0 404 Not Found
Content-Type: text/html

<head><title>Incorrect Request</title></head><body>
There is no entry in the URL database for '$TheSearch'.
This may indicate an error in our database of URLs.
If you are sure you got this message by simply choosing
one of the links on our page, please send email to
<a href=\"mailto:$WebPerson\">$WebPerson</a>.
</body>
EndNotFound
}
```

In order to use the redirection program in Listing 14-3, your Perl CGI program must be the only one sending any HTTP headers. However, this program doesn't work on all Web servers because it sends out its own headers. It won't work on a server that also sends out a set of headers because a Web client can only understand one set of headers. You may find that many servers enable you to prevent those servers from sending out headers for some CGI programs using special settings. (Check your Web server documentation to determine how you can prevent the server from sending out any HTTP headers for this particular program or any CGI programs.)

The *MicroTimes* Web site that I mentioned earlier in this section contains pages with links to a database. A portion of the HTML for the site's pages looks like this (plus some, for the hundreds of additional advertiser's URLs):

```
<h3>Computer Systems</h3>
<a href="ad-url?ACME">ACME Micro-System, Inc.</a><p>
<a href="ad-url?AdvancedComputer">Advanced Computers
and Technology</a><p>
<a href="ad-url?Airt"> AIRT Computers</a><p>
```

The advertiser database consists of a simple text file with lines of advertisers' names and the respective URLs for their home pages:

```
ACME  http://www.acmemicro.com/
AdvancedComputer http://www.plgrn.com/adv-comp.html
Airt  http://www.airtcomp.com
```

Security and CGI programs

You can do lots of stuff with Perl and CGI that will make your Web pages more interesting and versatile. However, you can also do plenty of stuff that's detrimental to the security of your Web site. When you write CGI programs, be careful when reading and writing files on your system. Hackers who enjoy breaking into systems and wreaking havoc with them are always on the lookout for poorly written programs that are easily cracked and manipulated. After hackers break in, they may alter your Web pages (in some cases, by adding offensive material) or they can steal private corporate information, such as customer records.

Keep an eye on any CGI programs that take input from a user and then use that input as a command for the Web server (I describe some of the pitfalls of doing this in Chapter 18). Before you write any Perl CGI program, read the Web Security FAQ document that you can find at

```
www.w3.org/Security/Faq/
www-security-faq.html
```

This document lists many of the common security mistakes that programmers make when creating CGI programs.

Exploring a Few Other Environment Variables

A number of environment variables, other than the ones that I mentioned earlier in this chapter, are available to your CGI programs. Frankly, some of those other variables aren't terribly useful, but the following sections describe a few worth adding to your CGI program mix.

Gathering additional client information

The CONTENT_TYPE variable holds the MIME type of the form handed to the CGI program. This variable is often left blank, but it can be set in the HTML <form> tag with the enctype attribute.

Most Web clients also send a few additional HTTP headers when they make requests. These headers appear in environment variables whose names have HTTP_ before the header name and hyphens changed to underscores. For example, the User-Agent header put out by most clients can be accessed from the HTTP_USER_AGENT environment variable.

Not all Web servers put values in every environment variable that Web clients give them.

Collecting server information

Table 14-2 lists the environment variables that provide information about the Web server from which a CGI program is launched.

Table 14-2	Server Information Variables
Variable	*Description*
SERVER_SOFTWARE	The name and version of the Web server software
SERVER_NAME	The domain name that the server is running from
SERVER_PORT	The TCP port on which the request was made
SERVER_PROTOCOL	The version of HTTP that the server is running
GATEWAY_INTERFACE	The version of CGI that the server is using

Some Web servers also create server-specific environment variables. Unfortunately, those variables don't have standard names, so you can't find them easily. For example, my favorite Web server software on UNIX is called WN. WN creates environment variables called WN_DIR_PATH and WN_ROOT; other servers create similar variables with their own non-standard names.

Authenticating the user

If your Web server supports user authentication, REMOTE_USER contains the name of the user. AUTH_TYPE is the protocol used to authenticate the user. If your Web server supports the Internet IDENT protocol, and the user's computer does as well, the REMOTE_IDENT variable holds the user's login name.

Don't rely on the IDENT protocol to provide you with any security. It's easy to fool an IDENT server into thinking that a user is someone he or she isn't.

SCRIPT_NAME is the path to the CGI program being run, in case you need to know what directory you're in.

Working with Apache and Perl

The Apache Web server is the most popular Web server software on the Internet. It combines simplicity of management with good security. More importantly, its source code is open to review by anyone (just like Perl's), which means that people can also add new features easily.

On systems that rely heavily on Perl CGI scripts, it makes sense to reduce the overhead of running Perl as much as possible. One way to do this is to embed Perl directly into the Web server. This isn't needed on Web sites that aren't being pounded all the time, but is quite useful for those busy Web sites that get dozens of hits a second.

Introducing mod_perl

In Apache, the preferred method for embedding Perl in the server is called mod_perl. The biggest advantage of using mod_perl is that it reduces the time that it takes to start up Perl in your CGI scripts, but that's only one of its features. mod_perl also lets you have access to the internals of Apache, which in turn gives you a way to write much more sophisticated programs, such as ones that keep track of a user as they visit different parts of your Web site.

You can find out much more about mod_perl on the Web at perl.apache.org.

Using mod_perl

To use mod_perl, it has to be built into the Apache server itself by the person who installed Apache on your server hardware. This means that end users can't just install mod_perl themselves; instead, they have to ask their system administrators to install mod_perl for them.

After mod_perl is built into Apache, you don't have to make any changes to your Perl programs in order to use mod_perl. However, you do need to change the way that Apache calls your program, which is specified in your httpd.conf file. Assuming that the name of your CGI script is GuitarChoice.cgi, you would add the following lines to your httpd.conf file:

```
<Files GuitarChoice.cgi>
   SetHandler perl-script
   PerlHandler Apache::Registry
   Options ExecCGI
</Files>
```

Basically, that's all you need. If you want to do more than just accelerate your Perl programs, you can add Apache modules that hook into your Perl scripts. The mod_perl Web site (perl.apache.org) has extensive lists of modules that are ready-to-use for all sorts of useful tasks.

Handling CGI and HTML with Mason

Although Perl's CGI module is fairly useful, you may also want to look at Mason. Although most people who use Mason do so as part of mod_perl, you can use Mason by itself. Its most interesting features include the ability to add conditional choices to your HTML and to create HTML templates that you can re-use in your scripts.

In some ways, Mason is just a much fancier replacement for the CGI module in Perl. That is, 90 percent of all Perl users who need to create CGI scripts do just fine with the CGI module. The CGI module doesn't require that you do anything different in your Web server, which is also handy for those of us who are not system administrators.

For the 10 percent of users who need something beyond what the CGI module can offer, Mason is probably their best bet for a high-end tool. Mason has the advantage of having been developed much later than the CGI module. The folks who wrote Mason could see what advanced Perl users wanted in a CGI processor, and could also see how the Web evolved over the hectic years near the end of the last century. Like mod_perl (and Perl itself!), Mason is free and its source code is open to read and modify.

The Mason project has a very complete Web site at www.masonhq.com.

Chapter 15

Perl Gets Cozy with the Web, E-Mail, and the Rest of the Internet

In This Chapter

▷ Using Perl's library of modules for grabbing stuff off the Web

▷ Creating your own Internet clients

▷ Checking POP mailboxes

*I*nternet users are now quite used to working with fancy point-and-click interfaces to the Web — thanks to browsers like Netscape Navigator and Microsoft Internet Explorer. Many Internet users also make use of graphical interfaces to read and send mail through programs like Eudora by Qualcomm, the mail program in Netscape Navigator, or one of the mail programs from Microsoft.

These Internet programs are easy to use, but they don't provide the flexibility that all users want. For example, they're difficult or downright impossible to program. For example, suppose that you have a list of 100 domain names that host Web sites and you want to download the home pages of each site for later viewing. Navigator and Internet Explorer don't have point-and-click interfaces for doing this sort of thing. Naturally, this sounds like a job for Perl.

Lots of good Internet tools are already written in Perl, so you don't have to reinvent the wheel. In fact, the tools are fairly easy to use, and you can write programs with just a few lines of code that do things like get FTP files. The result is not a graphical program. Instead, it's a very character-oriented one, but that may be just what you want.

This chapter covers how to use a few of the Internet tools from the Comprehensive Perl Archive Network (CPAN) library.

Using the libwww-perl Library

To many people, the Internet is the Web, and the way to get to the Internet is through their Web browsers. By the time you read this, more people may think that e-mail is more interesting than the Web, but (sadly) I doubt it.

You may have many reasons for wanting to create a Perl program that knows how to go out and snag pages from the Web. For example, you may want to create a robot to get all the available Web pages from one site or from many sites. Or you may want to send out a Web request every hour to see whether the information on a particular Web page has changed since the previous hour. Or you may want to check a list of Web links to make sure that they're still valid. All these tasks require some amount of programming and can't be done easily with a standard *Web client* (a program that requests information from a Web server), such as Internet Explorer.

The best means for accessing the Web is through a library of utility functions called *libwww-perl*. The library's name comes from the fact that the Perl library is based on the earlier libwww library written in C. (We don't want those C programmers mistaking our library for theirs, do we?) ActivePerl and MacPerl come with libwww-perl built in, but UNIX users must install it from the CPAN library on the Web if they want to use it.

You can use the libwww-perl library for more than just accessing the Web: It contains modules for accessing FTP, Usenet news, Gopher, files on your computer, and even for sending mail. In technical terms, this means that libwww-perl can handle all the following types of URLs:

- ✔ http:
- ✔ ftp:
- ✔ news:
- ✔ gopher:
- ✔ file:
- ✔ mailto:

Installing libwww-perl on UNIX

Readers who don't already have libwww-perl (namely those on UNIX systems) can find the libwww-perl library in its compressed form on the CPAN library on the Web. (I describe CPAN in more detail in Chapter 2.) When you download the latest version of libwww-perl from CPAN, it comes with detailed instructions on how to install it. Instead of repeating those instructions here, you can read them from the copy that you download because different versions of libwww-perl have different installation instructions.

Getting documents from the Web and FTP

libwww-perl is a set of Perl 5 modules, so you normally use Perl's object-oriented syntax (described in Chapter 19) when interacting with it. Luckily, libwww-perl includes a simple interface so that folks who aren't geared to object-oriented programming can easily use the library's basic parts. The interface is the LWP::Simple module. (*LWP* is an abbreviation for libwww-perl.) At the beginning of a program, you can tell Perl that you want to use the Simple package in LWP with the following statement:

```
use LWP::Simple;
```

Table 15-1 contains the four functions in the LWP::Simple module that get the contents of a document based on its URL.

Table 15-1	LWP::Simple Functions
Function	*Description*
get($URL)	Gets the document at the URL and returns it
getstore($URL, $Filename)	Same as get except that it writes the retrieved document to the named file
getprint($URL)	Same as get except that it prints the information returned to the function to standard file output
mirror($URL, $Filename)	Same as getstore except that it gets the document only if it is newer or of a different size than the file on disk

The get function returns the document into a string, getstore puts it in a file, getprint puts it out on standard file output, and mirror gets the file only if it needs to. For example, if you just want to print the contents of a Web page, you can use this little program:

```
use LWP::Simple;
getprint('http://www.dummies.com');
```

If you want to download a file from an FTP site, you can use this program:

```
use LWP::Simple;
getstore('ftp://ftp.internic.net/rfc/rfc822.txt',
'rfc822');
```

The preceding program gets the file from the FTP site and stores it on your hard drive with the name rfc822.

If you give an invalid URL to get or getstore, such as the name of a Web site that doesn't exist or a filename that's spelled wrong, LWP::Simple returns an empty string; getprint, on the other hand, fills the string with an error message.

Testing Web links with a Perl program

You're probably going to use Perl to get a whole group of Web pages instead of just one at a time. This section shows you how to get a group of pages or how to check multiple links in one fell swoop.

An extremely handy program is one that can check whether all the links from one Web page actually work. Listing 15-1 shows a program called linkchck.pl that reads a Web page, picks out all the links from the page, and then goes out on the Web and tests whether those links are valid. If you don't feel like typing in the program, you can find it on this book's Web site. Go to www.dummies.com/extras, and click on the link for this book.

Listing 15-1:   A program for checking the links from a Web page.

```
$TheURL = $ARGV[0]; # Get the URL from the command line

# Section A
use LWP::Simple;
$TheMain = get($TheURL); # Get the main page
if($TheMain eq '')
  { die "The starting URL was not valid.\n" }

# Section B
$TheMain =~ tr/A-Z/a-z/; # Lowercase everything
$TheMain =~ s/\"/'/g;   # Double quotes to single
$TheMain =~ s/\n/ /g;   # Get rid of the linefeeds
$TheMain =~ s/\s+/ /g;  # Compress spaces/tabs

# Section C
# First find any "base href='URL'" for relative URLs.
$BasePos = index($TheMain, '<base href');
if($BasePos > -1) {
  $OpenQuote = index($TheMain, "'", $BasePos);
  $BaseStart = $OpenQuote + 1;
  $CloseQuote = index($TheMain, "'", $BaseStart);
  $BaseLen = $CloseQuote - $OpenQuote - 1;
  $URLBase = substr($TheMain, $BaseStart, $BaseLen);
}
```

```
else { $URLBase = '' }

# Section D
# Keep a list of the URLs we find
@URLList = ();
while(1) { # Loop forever, rely on "last"
  $TheA = index($TheMain, '<a href'); # The next link
  if($TheA == -1) { last };
  # Find the URL in the quotes
  $OpenQuote = index($TheMain, "'", $TheA);
  $URLStart = $OpenQuote + 1;
  $CloseQuote = index($TheMain, "'", $URLStart);
  $URLLen = $CloseQuote - $OpenQuote - 1;
  $TheURL = substr($TheMain, $URLStart, $URLLen);
  # Put the URL into @URLList
  push(@URLList, $TheURL);
  # Chop off beginning of $TheMain to our position
  $TheMain = substr($TheMain, $CloseQuote);
}

# Section E
@CheckURLs = ();
foreach $TheURL (@URLList) {
  # Determine which URLs are relative. Absolute URLs
  #   start with 'http:' or 'ftp:' or 'mailto:';
  #   others are relative to the base. Relative URLs have
  #   $URLBase added to the beginning.
  unless($TheURL =~ /^(http:|ftp:|mailto:)/)
    { $TheURL = $URLBase . $TheURL }
  # Don't check URLs starting with 'mailto:'
  unless($TheURL =~ /^mailto:/)
    { push(@CheckURLs, $TheURL) }
}

# Section F
# Now check each URL in the list for error messages
foreach $TheURL (@CheckURLs) {
  $TheCheck = get($TheURL);
  if($TheCheck ne "") { print "OK:   $TheURL\n" }
  else { print "Fail: $TheURL\n" }
}
```

The first line of the program in Listing 15-1 tells Perl to get the URL for the page that you want to check from the command line. For example, you can run the program with

```
linkchck.pl http://www.mycompany.com/accts/main.html
```

The set of statements labeled Section A in Listing 15-1 loads the LWP::Simple package, gets the document, and loads it into the string $TheMain. The program then checks whether the $TheMain variable has anything in it and ends if the string doesn't.

The four lines labeled Section B employ techniques described in Chapter 12. These lines do the following:

- ✔ Convert the document to all lowercase characters so that you don't have to for each string that you're looking for.

- ✔ Change all the quotation marks to apostrophes. URLs can be in either single- or double-quotation marks, so this conversion makes them easier to find.

- ✔ Change all linefeeds to spaces to prevent any HTML tags being split over a line break.

- ✔ Change all multiple spaces and tab characters into a single space. This prevents the program from missing some tags if they have multiple spaces or tabs within them.

The program's next task, which is covered in the statements in Section C of Listing 15-1, is its search for an HTML base tag. If the page that you receive has a base tag, some of the URLs on the page may be *relative* URLs, meaning that they don't have the full URL — just the last characters of the URL. At the end of that set of lines, $URLBase is set to either the base URL or the null string if no base URL exists.

The statements in Section D then go through the $TheMain string and look for HTML a tags that are links. The loop is exited when no additional HTML a tags exist. This set of statements finds the beginning of the tag and then the quoted URL inside the tag. Each URL is added to the end of the @URLList. The $TheMain string is then shortened up to the point where the tag was found, and the loop begins again.

The next statements in Section E go through all the URLs that were found to determine whether they are *absolute URLs* (that is, ones with the full URL syntax) or relative URLs. In the latter case, the program tacks on the base URL to the beginning of the URL. The program also checks to see whether the URL is a mailto: URL. If it is a mailto: URL, the program ignores it because mailto: URLs are never relative URLs, so they don't need to be checked.

The statements in Section F go out and check each remaining URL. If the get function is successful, the program prints OK: and the URL; otherwise, the program prints Fail: and the URL. You can quickly see which of the URLs that came back without documents so you can investigate them.

Using libwww-perl with objects

I want to emphasize that libwww-perl does much more than what I show you with the LWP::Simple package covered in the preceding two sections.

The `LWP::Simple` package is a great example of what's inside libwww-perl because it allows those who aren't familiar with the object-oriented features in Perl 5 to use Perl to get documents from Web servers and FTP servers.

Even if you read Chapter 19, which describes object-oriented Perl and shows you a bit about how to use the libwww-perl objects, I strongly recommend that you take a look at the other parts of the libwww-perl package. The package contains many useful features that allow you to do the following:

✔ Make Web robots that can download all the documents linked from a particular Web page.

✔ React to different HTTP headers that are returned on Web requests.

✔ Convert HTML to a more readable format for humans.

✔ Traverse directory trees on FTP servers so that you can get every file found in a particular directory and in its subdirectories.

✔ Get and send Usenet news.

✔ Send e-mail.

Getting Your E-Mail

Much of the information on the Internet is available only through e-mail, and not through the Web or FTP. For example, many mailing lists contain valuable resources that are not accessible by any other means. And, of course, e-mail provides quick and efficient person-to-person communication over the Internet.

Many versatile, graphically based Web clients exist for viewing pages on the World Wide Web. Also, many versatile, graphically based e-mail clients read and send e-mail messages. But, like their Web client brethren, few e-mail clients can be programmed to do what you want.

Suppose that you're on ten active mailing lists — wouldn't it be nice to have a program filter the messages into a number of different files so that you can find the particular items in which you are interested? You may also want to have a program act as an interface for e-mail if you use e-mail to receive regular reports from other computers; you can use the program to look for the reports, pull out the needed information, add it to previous reports, and so on. If you get your e-mail from a Post Office Protocol (POP) server, you can perform all these tasks easily with the `Mail::POP3Client` module, which I describe in the following sections.

Accessing the Mail::POP3Client module

The `Mail::POP3Client` module provides a simple interface to POP servers. A *POP server* enables your mail client to get e-mail from the server's hard drive. You can use the module to check your mail or grab particular messages, for example.

You must install the module before you can use it. You UNIX users can get your system administrator to install it (hopefully). You can find the module easily on CPAN. ActivePerl users can install the module by using PPM, as described in Chapter 2.

Creating a simple client object

Unlike the libwww-perl module, `Mail::POP3Client` has only an object interface (that is, it doesn't have a simple function-based interface). However, you can still do a few neat things with the `Mail::POP3Client`. You can create useful mail-collecting programs even without knowing anything about object-oriented programming.

With any mail program, you need to know three things in order to talk to a POP server:

- ✔ Mail account name
- ✔ Mail account password
- ✔ Domain name of the mail server

Given these three things, your program may begin with a few variables, such as the following:

```
$Name = 'larry';
$Pass = 'AouerGyvvt';
$Serv = 'mail.yourisp.com';
```

To use the `Mail::POP3Client`, you must first include it in your program and create a *client object*. The client object communicates with the POP server. When you create a new client, you supply the user name, password, and server name as arguments. Therefore, you can start your program off with the following statements:

```
use Mail::POP3Client;
$Client = new Mail::POP3Client($Name, $Pass, $Serv);
```

At this point, your Perl program has logged into the POP server. The POP server is waiting for you to send it POP commands. You should know the following things about POP before writing your programs:

  ✔ After you have logged into a POP server, you can send it commands that give you information about either the entire mailbox or about individual messages. For example, you can ask for a count of all the messages or for the contents of a particular message.

  ✔ Each message in a POP mailbox has a message number. Message numbers start at 1, and not at 0, as you may expect by having worked with other Perl programs.

You use `Mail::POP3Client` methods to send POP commands to the POP server and to examine the results. Many of the `Mail::POP3Client` methods take one argument, namely the message number on which you want the methods to act. Table 15-2 contains a few of the more interesting `Mail::POP3Client` methods.

Table 15-2	Methods for the Mail::POP3Client Module
Method	*What It Does*
Count	Tells how many messages are on the server
Head(num)	Gets the header lines of the message
Body(num)	Gets the body of the message
HeadAndBody(num)	Gets the entire message
Delete(num)	Marks the message for deletion
List	Lists all the messages and their sizes
Close	Closes the connection, thus deleting any marked messages
State	Tells whether the connection is alive

Examining a program for processing reports in your mailbox

Suppose that you have a program that mails you a report every day. You want to process your mailbox to find out whether the report was sent and, if so, to save the report on disk and delete that message from your mailbox. That way, you can use your graphical client to read the rest of the messages but still process the report automatically. Listing 15-2 shows you how such a program is built. (The program is also on the book's Web site under the name `popcheck.pl`.)

Listing 15-2:   A sample program that checks for a report in a POP mailbox.

```perl
$Name = 'larry';
$Pass = 'AouerGyvvt';
$Serv = 'mail.yourisp.com';
$Subj = 'Subject: Daily logging report';

use Mail::POP3Client;
$Client = new Mail::POP3Client($Name, $Pass, $Serv);
$TheState = $Client->State;
if($TheState eq 'AUTHORIZATION')
   { die "Bad user name or password.\n" }
elsif($TheState eq 'DEAD')
   { die "Mail server unreachable or unavailable.\n" }
# Find out how many messages there are
$NumMsg = $Client->Count;
#Loop through the messages (starting at 1)
for($i = 1; $i<=$NumMsg; $i +=1) {
  $Headers = $Client->Head($i);
  @HeadList = split(/\n/, $Headers);
  foreach $Line (@HeadList) {
    if($Line =~ /^$Subj/) {
      # Found the message; get the body, then delete
      $Body = $Client->Body($i);
      $Client->Delete($i);
      # Process the report and leave
      &ProcessReport($Body);
      last;
    }
  }
}
# Close the connection so the delete happens
$Client->Close;
sub ProcessReport {
  my($Report) = pop(@_);
  # Do something here that is processing the report
  return;
}
```

The first few lines of the program in Listing 15-2 set up variables for use later on in the program. The following statement uses the State method on the client:

```perl
$TheState = $Client->State;
```

The three possible results of the State method are: TRANSACTION, meaning things are fine; AUTHORIZATION, meaning that the POP server is trying to authorize the client; and DEAD, meaning that the POP server wasn't found. If you end up in AUTHORIZATION after giving a username and password, this means that the combination didn't work. The program then gets the number of messages and loops through each one. The following statement gets the headers for the current message:

```
$Headers = $Client->Head($i);
```

The headers are then split into an array and checked for the subject header that identifies the message that you want. If that subject header is found, $Body gets the body of the message, the message is deleted, the report is processed, and the loop terminates.

Pinging with Perl

Sometimes, you don't want to do much with another computer other than to see if it is still connected to the Internet. The typical way to do this is by "pinging" it. The term *ping* comes from the name of the UNIX program that has been used for decades for this task. Starting with Perl 5.6, Perl makes it easy to do the same thing in your programs.

The Net::Ping module is pretty simple because it only has one interesting method: ping. To see whether a remote computer's connection to the Internet is working, you use that computer's domain name as the argument to the ping method. The method returns true if it reached the other system over the network, and returns false if it couldn't reach it.

Suppose that you want to see if the server www.whitehouse.gov (the Web site for the President of the United States) is up. To do so, you would use the following:

```
use Net::Ping;

$Pinger = new Net::Ping;
if($Pinger->ping('www.whitehouse.gov'))
  { print "www.whitehouse.gov is up\n"; }
else { print "www.whitehouse.gov is down\n"; }
```

The ping method also works with IP addresses (those four-number monstrosities that you sometimes still need to use when you want to connect to a system on the Internet, but you don't know its domain name). For example:

```
if($Pinger->ping('65.85.22.216'))
  { print "That site is up\n"; }
```

The ping method uses a method that often, but does not always, works. Some systems don't allow you to determine whether they are alive by using the ping method. Don't assume that getting a negative answer from the ping method means that the system is not active; it may only mean that the ping method couldn't reach the system.

Using Net::FTP to Grab Files

You can generally get files from the Internet in two different ways: using the Web and using FTP, which stands for *File Transfer Protocol*. FTP was around a long time before the Web was invented, and it is still used today for many file transfers.

Most computers come with FTP clients, which interact with FTP servers. FTP servers are usually set up so that you can only get files from them, but some FTP servers (such as inside a company) allow you to put files on them as well.

As you may expect, Perl makes it easy to interact with FTP servers. First, you have to get the Net::FTP module:

- ✔ **Perl 5.8:** If you are using Perl 5.8, getting the Net::FTP module is no problem, because it is already built in.
- ✔ **Perl 5.6:** If you are using Perl 5.6 on UNIX, you need to download the libnet library, which includes many modules, including Net::FTP. (Windows-based Perl users already have libnet built in).

As you saw earlier in this chapter, you can access FTP servers with the libwww-perl package, but only if you have a specific URL for the file that you want to get; Net::FTP gives you much more flexibility.

The libnet package has to be installed before you can use it. UNIX users can get your system administrator to install the libnet package (hopefully). You can find the package easily on CPAN (which is described in Chapter 2). ActivePerl users already have the module installed.

FTP servers require you to give a username and password to get access to their files. However, FTP servers that allow anyone to have access standardly use "anonymous" as the user name and any e-mail address as a password. (This doesn't have to be your own e-mail address; it could be anyone's).

After you get to an FTP server, you can look around the directories like you look around the directories on your own computer. When you find a file that you want to get, you tell the FTP server the name, and it sends it to you.

Doing all this in Perl with the Net::FTP module is pretty simple, and it follows the same patterns as you have seen with the other modules in this chapter. For example, suppose that you want to get the file SaturdayNight.mp3 that is in the /Music directory on the open FTP server whose domain name is ftp.example.com. The following program does that for you:

```
use Net::FTP;
$ThisFTP = Net::FTP->new('ftp.example.com');
$ThisFTP->login('anonymous', 'me@you.com');
$ThisFTP->cwd('/Music');
$ThisFTP->binary;
$ThisFTP->get('SaturdayNight.mp3');
```

The `$ThisFTP->binary` command is quite important in this case. FTP has two ways that it can transmit files to you: ASCII and binary. You only want to use ASCII mode when you are getting files that are all text, and use binary mode for everything else.

The `get` method can take either one or two arguments. The first argument is the name of the file on the FTP server that you want to get. If you include a second argument, it tells Perl what to name the file on your computer. This lets you get files and change their names before saving them locally.

If you are connected to an FTP server that lets you upload files (that is, to copy them from your computer to the FTP server), you can use the `put` method:

```
$ThisFTP->put('MyFile.doc');
```

Like the `get` method, the `put` method can have two arguments. In the case of `put`, however, the first argument is the name of the file on your computer, and the second argument is the name that you want the file to have on the FTP server.

`Net::FTP` has many other methods that have names similar to the commands that you see in many FTP clients. For example, the `dir` method returns an array that is a directory listing of the current directory. This is not just a list of files: Depending on the server, it can also include the size of the files, when they were last modified, and so on.

Delving into Domain Names with Perl

The Internet's domain name system (DNS) is one of the wonders of modern technology. The Internet today is thousands of times larger than when the DNS was invented, but the DNS still works just fine with almost no significant changes. Domain names are so ubiquitous that many people don't even think about them.

Perl uses domain names in the modules that you have already seen in this chapter. For example, you give a host name as part of the URL in the `get` function in `LWP::Simple`, in the `new` method in `Mail::POP3Client`, and so on. Many standard Perl functions also use domain names.

Generally the only thing that you want to do with a domain name in Perl is to get the IP address associated with it. You don't need any modules to do that; you can just use the gethostbyname function. You should use this function in scalar context (described in Chapter 7) because that's what gets you the IP address most easily. The address returned is four bytes smooshed together; you use the unpack function to split them apart. For example:

```
$DummyIP = gethostbyname('www.dummies.com');
($a1, $a2, $a3, $a4) = unpack('C4', $DummyIP);
print "$a1.$a2.$a3.$a4\n";
```

The DNS is much more than just domain names that translate to IP addresses, however. For example, many domain names also have additional records of information associated with them, such as information on where you would find an SMTP server that is associated with a domain name. To get that kind of information, you need to use the Net::DNS module in Perl.

The Net::DNS module gives you access to all the guts of the DNS. This admittedly is not something that most people want to see, which is why the module is not covered here. However, if you learn more about the intricacies of the DNS and want to write Perl programs to explore, the Net::DNS module will come in very handy.

Chapter 16

Using Perl as a Gateway to XML and Web Services

M ost of the text documents on the Web are formatted with HTML, the language that allows you to specify how your Web page text will be styled. HTML has served the Web very well since the Web's inception in the early 1990s, but many people believe that HTML needs to be replaced with something better in order for the Web to reach its full potential.

In 1996, the World Wide Web Consortium (W3C) started doing serious work on the follow-up to HTML. XML (eXtensible Markup Language) has capabilities well beyond those of HTML, which is why so many people are interested in it. HTML is really only good at determining how text will look when it's displayed. XML, on the other hand, describes each part of a text document so that the displaying program (which is usually your Web browser) can decide on its own how to display the document.

Exploring the Role of Perl and XML in Web Programming

If you think of content on the Web as stuff created and formatted by hand, you may be confused by the idea of Web programming. However, if you realize that most of the formatting and searching for the Web is done by programs (again, usually Web browsers), you can see how Web programming can be useful. Take a look at the home pages for CNN at www.cnn.com, and you can see how hard it would be to get the formatting correct if it was done by hand and constantly updated.

The same is true for the Web's (still-limited) use of XML. XML can indeed be created by hand, but it is much easier to do that with a program. And Perl is quite possibly the best program to use when working with XML because of its excellent text-handling abilities.

Introducing XML

Don't think of XML as just another Web-related technology that gets hyped in the media but then never amounts to much. Although XML is still somewhat new, it is of special importance to programmers for a number of reasons. XML is useful for many things other than displaying text on the Web: XML can be used as a mechanism for exchanging databases, such as medical records, or for conducting commercial transactions between individuals who have never met face to face, among many other applications.

XML is a method for adding text to a document that makes the document richer. The XML *tags* that you add to a document allow a program that is processing that document to understand more about the content, such as what part is the title of the document, what part is a table, what parts are footnotes, and so forth. Although a human can read an XML document and absorb some of this information, XML is designed so that its documents are processed by programs.

XML is complex and powerful, and the subject could fill a whole book, which in fact it has — *XML For Dummies*, 3rd Edition, by Ed Tittel published by Wiley Publishing, Inc. Because many people think that XML is so important for the future of the Web, people developing Web sites may want to find out more about XML.

Examining an XML document

Most elements in XML have a start tag and an end tag. For example, you may see the following in an XML document that may be used to control a sound system:

```
I want that cake <yell>now</yell>!
```

The expression <yell> is the start tag and </yell> is its matching end tag.

Some tags have attributes in them. For example, note the difference between the tags in the following example from those in the previous one:

```
I want that cake <yell volume="loud">now</yell>!
```

In the second example, volume is the name of the attribute and loud is the value of that attribute. A tag can have many attributes.

XML elements can be inside another element. For example, suppose that you have a database of customer orders. Each order in the database is its own record, and an order can have any number of sub-parts. The "order" entity would look like this:

```
<order> . . . some stuff . . . </order>
```

The "stuff" in the order entry would also be XML. For example, the item whose part number is 13572 may look like this:

```
<item><itemid>13572</itemid></item>
```

In XML, you can freely break a line of XML tags into separate lines, or add space between them. If the order described previously contained just the one item, it may look like the following:

```
<order><item><itemid>13572</itemid></item></order>
```

Or, it could have some spaces added:

```
<order>  <item>  <itemid>13572</itemid> </item>  </order>
```

Or, it could even be broken up:

```
<order>
   <item>
     <itemid>
        13572
     </itemid>
   </item>
</order>
```

Don't forget that entities can also have attributes. When using XML for databases, you will find that attributes are incredibly handy. For example, the same example, with descriptive attributes, may look like the following:

```
<order order_number="4377821">
   <item>
     <itemid quantity="20" color="sapphire">
        13572
     </itemid>
   </item>
</order>
```

One note of caution: XML isn't found on the Web yet. At the time of this writing, no major Web site is based on XML even though many of the popular Web browsers are able to display XML. Thus, this chapter emphasizes how to create XML for databases and other Web services, but not for display on the Web.

Even though you don't see XML pages on the Web yet, XML documents are floating all over the Internet. For example, the documents that Web log sites (commonly called "blogs") use to tell readers what their new articles are about are XML documents. The Jabber instant-messaging system uses XML both for controlling access to messages and for the messages themselves. Literally thousands of examples of XML are being used for moving data, even though you almost never see it when you wander around the Web.

Combining XML and Perl

Perl is a particularly good language for processing XML documents. One of Perl's biggest strengths is its ability to process text, and XML documents are all text. Another of Perl's strengths lies in its list handling, and programs that process XML documents need to keep many lists as they work, particularly when checking whether the XML markup in the document is valid (that is, no XML language mistakes are in the document). A third important feature of Perl that is relevant to XML is Perl's native handling of Unicode characters, which is described in Chapter 5.

Because of the good match between the demands of XML and the features of Perl, the Perl programmer community is busy creating Perl modules that work with XML. Larry Wall, Perl's creator, has been involved since the early days of XML, and many other Perl programmers have contributed to the effort. Some folks in the XML industry (notably Tim Bray, one of the inventors of XML) have also been involved in creating Perl modules for processing XML.

Perl's interaction with XML comes in two flavors: reading XML files and creating XML files. For the first few years of XML's existence, most of the emphasis on Perl tools for XML was on reading XML files and extracting data out of them. More recently, Perl's tools for creating XML files have become much better. In this chapter, I cover reading XML files first (and in more depth), and then I cover writing XML files.

People who talk about XML see it being used primarily for text processing and data interchange. Although text processing is the area that gets the most attention, I think that using XML in data interchange is the much more exciting Web application, particularly in the area of commercial transactions.

The following example involves processing a data file in XML format. Suppose that you have a Web server that receives data files from Web users, and the data files consist of customer orders for houseplants. Additionally, suppose that the data files are in an XML format that you define. Such a data file may look like this:

```
<order>
  <purchaser name="Chris Chambers" id="CC230"/>
  <shipping method="ground"/>
  <item>
    <itemid quantity="20" color="sapphire">13572</itemid>
  </item>
  <item>
    <itemid quantity="3" size="3 feet">72400</itemid>
  </item>
</order>
```

I recommend entering this XML document into a file called `theorder.xml`. Also, remember that the indentation is not important in an XML file.

Checking a Document for Accuracy

XML defines two types of documents, *well-formed* and *valid.* A document is well-formed if it follows all of the basic XML rules for tags, elements, and so on; a document is valid if it also follows additional rules that are specified in a *document type definition,* or DTD. A valid document has to conform to more stringent rules than well-formed documents. The previous example is well-formed but not valid, but that's not a problem in this scenario because you can use XML documents that conform to the XML structure that you've already defined for your orders.

Analyzing a document to see if it is well-formed or valid (or not valid!) is an easy task for Perl. A few different modules for parsing XML documents have been written for Perl. (*Parsing* is just a fancy computerese word that means "reading and splitting apart.")

Introducing XML::Parser and XML::Simple

The XML::Parser module is the most popular module for reading XML files into your Perl programs. Other modules are available, but many of them are just extensions of XML::Parser. The XML::Parser module uses the expat program, which must also be installed for XML::Parser to work.

Windows users who are running ActivePerl 5.8 already have XML::Parser and XML::Simple loaded. UNIX users can download the XML::Parser and XML::Simple modules from CPAN and can find more about expat, including download information, at the Web site for the program at expat.sourceforge.net. (CPAN and PPM are described in detail in Chapter 2).

Parsing an XML file

The following short program checks whether your file (`theorder.xml`) is well-formed:

```
use XML::Parser;

$p = XML::Parser->new;
eval { $p->parsefile('theorder.xml', ErrorContext => 1); } ;

if($@) { print "There was an error\n" .
  "$@\n"; }
else { print "The XML is well-formed.\n" }
```

The `parsefile` method parses the file, and returns whatever `expat` returns. The `ErrorContext => 1` in the `parsefile` method tells the module to show both the error and one line before the error so you can figure out both where the error occurred and possibly why.

If `expat` doesn't return anything, the program tells you that the file is well-formed. If an error is present, however, the program shows you the problem. For example, if you change the last line of your file from `</order>` to `<//order>`, you make the file invalid XML. Running the program gives the output:

```
There was an error

not well-formed (invalid token) at line 10, column 2, byte
              238:
   </item>
<//order>
=^
  at /usr/pkg/lib/perl5/site_perl/5.8.0/i386-
              netbsd/XML/Parser.pm line 185
```

That last line is kind of unnecessary: It tells you the full path name of the module (in this case, the `XML::Parser` module) that called `expat`. The line above it, however, is quite useful because the little arrow points to the exact part of the line that contained the error that made your XML file not well-formed.

You can experiment with this program with other XML files that you create as you work with Perl. You can also experiment with your `theorder.xml` file, changing various parts to see whether your changes cause an error. Of course, keep a copy of the file around for later use.

Incidentally, the input to the `XML::Parser` module doesn't have to be a file on disk. It is common to give it some XML that exists in a string variable. In that case, you use the `parse` method instead of the `parsefile` method, as in the following example:

```
$MyXML = <<EOF;
<order><purchaser name="Chris Chambers" id="CC230"/>
<shipping method="ground"/><item>
<itemid quantity="20" color="sapphire">13572</itemid>
</item><item>
<itemid quantity="3" size="3 feet">72400</itemid>
</item></order>
EOF

use XML::Parser;

$p = XML::Parser->new;
eval { $p->parse($MyXML, ErrorContext => 1); } ;

if($@) { print "There was an error\n" .
  "$@\n"; }
else { print "The XML is well-formed.\n" }
```

How Do You Want to Read It?

The XML::Parser module is useful for much more than just checking whether a file is well-formed, of course. Its real task is to make the contents of XML files available to your Perl programs for easy handling. The module has many styles of parsing, but they fall into two broad categories: *stream* style and *tree* style. (Kind of makes you want to go outdoors to read the rest of this chapter, doesn't it?)

The stream style of parsing has XML::Parser look through your file for XML items and causes some other Perl code to execute for each item. For example, when it sees a new entity, it runs some Perl code that you have specified to run for new entities. In the orders database that's used throughout this chapter, the first entity is the order, the next is purchaser, and so on.

The tree style of parsing causes the XML::Parser module to read the whole file at once. The output of the parse or parsefile command is a single Perl variable (a hash or a list) that contains a tree-based structure of your XML. You can then use your own Perl code to read through the variable.

As you can see, these are very different styles of programming. Stream-style parsing is useful if you think of parsing as a series of events that have to be dealt with as they come up. Tree-style parsing is more useful if you want to treat your XML document as a single item that you handle all at once. The next two sections show how to use XML::Parser to do each of these styles.

Parsing XML as a stream

Listing 16-1 presents a program that parses an XML document that consists of customer orders. The program assumes that the document has the same XML format as the order database used throughout this chapter. The program prints out information from the order.

If you don't feel like typing in the program, you can find it on this book's Web site. Go to www.dummies.com/extras, and click on the link for this book.

Listing 16-1:   A sample program that parses XML streams.

```
# Section A
use XML::Parser;

$ItemCount = 0;
@ItemList = ();

# Section B
$parser = new XML::Parser(Style => 'Stream');
$parser->parsefile('theorder.xml');

# Section C
print "The total number of items ordered was $ItemCount\n";
for($i = 1; $i <= $ItemCount; $i+=1) {
  print "Item $i is $ItemList[$i][3]\n",
    "  Quantity: $ItemList[$i][0]\n",
    "  Color: $ItemList[$i][1]\n",
    "  Size: $ItemList[$i][2]\n\n";
}
exit;

# Section D
sub StartTag {
  my $Handler = shift(@_);
  my $Name = shift(@_);
  my %Attr = %_;
  # Section D1
  if($Name eq 'order') { } # Nothing to do
  # Section D2
  elsif($Name eq 'purchaser') {
    $PurchName = $Attr{'name'};
    $PurchID = $Attr{'id'};
    if($PurchID eq '')
      { die "There was no purchaser ID\n" }
  }
  # Section D3
  elsif($Name eq 'shipping') {
```

```
        $ShipMethod = $Attr{'method'};
    }
    # Section D4
    elsif($Name eq 'item') {
        # Add 1 to the count of items ordered
        $ItemCount += 1;
    }
    # Section D5
    elsif($Name eq 'itemid') {
        $ItemList[$ItemCount][0] = $Attr{'quantity'};
        $ItemList[$ItemCount][1] = $Attr{'color'};
        $ItemList[$ItemCount][2] = $Attr{'size'};
    }
    # Section D6
    else { # Here if there was an unknown start tag
        die "Found an unknown start tag:\n$_\n";
    }
}

# Section E
sub Text { $TheText = $_ };

# Section F
sub EndTag {
    my $Handler = shift(@_);
    my $Name = shift(@_);
    if($Name eq 'itemid') {
        $ItemList[$ItemCount][3] = $TheText;
    }
};
```

Examining the program

The first line in Section A of Listing 16-1 loads the XML::Parser module. The following two lines in the section initializes the $ItemCount variable, which keeps track of how many items are in this order, and the @ItemList variable, which holds a multidimensional list that has the information about a particular item in the order. (I cover multidimensional lists in Chapter 7.)

The two lines in Section B do almost all the work of the program. The first of these two lines initializes the XML parser by creating a new parser object. Note that the style is "Stream." This lets the module know what you want to do with the parsed XML. The second line uses the parser object that was just created to parse the file that contains the XML document. After this line has been executed, the file is completely parsed.

Section C contains the statements that tell your program what to do after it has parsed the XML document. These lines display information about the order, including the number of items ordered and a description of each item. If you were using this program in a real order-entry system, you would probably add statements for printing out a mailing label or telling the warehouse what had been ordered. After this section is run, the program exits.

You may think, "Hey, how does the parser know how to handle each of those XML tags?" That's where the rest of the program sections come into play. In the "stream" style of XML::Parser, your program is expected to have subroutines that tell the parser what to do when it comes to a start tag, an end tag, and the text in between:

- StartTag **subroutine:** Called each time the parser comes across a start tag

- EndTag **subroutine:** Called each time the parser comes across an end tag

- Text **subroutine:** Called each time the parser comes across text that is between a start and end tag

You can also define a couple of other subroutines that we didn't care about for this program:

- StartDocument **subroutine:** Called when the parser starts parsing

- PI **subroutine:** Called each time the parser comes across an XML processing instructions

- EndDocument **subroutine:** Called when the parser finishes parsing

Section D and its subsections describe what the parser should do when it comes to a start tag. The first three lines of the subroutine define the variables that are passed to the subroutine from the parser. (I describe subroutines and their variables in Chapter 13.) The two variables of note are $Name, which holds the name of the tag, and %Attr, which is a hash of the attributes of the tag.

The six subsections of Section D in Listing 16-1 describe the five kinds of start tags that you can find in the XML format in this scenario:

- **Section D1 shows the** order **tag.** The program has nothing to do at this point because you don't need any special processing at the beginning of the order.

- **Section D2 contains the** purchaser **tag.** This tag sets the two variables $PurchName and $PurchID based on the attributes of the tag. The if function checks to see whether a purchaser identifier exists and, if not, aborts the program.

- **Section D3 contains the** shipping **tag.** This tag sets the $ShipMethod variable.

   ✔ **Section D4 contains the** item **tag.** This tag increments the $ItemCount variable so that you know how many items are in the order.

   ✔ **Section D5 contains the** itemid **tag.** This tag fills in the slots in the @ItemList multidimensional list.

   ✔ **Section D6 gets run if the tag isn't any of the ones in this list.** It causes the program to abort with a message.

In every XML program that parses using streams, you have to decide what to do if you find a start tag of a type that you don't expect. Generally, you do one of two extreme things: ignore it or stop the program. In section D6, the latter is chosen.

Section E contains the subroutine that tells the parser what to do with any text that it comes across. Because the end tags deal with any text that precedes them in the program, this subroutine simply stuffs the text into the $TheText variable, which will be used by the end tag processor.

Speaking of the end tag processor, it appears in Section F. The only tag that has text that needs to be processed by the end tag is the itemid. In this subroutine, the value of the text that appears before the end tag for the itemid is put into the multidimensional list for the current item.

Looking at the output

When you run the program, it produces the following output:

```
The total number of items ordered was 2
Item 1 is 13572
   Quantity: 20
   Color: sapphire
   Size:

Item 2 is 72400
   Quantity: 3
   Color:
   Size: 3 feet
```

You can probably see many easy ways to modify this program. For example, you could total the quantities, keep sub-totals by color and size, and so on.

Parsing XML as a tree

Using XML::Parser's tree style leads to very short programs. However, the XML::Simple module is even easier and the output is easier to understand. Both modules parse XML text into a multi-dimensional lists and hashes. (Multi-dimensional lists and hashes are described in Chapter 7.)

For example, the following program simply reads the XML into an array, and prints the array using the `Data::Dumper` and `Dumpvalue` modules that come with Perl. The `Data::Dumper` and `Dumpvalue` modules take a variable and turn it into a string for display. This makes it easier to see what you have in a multi-dimensional array.

```perl
use XML::Simple;
use Data::Dumper;
use Dumpvalue;

$p = XML::Simple->new();
$MyTree = $p->XMLin('theorder.xml');

$OutString1 = Dumper($MyTree);
print $OutString1, "\n\n";

$dv = Dumpvalue->new();
$OutString2 = $dv->dumpValue($MyTree);
print $OutString2, "\n\n";
```

The result is:

```
$VAR1 = {
        'purchaser' => {
                'name' => 'Chris Chambers',
                'id' => 'CC230'
                },
        'item' => [
                {
                  'itemid' => {
                         'color' => 'sapphire',
                         'content' => '13572',
                         'quantity' => '20'
                     }
                },
                {
                  'itemid' => {
                         'content' => '72400',
                         'quantity' => '3',
                         'size' => '3 feet'
                     }
                }
                ],
        'shipping' => {
                'method' => 'ground'
                }
        };


'item' => ARRAY(0x83012d0)
   0  HASH(0x820a754)
        'itemid' => HASH(0x82104cc)
           'color' => 'sapphire'
```

```
        'content' => 13572
        'quantity' => 20
 1  HASH(0x821052c)
    'itemid' => HASH(0x82105d4)
        'content' => 72400
        'quantity' => 3
        'size' => '3 feet'
'purchaser' => HASH(0x820a76c)
  'id' => 'CC230'
  'name' => 'Chris Chambers'
'shipping' => HASH(0x820a760)
  'method' => 'ground'
```

Writing programs that use trees is a fairly tricky task. You need to know the structure of the tree in advance, which is rarely the case in the real world. You are much more likely to find yourself using XML::Parser in its stream style.

Writing an XML Document

Chapter 14 is mostly about parsing CGI, and only a little about writing HTML. Well, the same is true in this chapter. There simply isn't much to say about writing XML, and there's only one interesting module to do it. That module is appropriately named XML::Writer, and is available from CPAN (for UNIX users) and PPM (for Windows users).

XML::Writer has a slew of methods, shown in Table 16-1. The table shows the methods that are used for output, and it omits some of the optional arguments used for making advanced XML files.

Table 16-1	Output methods used in XML::Writer
Method	*Description*
xmlDecl	Puts an XML declaration in the document. This should be the first thing you have in your document.
doctype(*type*)	Puts a DOCTYPE declaration in the document. This has to appear before you start your XML elements.
startTag (*name* [, *attribute* => *value*, ...])	Adds a start tag. This can have one or more pairs of attributes and values.

(continued)

Table 16-1 *(continued)*

Method	Description
`endTag`	Adds an end tag. The module figures out which is the most recent open start tag, and makes this end tag match it.
`emptyTag(`*name* `[,`*attribute =* `>` *value*`, ...])`	Adds an empty tag. This can have one or more pairs of attributes and values. Empty tags are elements that do not have end tags.
`characters(`*data*`)`	Adds text. This method automatically changes XML special characters into their proper form.
`dataElement(`*name*`, data [,` *attribute => value*`, ...])`	Shorthand method for adding an element with character data. It is the same as calling the startTag method, characters, and the endTag method all at once.
`comment(`*text*`)`	Adds an XML comment.
`pi(`*target*`, [`*data*`])`	Adds an XML processing instruction.
`end`	Finishes the document.

Using the `XML::Writer` module is pretty simple. The following program creates an XML file that has the same structure as the database that has been used throughout this chapter.

```
use XML::Writer;
use IO;

$Output = new IO::File('>newdata.xml');
$w = new XML::Writer(OUTPUT => $Output);

$w->startTag('order');
$w->emptyTag('purchaser', 'name' => 'Chris Chambers',
  'id'=> 'CC230');
$w->emptyTag('shipping', 'method' => 'ground');
$w->startTag('item');
$w->dataElement('itemid', '13572', 'quantity' => '20',
  'color' => 'sapphire');
$w->endTag;
$w->startTag('item');
$w->dataElement('itemid', '72400', 'quantity' => '3',
```

```
    'size' => '3 feet');
$w->endTag;
$w->endTag;
$w->end;
```

The `XML::Writer` module requires its output to go to an object that was created with the `IO` module. This explains the somewhat mysterious second and third lines of the program.

You may find the output of the module unsatisfying. For example, the previous program produces the following:

```
<order><purchaser name="Chris Chambers" id="CC230" />
<shipping method="ground" /><item><itemid color="sapphire"
quantity="20">13572</itemid></item><item><itemid quantity="3"
size="3 feet">72400</itemid></item></order>
```

You can't see it here, but that comes out as a single line! You do have an option when you create a new writer that lets you add line breaks. It looks like this:

```
$w = new XML::Writer(OUTPUT => $Output, NEWLINES => 1);
```

However, even with the `NEWLINES` attribute, the output is not terribly pleasant:

```
<order
><purchaser name="Chris Chambers" id="CC230"
 /><shipping method="ground"
 /><item
><itemid color="sapphire" quantity="20"
>13572</itemid
></item
><item
><itemid quantity="3" size="3 feet"
>72400</itemid
></item
></order
>
```

The upshot of this is that you are probably better off using your own Perl programming to make your XML output.

Reading and Writing XML in Other Ways

`XML::Parser`, `XML::Simple`, and `XML::Writer` are just a few of the dozens of Perl modules that have been created over the past few years to help you handle XML just the way you want. As you get more comfortable with XML, you may want to explore some of the other modules.

To whet your appetite, I list a few of the better-known XML-related modules here. All of them are available from CPAN, and some of them are available through PPM for ActivePerl users:

- ✔ `XML::Generator` writes out XML documents, but in a way very different from `XML::Writer`.

- ✔ `libxml` is an extensive library of functions and modules. It feels like a Swiss army knife for XML programming.

- ✔ `XML::SAX` is a wonderful system for creating your own, extensible parser for XML. If you start feeling constrained by `XML::Parser`'s limitations, you should definitely check out `XML::SAX`.

- ✔ `XML::DOM` is a parser that converts your XML into DOM (Document Object Model) format. DOM is a popular standard that describes the structure of text documents.

- ✔ `XML::RSS` is an interface to RSS files, which are the standard method for transmitting information about Web logs (commonly called "blogs").

- ✔ `SVG::Manual` and `SVG::Parser` are two modules for writing and reading Scalable Vector Graphics (SVG) files. SVG is a new standard for describing graphics that are based on lines, areas, and text. SVG files are in XML, so creating them and reading them is an extension of what you have learned so far about XML.

Looking into Web Services

A few years ago, many people said that XML was going to be the buzzword of the decade. Well, it didn't happen that way, but XML is the central part of the corporate Internet's latest buzzword: *Web services.*

Web services doesn't have a single definition, but most of the descriptions these days are something like "a group of modular applications that can be accessed over a network through a single interface based on XML." Yes, that's pretty vague, but it gives the Web services industry plenty of leeway in claiming that this or that particular product belongs in the term. Another way to think of the definition is "anything that inputs or outputs XML as data."

Some of the excitement over Web services is because XML is so flexible that integrating very different data becomes much easier than, say, using traditional databases. Even a little Perl program that took an hour to write can exchange data with a massive database inventory program. In some ways, Web services can be thought of as business processes, and not just data, because the movement of the XML-based data can resemble the way that data moves in a corporation. XML is definitely the glue for everything being touted as Web services today.

An additional component of Web services is important to understand. It's not just about XML, it is also about how XML is transferred between programs. The most common method for communication in Web services is called *SOAP* (an overly-cute acronym for Simple Object Access Protocol). SOAP moves XML over the Web by using well-defined methods so that it is easy to create programs (particularly Perl programs) to send and receive XML data in a predictable fashion.

A second important component in Web services communication is the Web Services Description Language, commonly called *WSDL*. When you create a modular Web service, you need a way to describe what it is, what kind of data is in it, and so on; WSDL is the format that is commonly used for these tasks.

Connecting Web Services and Perl

This chapter is primarily about how to read and write XML with Perl. If that's all that Perl did, it would be considered a minor player in the Web services field. Of course, Perl does much more. For starters, Perl is also superb at working with the Web.

Chapter 14 showed how easy it is to integrate Perl with CGI, the standard method for making Web requests. Combine that with Perl's ability to read and write XML, and you have a much more complete solution for Web services. Modules are even available for using CGI specifically with XML.

But the wonderful freeware authors of the Perl community didn't stop there. You can also access many different modules for creating SOAP clients and servers. Similarly, you can choose from modules for creating and reading WSDL. In fact, when a new acronym gets created in the Web services world, you can usually find a Perl implementation of it in a matter of days.

So, how do you integrate all of this into a Web services program? Ah, if it were only so easy to describe. Because the world of Web services is still changing at a rapid pace, it is impossible to make a recipe like "read your database, use `XML::Writer` to create a file from it, and then use `SOAP::Transport::HTTP` to make it available to others, and be sure to also use `WSDL::Generator` to make its description public. (Those are actually the names of the modules you can use, by the way.)

Instead, you have to sit down with specifications for all the different standards that are in use and see which ones work for what you want to do. For example, you may not care about describing your Web service because it will only be used by people who already know what's in it. On the other hand, you will have to decide which of the many features of SOAP are and are not appropriate for the way that you want to publish your data.

The book I mentioned near the beginning of this chapter, *XML For Dummies, 3rd Edition,* by Ed Tittel, covers many of these topics in much more depth than I could cover here. Although that book doesn't talk much about Perl, you can see how the various Perl modules can be used as you read more about the services.

Chapter 17

Dancing with Databases

In This Chapter

▶ Storing data on disk

▶ Gaining quick access to keyed data

▶ Closing databases after you're done with them

I've used probably a dozen different database-management software packages in my life. Among them, I've seen the good, the bad, and the ugly. How Perl accesses databases is so amazingly simple that at first I couldn't believe it would even work. However, I can assure you that Perl does an admirable job of managing databases, as this chapter shows you.

Managing Databases Using Hashes

In order to use Perl with database files, you first need to understand how hashes work (I cover that topic in Chapter 7). In fact, that's about all the basic information you need, besides a couple of Perl functions for opening and closing databases — dbmopen and dbmclose.

How does Perl dispense with the dozens of different commands that are common to most database-management programs? Perl binds a hash to the database file so that any changes you make to the hash are also made to the database. When you look up a key in the hash, Perl actually gets the value from the database. (I describe hashes and keys in Chapter 7.)

Perl uses *DBM files* for its databases stored on disk. DBM is a UNIX standard (that is, a traditional way of doing things on UNIX systems) for simple *key-value databases* (databases in which every record has a key that is usually used for getting to the record). Many varieties of DBM files exist, and Perl can handle most of them. At the time of this writing, the flavors of DBM files that Perl comprehends include GDBM, BSD-DB, SDBM, NDBM, and ODBM. The bottom line: Perl saves you from having to program DBM.

Built for speed

The biggest advantage of using the Perl database functions, as opposed to reading a text file from disk into a hash, is sheer speed. Imagine if you had an inventory database that was a text file 10,000 lines long. Reading the entire file and parsing it into a hash takes a significant amount of time. If you want to look at just one item, the whole process eats up work hours and computer resources.

Instead, you can use Perl database functions to open a DBM file on disk. For example, a program designed to look up the record for a key that is given in `$ReqKey` may look like this:

```perl
# Open database for read-only
dbmopen(%AllInv, "/usr/
    general/inventory", 0400);
. . .
$TheRec = $AllInv{$ReqKey};
($Loc, $PartName, $Quant) =
    split(/\t/, $TheRec, 3);
. . .
dbmclose(%AllInv);
```

If you want to add a record to the database or change the value associated with a key that's already in the database, you can use something like the following statement:

```perl
$AllInv{$MyKey} = join("\t",
    ($Loc, $PartName, $Quant));
```

Opening Databases

The dbmopen function takes three arguments: the name of the hash, the name of the database on disk, and a mode, as shown in the following line:

```perl
dbmopen(%AllInv, "/usr/general/inventory", 0600);
```

The *mode* is the numeric UNIX file mode in which you want to open the file. If you aren't a UNIX grunt, or you are and you tend to get the file modes mixed up, the two modes that you're most likely to use are 0600 if you want to read and write to the database and 0400 if you just want to read it.

When you use the dbmopen function, every time you access the hash in the function, you actually access the database on disk.

Closing Databases

After you're done working with a database, use the dbmclose function, whose argument is the name of the hash. This function closes the file on your hard drive. For example:

```perl
dbmclose(%AllInv);
```

Tips on Opening and Closing Databases

Opening and closing a DBM database takes time (although not as much time as reading through a long text file), so you don't want to open and close the database for each record that you are examining or updating. However, if you access a database that others are also using, you should close the database as soon as you finish.

The dbmopen and dbmclose functions are special instances of the Perl tie and untie functions. Although I don't get into the specifics of tie and untie in this book, it's worth knowing that these functions provide useful ways to associate Perl variables with an action. In the case of dbmopen and dbmclose, they allow access to a hash to be associated with a set of calls that reads and sets values in DBM databases.

Chapter 18

Controlling Your Computer from Perl

In This Chapter

▷ Understanding Perl's system-level functions

▷ Using Perl to control PCs and Macs

▷ Digging into Perl's UNIX roots

*P*erl interacts with you and your computer in a number of ways. This chapter covers some of the system-level tasks that you can perform with Perl. For example, you can use Perl to run other programs or to monitor programs that are running on your computer. This chapter also discusses the functions that can help you to gain control over your Windows or Mac systems. Throughout this chapter, any discussion of UNIX also applies to Mac OS X.

Getting with the System

Perl makes it easy to run commands on your computer — just as if you had entered them on the command line. Perl's system function is designed to execute a command. On a UNIX system, for example, you can use the system function to execute the ls command (which is UNIX's command to list the files in a directory):

```
system('ls');
```

The program that you name in the ls statement argument can contain command-line arguments, such as

```
system('ls -la /var/spool');
```

Under the various versions of Windows on which Perl runs, you can use the system function to give DOS commands, such as the DOS DIR command:

```
system('DIR');
```

The system function causes Perl to run the named program and wait for that program to exit. That sounds logical, doesn't it? However, Perl has another function, exec, which doesn't wait for the program to exit. The exec function acts like the system function except that it causes Perl to immediately stop and run the named program — never to return to run the statements after the exec statement. The only way any lines after the exec statement will ever be run is if the named program isn't found. Therefore, the second line of the following program won't be seen unless an error occurs while Perl looks for the program that you name:

```
exec('myprogram');
print "Hmmm, my program didn't seem to run.\n";
```

Getting output from a program

At times, you may want to capture the output of a program within a variable and use that information later in the program. In this case, you should use Perl's ` operator, which is known as the *backtick operator*. (Note that this operator is a left-slanting single quote, usually found to the left of the number 1 on a keyboard.) Enclosing a program name with the backtick operator causes the output to be returned. Here's an example of how it's used:

```
$TheOutput = 'myprogram';
```

If you use the backtick operator in a scalar context, all output is written into the string variable. If you use the backtick operator in a list context, each line of the output is stored in a list item.

Using backtick operators takes the standard file output (described in Chapter 11) of the program and passes it into the variable. It does *not* cause the standard error output from the program to go into the variable — only the standard file output. This means that error messages may not appear in the variable.

Perl 5 introduced the qx// operator, which acts just like the backtick operator. The qx// operator works like Perl's other quoting operators in that you put a string between the two slash characters, as I describe in Chapter 5. Here's an example of using qx//:

```
$TheOutput = qx/myprogram/;
```

or:

```
$TheOutput = qx(myprogram);
```

Using the open function

The open function can also work somewhat like the backtick operator described in the previous section, except that instead of sending the output to a variable, it sends it to a file handle (I describe file handles in Chapter 10). To use open in this fashion, the command is followed by a vertical bar (|) character (which is sometimes called a *pipe* character) as the second argument to the open function. For example:

```
open(THEOUT, "myprogram |");
```

In the previous statement, you can then treat THEOUT like any other file handle that has input that you want to read from. You don't need to use the close function to close programs that send output to Perl.

You can also use open in the opposite fashion: to pass data to the standard file input of the program. In this case, you place the | (pipe character) in front of the name of the program in the second argument. You can then treat the file handle of the open function like any file that you're writing to. For example, if your program takes data from the standard file input, you can enter something like this:

```
open(THEPROG, "| myprog");
print THEPROG $a1, $a2, "\n";
close(THEPROG);
```

After the close function executes, the program then has all of its input and runs with it.

Using the open function to pass data to the standard file input of a program is done much more frequently on UNIX systems than on Windows because few DOS programs are written to take input from standard file input.

Running programs in MacPerl

Programs running on a Macintosh work differently from programs running on UNIX or Windows. Because of these differences, backtick operators and the system and exec functions normally don't work in MacPerl.

A few commands that you would put inside the backtick operator *do* work under MacPerl (see Table 18-1). They make converting some UNIX-based Perl programs easier to do because you don't have to change statements with these commands.

Table 18-1 Backtick Operator Commands that Work under MacPerl

Backtick Statement	Value Returned
`pwd`	The current folder, followed by a new line. You can also use `Directory`.
`hostname`	Name of the Macintosh.
`glob <argument>`	List of all files matching the argument. You can use * and ? (for example, *.c).

Controlling a Windows or Mac Computer with Perl

Although the user interface for ActivePerl is meager (to say the least), it offers a fair number of Windows-specific functions and features. They enable you to monitor system activity, change system parameters, and perform other system-management chores. Most of the functions and features are geared more toward Windows NT, Windows 2000, Windows Me, and Windows XP rather than Windows 95/98, but some features work fine on both platforms.

Every extension that comes with ActivePerl has the prefix Win32::. Between the time of this writing and the time you read this book, more extensions may exist in the most recent version of ActivePerl. The extensions fall into three categories: variables, functions, and modules. The following sections contain brief introductions to these features (the documentation that comes with ActivePerl goes into much greater detail).

ActivePerl was originally developed for Windows NT (although it also works well on Windows 95 and Windows 98). Because of this NT-and-later orientation, many of the extensions in ActivePerl are used for system administration that only works under modern versions of Windows, and not under Windows 95/98. For example, Windows 2000 is a multiuser system, so many ActivePerl extensions exist for adding, removing, and controlling user accounts; none of these have any relevance if you are running ActivePerl on Windows 95/98.

Mac users need not fear that they have been left behind: the MacPerl package comes with many useful modules for controlling your Macintosh. Some are for advanced users only (such as those that control the network interfaces), but others are for all Perl programmers and give access to Macintosh user interface features.

Using UNIX-Only System Functions

UNIX, quite naturally, has its own set of system control functions. These functions interest system administrators the most because the functions are used primarily to examine information on users and user groups.

Reading user databases

The getpwent function reads the user database. On UNIX systems, this database is usually the file /etc/passwd. The getpwent function starts at the beginning of the database and keeps track of which record in the database it last read. When you include this function in a program, the function returns a list that contains the following items:

- ✔ Username
- ✔ Encrypted password (or asterisk)
- ✔ User number
- ✔ Group number
- ✔ Quota field
- ✔ Comment field
- ✔ gcos field (an obscure UNIX feature that is almost never used)
- ✔ Home directory
- ✔ Default shell

Because the getpwent function gets the next record, using getpwent in a loop is common, such as in the following while statement:

```
while(@PWList = getpwent) { print "$PWList[0]\n" }
```

You can reset getpwent to start reading from the top of the user database with the setpwent function and close the database with the endpwent function (although you don't have to).

Another pair of functions, getpwuid and getpwnam, returns a list that has the same format as the list that getpwent returns. However, these functions take a single argument (a user ID or a username, respectively) and return the list for that argument. For example, to get the list for user phoffman, you can enter the following statement:

```
@PWList = getpwnam('phoffman');
```

The getlogin function returns the login name of the user running the program. You can obtain this name from the /usr/utmp file.

Accessing group databases

The getgrent function acts like the getpwent function, except that it walks through the *group* database instead of the user database. The getgrent function returns the following:

- ✔ Group name
- ✔ Encrypted password (or asterisk)
- ✔ Group number
- ✔ String of member names

As you may have guessed, Perl also has setgrent and endgrent functions, which set the location from which to read the next record in the group database. And, as you may also have guessed, you can use the getgrgid and getgrnam functions, both of which take a group ID as an argument and return a list that has the same format as the list returned by getgrent.

Chapter 19

Object-Oriented Perl

*T*he programming industry is much less prone to flash-in-the-pan fads than the rest of the computer world. Programming languages stick around forever — long after they should have died a quiet death. The one major fad to hit the programming world in the last decade is *object-oriented programming*. Clearly, object-oriented programming is here to stay and Perl has embraced it in a very Perl-like fashion. That is to say, you can use objects if you want to, but Perl doesn't make it a requirement.

In this chapter, I cover Perl's object-oriented programming features so that you can read and use object-oriented programs written by other Perl programmers. Most Perl programmers who write programs for others to use incorporate the object-oriented parts of Perl. In fact, much of the CPAN library uses object-oriented Perl. If you know how to use objects, you can tap into the wealth of prewritten Perl programs, which can save you loads of time.

Understanding the Advantages Object-Oriented Programming

When people started talking seriously about object-oriented programming in the mid-1980s, many programmers were openly skeptical of it. Its acronym, OOP, didn't help matters; it became the butt of jokes. Nevertheless, over time, more and more programmers became enthralled with the promise that object-oriented programming holds, even though it involves learning some new programming concepts and ultimately requires more work. All in all, OOP has a number of benefits:

- ✔ The most important benefit of object-oriented programming is that it allows programmers to reuse prewritten programs for their own applications, which saves them the time and trouble of starting from scratch. (Of course, you still need to obtain legal permission from the original author before reusing his or her work.) For example, you can write a program designed to do a particular task on the Internet, and others can easily include what you've written as part of their programs. Without object-oriented programming, using prewritten programs is still possible, but requires so much work that it's impractical.

- ✔ Another significant benefit is that team programming projects are much easier to coordinate when the programmers are all using object-oriented programming. It forces programmers to use a consistent interface on the code that they write, and each piece of the larger project can be more easily integrated with the rest.

- ✔ Object-oriented programming also simplifies hierarchical program development in which a program is built from general concept to detailed specifications. If your customer has a general idea of what the program is supposed to do, but he or she is fuzzy on the specifics, you can start with the basics and then fill in the details at the various levels of the program as the customer provides more information or as the customer's needs change.

- ✔ Object-oriented programming helps you to manage complex projects. For example, some projects may not be well-defined and therefore require some trial and error; or turnover in your company's programming staff may mean that too many chefs have been seasoning the program "soup." In addition, programs tend to evolve as they're written and large programs are inherently complex, just because they're designed to do a bunch of stuff. Because the goal of object-oriented programming is to make the programming process *modular* (meaning that it's broken into smaller chunks), performing one task at a time becomes easier to do.

Object-oriented programming techniques are great for large programs, and even for some medium-sized programs, but they aren't so great for the kinds of small programs that Perl is often used for. The fact that many Perl programmers employ object-oriented programming is a boon for everyone because their programs can be more easily recycled. However, for most one-person projects, object-oriented programming is not necessary (unless those projects develop into a team effort).

Defining Objects, Methods, and Arguments

In Perl programs, most of the action takes place within variables. You set a numeric variable here, you add items to a list variable there, you split a string variable into other string variables, and so on. *Variables,* in essence, hold the information in a Perl program.

In an object-oriented program, you do have variables, of a sort. The things used to hold information are called *objects* and objects are much more than just a variable. An object is a collection of variables combined with a collection of actions (called *methods*) that the object is capable of performing. You don't examine or change the variables in an object by using the standard Perl commands. Instead, you use an object's methods to handle its variables.

You can think of an object as a black box that's attached to a microphone through which you give the object directions. The box also has a list of instructions that you can paste on it and a slot through which various items may emerge (somewhat like a restaurant drive-through window). You don't know exactly what's inside the box or how its innards work, and you don't even know whether the instructions are complete. You know only that you give instructions to the object and that you expect a certain result, but you don't necessarily know all the choices that are available to you.

For example, imagine that you have a black box that functions as a bicycle object. The instructions on the side of the box provide a list of *methods,* including TellColor, GoForward, FallOver, and so on, that you apply to the object. You announce "TellColor" into the microphone, and out comes a slip of paper saying "blue." You say "GoForward 7" into the microphone, and the box jumps forward seven inches. Some methods have *arguments,* which are additional instructions to the object, and some don't; some methods return a value, while other methods just tell the object what to do.

The concept of objects may seem a bit confusing at first because they're so dissimilar to variables. But it's the difference between an object and a variable that enables object-oriented programs to manage complexity. If you could change the innards of an object's variables at whim, writing object-oriented programs with predictable results would be almost impossible. Objects force program developers to use only those methods associated with a particular object, which assures consistent results.

Objects also give you a degree of flexibility. You can change how a method works in an object without changing all the programs that use that object. Take the bicycle object that I describe earlier, for example. Suppose that some of your colleagues are using this object in their programs. You later discover a much faster way to implement the GoForward method. You can change that method without forcing everyone who is already using your object to change anything that they're already doing with their programs.

Objects don't just appear out of nowhere. They're created from *classes*. You can think of a class as a cookie cutter that stamps out many identical objects from one mold. The cookie cutter (the class) and the cookie (the object) are two very different things. (To say that objects are "created from" classes isn't absolutely correct. Technically, an object is *instantiated* from a class, meaning that it has the same features as the class.)

Perl's Objects Made Easy

At this point, you're probably asking, "So, how do I use Perl's object-oriented features to build a Perl program?" Fortunately, the answer is, "Very easily." But first, you need to keep in mind three important things about object-oriented programs: classes, methods, and objects. Beginning in Perl 5, a class is a called a *package*. Located inside each package are definitions of the various methods of that class. These methods are, in fact, *subroutines* (which I also describe in Chapter 13).

One tricky aspect of using Perl's object-oriented features is a part of Perl called *references* that are used to create the objects themselves. The topic of references is beyond the scope of this book, but fortunately, you can use objects without knowing exactly how references work.

The remainder of this chapter refers to the object-oriented interface of the libwww-perl library, which I cover in Chapter 15. You can use the library while following along with the discussion (assuming that the library has been installed on your system as covered in Chapter 15), or you can follow along without it.

Opening a Perl module with the use function

Before you can create objects, you have to open the latest version of the Perl module that contains the classes you want. To open a Perl module, you need the use function. The use function normally takes only one argument, the module name. Module names are not placed in quotation marks, and if a module's name ends with .pm, you may leave off the .pm part of the filename. For example, you can use the following statement to open a Perl module:

```
use(LWP::UserAgent);
```

More frequently, the use function appears without the parentheses. For example:

```
use LWP::UserAgent;
```

It's rarely used, but you can also include additional arguments in the use statement if you want particular variables from the module.

Making new objects with the new subroutine

After you specify one or more modules for Perl to open, you're ready to create objects. Remember that each object comes with its own methods; therefore, you have to create an object before you can use its methods. In Perl, you almost always use the new subroutine of a package to create a new object, as shown in the following statement:

```
$TheAgent = new LWP::UserAgent;
```

The new statement creates a new object from the LWP::UserAgent class and makes $TheAgent a reference to the new object.

Think of $TheAgent not as the object, but as something that points to the object. For example, someone may say to me, "You are Paul Hoffman," when what they mean is, "You are the person who is named Paul Hoffman." I'm the person — not the name — but it's simpler to just think of me by my name.

The new subroutine of a package sometimes requires arguments. The arguments are listed after the name of the module, as the following statement shows you:

```
$Req = new HTTP::Request 'GET', 'http://www.dummies.com/';
```

Most Perl object libraries enable you to invoke the new subroutine with no arguments and use methods instead of arguments to supply what would have been the arguments. Here is an example of a new subroutine with no arguments:

```
$Req = new HTTP::Request;
```

Invoking an object's methods

After you create an object, you can use its methods. You invoke Perl methods with the following format:

```
$OBJECTREF->METHODNAME(ARGUMENTS);
```

For example, in the preceding section of this chapter, you can see an HTTP::Request object set to the name $Req. All HTTP::Request objects have a method called url that tells the object which URL to use. You can invoke this method with a statement like the following:

```
$Req->url('http://www.dummies.com/');
```

Note that to the left of the -> operator is the reference to the object whose method you want to invoke, and to the right of the -> operator is the method name. Some methods take arguments (in parentheses, of course), and others just appear on their own, as in the following example:

```
$Req->url;
```

Considering a Real-World Object Example

The libwww-perl set of modules is a good example of an object-oriented Perl program that does real work (some modules perform only small tasks). As described in Chapter 15, libwww-perl enables you to create Perl programs that act like Web clients.

This section gives you an idea of what you can do with the LWP::UserAgent object that acts like parts of a Web browser. (See the Perl documentation that comes with the LWP::UserAgent module for a complete list of methods.)

Three types of objects are used in simple LWP::UserAgent programs:

- **HTTP user agents:** Created with a new LWP::UserAgent statement
- **HTTP requests:** Created with a new HTTP::Request statement
- **Responses from requests:** Returned from calls to the request method used on HTTP user agents

Each of the three different objects has its own methods, some of which are listed in Table 19-1. The table lists some example-specific methods that are used in a simple `LWP::UserAgent` program.

Table 19-1 Examples of Methods Used in a Simple LWP::UserAgent Program

Object	Sample Methods
`LWP::UserAgent`	`request, time-out, proxy`
`HTTP::Request`	`method, url`
`HTTP::Response`	`content, is_success, is_error, code`

To start a libwww-perl program that acts as a Web client, you must create an agent object and a request object. For example, the following statements open the `LWP::UserAgent` object, create a new agent, and create a new request:

```
use LWP::UserAgent;
$TheAgent = new LWP::UserAgent;
$Req = new HTTP::Request;
```

In this example, `$TheAgent` points to the agent object and `$Req` points to the request object.

The request object has a method that specifies the HTTP request method and a method that allows you to specify the URL to which you want to make the method. These methods are called `method` and `url`, respectively. If you just want to get the contents of a Web page, you use the `HTTP "GET"` method. For example, the following two lines

```
$Req->method('GET');
$Req->url('http://www.dummies.com/');
```

assign the kind of method and URL that you want to use.

You're now ready to make the request over the Web. To do so, you need to tell your agent the request to use with the `request` method. Perl returns the Web page as a response object:

```
$TheResp = $TheAgent->request($Req);
```

Programming with pragmas

Some built-in Perl modules, called pragmas, affect the way that Perl compiles your program before executing it. These modules can be of use in debugging your code or can force you to program more effectively (you can make the Perl compiler alert you more often about possibly unsound programming practices).

You can turn on Perl's pragmas by using the use function, just as you do with other modules. Pragmas usually apply only to the current block in which they're set. Therefore, you can turn on a pragma within a block; then when it reaches the end of the block, Perl returns to its normal mode of operation. For example, to start using the diagnostics pragma, you can enter the following line in your program:

```
use diagnostics;
```

After you turn on a pragma, you can turn it off with the no function. It is essentially the opposite of use. For example:

```
no diagnostics;
```

The most useful built-in pragmas include:

✔ diagnostics: Causes Perl to produce lengthier and more descriptive error messages

✔ english: Enables you to use easier-to-read names for built-in variables (names such as $ARG and $MATCH instead of cryptic variable names, such as $_ and $&)

✔ integer: Forces integer arithmetic on calculations

✔ strict: Causes compile errors for some possibly unsafe programming practices; this prevents the program from running until you change it

✔ utf8: Causes Perl to recognize Unicode characters in strings (in Perl 5.6 and Perl 5.8)

The strict pragma checks for symbolic references, and variables that weren't declared with the my function (covered in Chapter 13). It helps to find some other subtle programming mistakes. Perl 5.6 includes a new function, our, that makes this strict checking a bit more manageable if you want to bend the rules.

With the previous statement, you create a response object that is pointed to by the $TheResp variable.

Naturally, after you put together a Web page, you want to look at it. Remember that $TheResp points to a response object, and not to the content itself. Response objects have a method, namely content, that enables you to examine the page's content. For example, the following statement assigns the value of the content to a variable:

```
$TheRespContent = $TheResp->content;
```

$TheRespContent is now a string that contains the content.

Response objects have other interesting methods that can give you more information about the response you get from a Web server. For example, is_success and is_error tell you whether your Web request was successful. Instead of assuming that any content exists, you may want to check first by using the following:

```
if($TheResp->is_success)
   { $TheRespContent = $TheResp->content }
```

If you get an error, the response object can format the error message for you as an HTML document by using the error_as_HTML method. For example:

```
if($TheResp->is_success)
   { $TheRespContent = $TheResp->content }
else { $TheRespContent = $TheResp->error_as_HTML }
```

Many different methods for these objects exist, and the best way to find out more is by reading their documentation. You can usually find the documentation for modules by using the perldoc command that comes as part of Perl.

Part V
The Part of Tens

The 5th Wave   By Rich Tennant

VISUAL WEB DEVELOPMENT TEAM

"Give him air! Give him air! He'll be okay. He's just been exposed to some raw HTML code. It must have accidently flashed across his screen from the server."

In this part. . .

*B*ecause I bet you love lists as much as I do, I present the chapters in this part as lists of top-ten items worth knowing about Perl. A lot of good, quick information is yours if you read these chapters, so take a break in your Perl programming to spend a bit of time with them.

Chapter 20

Ten Guidelines for Programming with Style

▶ Making your programs easier to read and use

▶ Taking advantage of mnemonic variable names

▶ Inserting comments and blank lines as needed

*E*very programming language has its own hard-and-fast rules for how you must structure a program, as well as many optional guidelines that you should follow. Perl certainly has plenty of both. For example, this is a Perl absolute: You must use correct capitalization for function names. (For example, the statement `Print $SomeVariable;` generates a Perl error because of the capital P in `Print`.)

If you violate the "should" guidelines for Perl program writing, you probably won't get an error message, and your program will likely work just fine. However, when you follow the "should" rules, your programs are easier to read by you and others, and maintaining your programs is much easier.

Examining the Perl Creator's Style Preferences

Larry Wall, Perl's originator, laid down some of his style preferences early on in Perl's life. A few other early and active Perl users have added to Larry's list. Many programmers take these preferences as gospel, although others more or less follow them by making changes to suit their own tastes. (I'm part of the latter group.)

The Perl documentation offers a useful list of style guidelines; I mention some of them here:

✓ Indents should consist of a group of four spaces.

✓ The opening curly brace should be on the same line as the keyword, if possible; otherwise, it should line up with the indentation.

✓ A space should be inserted before the opening curly brace of a multiline block.

✓ A one-line block may be put on one line, including its curly braces.

✓ Do not put a space before the semicolon at the end of a statement.

✓ You can omit the semicolon in a short, one-line block.

✓ Insert a space on either side of most operators.

✓ Insert blank lines between the chunks of your program that have different uses.

✓ No space should exist between a function name and its opening parenthesis.

✓ Insert a space after every comma.

✓ Break long lines after an operator (except and and or, which should be followed immediately by the rest of the statement).

✓ Insert a space after the last parenthesis on the current line.

✓ Line up corresponding items vertically.

An example of being able to choose your own style is the placement of curly brackets in one-line blocks. The guidelines I just listed would have you write something like the following:

```
if($Num < 10) {
   print "$Num is too small.\n"; exit;
}
```

However, the following makes more sense to me because the print and exit statements are small:

```
if($Num < 10)
   { print "$Num is too small.\n"; exit }
```

In cases like the preceding example, I even use the following construction just because it looks good to me:

```
if($Num < 10) { print "$Num is too small.\n"; exit }
```

Choosing Your Operator

Because Perl has a wealth of operators, you often have a choice between two equivalent operators for the same task. I always recommend that you choose the operator that will make the most sense when you read the program later.

For example, should you use the ++ or += 1 operator after a variable? Compare the following two statements:

```
if($Done) { $Count++ }
```

```
if($Done) { $Count += 1 }
```

In my mind, the second construction looks more like "add 1 to $Count" than the first one does. Nevertheless, most Perl programmers use $Count++ instead. Both formats do the same thing, and I can certainly recognize that $Count++ means "add 1 to $Count"; however, I sometimes prefer to see the numeral 1 in the program, and sometimes I'm happy with just ++.

The preceding example brings up another interesting stylistic preference: Should you use assignment operators, such as += and .=, or specify the actual assignment? Compare the following:

```
if($Done) { $Count += 1 }
```

```
if($Done) { $Count = $Count + 1 }
```

To me, the latter statement is clearer, but using $Count twice on the same line seems redundant. I almost always prefer using the assignment operator +=, but some folks prefer to be more explicit by spelling everything out.

Parentheses Are Your Friends

In many cases, parentheses are optional in Perl programs. In mathematical equations, you can omit the parentheses if you're sure that you understand the order in which the operators will be evaluated. However, it's safer to include them so that you or some other person reading the program can understand what's going on.

You can also omit the parentheses around functions, but doing so makes many Perl statements difficult to read. For example, the following two statements essentially say the same thing:

```
mkdir("/usr/home/paul/Temp", 0700);

mkdir "/usr/home/paul/Temp", 0700;
```

To me, the first is much more readable than the second because you can see the arguments grouped together in the parentheses. Another Perl programmer may tell you that the parentheses just get in the way and don't add anything to the program.

Sometimes, I don't even use parentheses, namely with the `print` function. For example, throughout this book I use statements like

```
print "The name is $Name\n";
```

instead of

```
print("The name is $Name\n");
```

I don't know why I started using `print` without the parentheses, but once I started, I kept it up. Every Perl programmer I know uses `print` without parentheses, so I'm in good company.

Flexible Ordering for Conditionals

Throughout this book, you see conditional statements (`if` and `unless`) written with the condition appearing first:

```
if($Done) { $Count += 1 }
```

If the block that follows the conditional has exactly one statement in it, such as in the preceding line of code, you can place the statement first, followed by the conditional. You can even pull the expression outside of the parentheses if you want. Therefore, you can replace the preceding example with either of the following statements:

```
$Count += 1 if($Done);

$Count += 1 if $Done;
```

To some people, the preceding statements sound a bit more like English: Do this if that is true for you. However, I find this setup confusing because it violates the left-to-right reading patterns to which we're all accustomed. The left part is executed only if the right part is true, so you have to read from right to left on lines like the preceding ones. Also, having the conditional test outside of the parentheses just plain bugs me because you can't construct the statement that way if the conditional comes first.

You can use the "statement first" form for `while` and `until` as long as you have only a single statement. For example, the following statement is perfectly legal:

```
&MySub while $Count < 0;
```

The previous statement causes the `&MySub` subroutine to execute repeatedly until `$Count` is greater than or equal to 0. This statement is equivalent to the following statement:

```
while($Count < 0) { &MySub }
```

Just because I always put the conditional first doesn't mean that you have to do likewise. In fact, you can find lots of examples of Perl programs (written by very good programmers) that have the conditional second. Because that treatment always makes me stop and stare when I come across it, I choose not to use it.

Commenting about Comments

Programming style is all well and good, but a program without comments is essentially worthless. Yes, that's a strong statement. But yes, I really mean it. And yes, I sometimes violate this rule myself.

Unless a program has five lines or fewer, you should always start it with at least one line of comments. Even on a little three-line program, adding one line of comments may take you all of 15 seconds and will make the program much more useful in the future.

For multiline comments, I usually indent the second line a few extra spaces to make it clear that it is a continuation of the previous line:

```
# empdata1.pl: a very simple employee database application.
#   This program reads a text file that is an employee
#   database and lets you query it by ID number.
```

Then again, other programmers don't indent run-over lines:

```
# empdata1.pl: a very simple employee database application.
# This program reads a text file that is an employee
# database and lets you query it by ID number.
```

Standout Line Treatments

Some folks like to embellish the comments at the beginning of their programs (and sometimes at the beginning of their subroutines) with long lines of characters to make them more noticeable:

```
##############################################################
# empdata1.pl: a very simple employee database application.
##############################################################
```

As long as a line starts with a # character, it's a comment. Some people, however, get a bit carried away:

```
#--*--*--*--*--*--*--*--*--*--*--*--*--*--*--*--*--*--*--#
# empdata1.pl: a very simple employee database application.
#--*--*--*--*--*--*--*--*--*--*--*--*--*--*--*--*--*--*--#
```

Some time ago, I came across the following lines written for another language. I think that they demonstrate an art deco influence coupled with a Southwestern motif (all of which are completely useless):

```
#_____.__...----~~~****\/\/|||\/\/****~~~----...._____
# empdata1.pl: a very simple employee database application.
#_____....----~~~****\/\/|||\/\/****~~~----...._____
```

But if this kind of artistry helps you to write clear comments, by all means use it.

Comments Cohabitating with Code

As if we didn't have enough to argue about, you'll also hear some disagreement about which of the following constructions is better:

```
if($Signature ne 'Dave') { next } # Wasn't what we wanted
```

or

```
# Check if signature is correct
if($Signature ne 'Dave') { next }
```

I'll admit that I can go either way on this. Sometimes, I put the short comment on the same line as the test, and sometimes I insert it before the test. Other folks insist that you should never put a comment on the same line as Perl code because it's harder to read. My suggestion: Try both and see which suits you best.

Naming Your Variables Descriptively

Another common way to "comment" a program is to use descriptive names for your variables. Throughout this book, the variable names (even in the short snippets) often suggest their actual usage — for example, $Count and $TheLine.

Generally, the longer the program, the more variables you have. The more variables you have, the more important it is for you to know what each variable does. In short, the variable names become extremely important.

A long history exists of programmers using short, non-mnemonic names for variables, such as $i, $j, $x, and the venerable $foo and $bar. This practice is fine if you never have to look at the program again after you write it and if you're able to remember what each of those arbitrarily named variables stands for.

You may notice that I use $i and $j in this book. It's okay to use short names like these in places where the variable is used for only one or two lines, such as in a short for statement. In fact, I think it is a good practice because it gives you a visual reminder that this is a short-lived variable. However, if the variable will be "alive" for more than four or five lines, I recommend giving it a more memorable name.

Capital Offense, or Not?

Another area of controversy among programmers is in the capitalization of variable names. In Perl, capitalization counts — the variable $OldFileHandle is different from $OldfileHandle (note the f). Some folks like to use mixed case in a variable name because it helps to decipher a jumble of characters; others don't like using mixed case because it can introduce typing errors. Those in the latter group usually use all lowercase characters (such as $oldfilehandle) or just an initial capital (such as $Oldfilehandle).

I personally like using internal capital letters in variable names (the dweeb-speak term for those letters is *intercaps*). However, I have to agree with the people who say that intercaps can result in increased typos. That type of error is often difficult to find in Perl programs because you don't have to pre-declare your variables.

Some programmers avoid intercaps by using all lowercase letters and inserting underscore (_) characters between the parts of the variable name. These folks may have a variable called $old_file_handle, for example. I have a hard time with this treatment because you have to use the Shift key to get the

---

Seek and ye shall find errors: The -w switch

This is a good place to remind you about Perl's -w command-line switch. Running Perl from the command line with the -w switch causes Perl to scan your program and print warnings about simple errors that you may have made before it runs the program. If you are using UNIX, you can also put the -w switch on the first line of your program, after the #!/usr/bin/perl invocation.

Inserting the -w switch on the Perl command line is a good way to avoid many common errors, but it's not foolproof. It is often good at finding mistyped variable names. For example, if you enter the same typo twice, it will probably miss both errors because it thinks that the mistaken variable is the one that you really want.

---

underscore, and you may as well make a capital letter out of a lowercase one. Also, underscores just don't look right to me, whereas intercaps do. Clearly, you can make your own choice on this.

The Beauty of Blank Lines

The lowly blank line is one of the most neglected types of comment. It doesn't have anything in it, so why bother with it? To me, a blank line is extremely helpful, particularly when I'm reading a program by an author who rarely uses descriptive comments.

A blank line tells you where one operation stops and another begins. You may be able to figure out what's going on by reading the statements in the program, but it helps to be able to scroll down a long program and see where the programmer intended the "sections" to be.

Having said that, I rarely use two blank lines together. One is enough to break the visual flow of a program; two lines can look like a chasm.

Chapter 21

Ten Really Short, Really Useful Perl Programs

In This Chapter

▶ Seeing just how short a really good Perl program can be

▶ Printing, sorting, and listing files and directories

▶ Working with passwords and calculators

Some people believe that short programs aren't good for very much, but that's just not so with Perl. Just a couple lines of Perl code can go a long way. This chapter lists some of my favorite teeny, tiny Perl programs.

Collecting Unique Lines

If your text file has many lines that are duplicates and you only want to see the unique lines, you can collect them into an array (in this case, it's called @Unique) with the following program:

```
open(IN, "somefile.txt"); @Unique=();
while(<IN>) { unless($i{$_}++) { push(@Unique, $_) } }
```

The trick here is that $i{$_}++ returns 0 the first time you create a key-value pair with $_ as the key, and some nonzero value after that.

Getting Rid of Multiple Blank Lines

Some text files have multiple, consecutive blank lines, which make them hard to read, particularly on small screens. The following program prints a text file, compressing all instances of two or more blank lines into a single blank line.

A blank line can have whitespace characters in it, such as spaces and tabs, but no displayable characters.

```
open(IN, "somefile.txt"); $PrevBlank = 0;
while(<IN>) {
  if(/\S/ or !$PrevBlank) { print $_ }
  $PrevBlank = /^\s*$/;
}
```

The if statement in the preceding example is true if there are nonblank characters on the line or if the previous line was not blank. The $PrevBlank assignment tells you whether the current line is blank, meaning that it has zero or more whitespace characters and nothing else.

Printing Lines from a File in Sorted Order

It's easy to forget how useful Perl's sort function is. The following program reads the entire file into an array, sorts the array, and prints the result. Short and sweet, and pretty efficient to boot:

```
open(IN, "somefile.txt");
print sort(<IN>);
```

Printing a Range of Lines from a File

Have you ever wanted to read just a few lines from a file, and not the whole thing? The following program prints just a range of lines. You run the program with two arguments: the range that you want and the filename. For example, if you name your program "showline" and you want to see lines 10 through 20 of the somefile.txt file, you use the following command line:

```
showline 10-20 somefile.txt
```

The following program prints a range of lines:

```
open(IN, $ARGV[1]) or die "Could not read $File.\n";
($Start, $Stop) = split(/-/, $ARGV[0]);
for($i=1; $i<=$Stop; $i += 1)
  { $Line = <IN>; if($i>=$Start) { print $Line } }
```

Listing Just the Files in a Directory

At times, you may want to ignore the subdirectories in a directory and just focus on the files. You can use the following -f file test to list all the files in a directory:

```
foreach $f (<*>) { if(-f $f) { print "$f\n" } }
```

Listing a Directory by Size

To sort a directory listing by anything other than its filenames, your program has to keep a list of records consisting of the names and other items in the listing. Hashes are great to use for this kind of list that has records with a key (the filename) and a value (the other directory information). The following program creates a hash that lists the size of each file in the directory and then sorts the items for output. (You can easily modify this program to sort by date instead of by size.)

```
foreach $f (<*>) { $i{$f} = -s $f };
foreach $k (sort{ $i{$b} <=> $i{$a} } keys %i)
  { printf "%8d %s\n", $i{$k}, $k }
```

Sorting Directories by Extension

Sorting by a portion of a filename is a slightly more difficult process than sorting by file size or by the date the file was modified. The following program breaks the filename into two and sorts by the second part. If you're running Perl on a UNIX or Macintosh system, this program works predictably only if the filenames have no period or one period:

```
foreach $FullName (<*>) {
  ($Name, $Ext) = split(/\./, $FullName, 2);
  push(@Temp, "$Ext\t$FullName");
}
foreach $Val (sort(@Temp)) {
  ($Ext, $FullName) = split(/\t/, $Val);
  print "$FullName\n";
}
```

Creating a Simple Calculator

Ever needed a simple-to-use calculator to knock off some quick-and-dirty math? The following program uses Perl's `eval` function to print out the answers to any equation that you enter. To end the program, enter a blank line. Here's the program for creating your own calculator:

```
while(<STDIN>) {
  $i = $_; chomp($i); unless($i) { last }
  $o = eval($i); print "Answer = $o\n";
}
```

When you run the program, you can enter something like the following:

```
((2**8) + (3**8))
```

and you get this result:

```
Answer = 6817
```

Randomizing a List

In Perl, generating random numbers is easy, but randomizing the order of an array isn't as simple. Nevertheless, you can use the `splice` function to pull a random element from an array and then place the element in another array. The following program randomizes the list @MyList:

```
my @TempList = ();
while(@MyList)
  { push(@TempList, splice(@MyList, rand(@MyList), 1)) }
@MyList = @TempList;
```

The trick here is that `rand(@MyList)` picks a number between 0 and the number of elements in @MyList, and `splice` changes this random number to an integer.

Generating Random Mnemonic Passwords

Trying to convince computer users to come up with passwords that aren't easily guessed is one of the most challenging jobs for a system administrator. People always seem to insist on using their birthdates or pets' names for passwords — breaching security then becomes child's play.

The following program generates random passwords. Instead of a jumble of hard-to-remember letters, however, the passwords are somewhat mnemonic because they appear in pairs of consonants and vowels that are pronounceable. By stringing together a few goofy-sounding syllables, you can generate easy-to-remember nonsense phrases.

Each syllable of the password can represent any one of 100 numbers; therefore, a single four-syllable password, such as *votahubo,* is one of 100 million (100 to the fourth power) possible passwords that the program generates. Having a system administrator assign these passwords provides more security than letting users pick their own, easily-guessed passwords:

```
print "Enter a seed number: "; $s=<STDIN>;
srand($s ^ time);
@c=split(/ */, "bcdfghjklmnprstvwxyz");
@v=split(/ */, "aeiou");
for($i = 1; $i <=4; $i += 1)
  { print $c[int(rand(20))], $v[int(rand(5))] }
```

The first two lines of this program initialize the seed for the random numbers (see Chapter 9), and the next two lines create lists containing the 20 consonants (minus *q*) and 5 vowels of the alphabet. The `for` loop simply prints the four syllables.

Part VI
Appendix

The 5th Wave   By Rich Tennant

WANDA HAD THE DISTINCT FEELING HER HUSBAND'S NEW SOFTWARE PROGRAM WAS ABOUT TO BECOME INTERACTIVE.

In this part. . .

This part covers the topic that always gets pushed to the end of computer books. Appendix A is the reference to Perl, with tables to help you in your programming.

Appendix

The Great Perl Reference

Perl Operators

The following table lists Perl's operators — those symbols that allow you to perform some sort of action on program data:

Operator	Description
x	Character repeat and list repeat.
.	String concatenation.
=	Assignment.
+	Add.
-	Subtract.
*	Multiply.
/	Divide.
%	Modulo divide.
-	Unary negation: negates the number that it precedes.
+	Unary plus: does nothing.
*	Raise to the power.
++	Unary increment; can be used before or after a variable to increment before or after the variable is evaluated. Therefore, if $a is 5, $a++ is 5 until it is evaluated, and then $a becomes 6; ++$a is 6 when it's evaluated.
—	Unary decrement; can be used before or after a variable to decrement before or after the variable is evaluated. Thus, if $a is 5, $a— is 5 until it's evaluated, and then $a becomes 4; —$a is 4 when it's evaluated.
+= . = etc.	Assignment after operation. For example, $a += 3 means "add 3 to $a and store that value in $a."

(continued)

Operator	Description
,	List separator.
..	Range.
< > <= >= == != <=>	Numeric comparisons: less than, greater than, less than or equal to, greater than or equal to, equal to, not equal to, comparison.
lt gt le ge eq ne cmp	String comparisons: less than, greater than, less than or equal to, greater than or equal to, equal to, not equal to, comparison.
not	Logical not. Can also be !.
and	Logical and. Can also be &&.
or	Logical or. Can also be ||.
xor	Logical xor.
?:	Conditional comparison: TEST ? IFTRUE : IFFALSE.
~	Bitwise logical not.
&	Bitwise logical and.
|	Bitwise logical or.
^	Bitwise logical xor.
<< >>	Bit shift to the left and to the right.
<>	I/O operator, such as <STDIN>.
=~ !~	Binds a scalar on the left to a pattern match, substitution, or translation on the right. !~ returns the inverse of the bound value.
m/pattern/modifiers	Searches for the pattern and returns true if found. Can also be specified without the m.
s/pattern/replacement/modifiers	Searches for the pattern and replaces it with the specified .text
tr/fromrange/torange/	Returns a string with letters translated from one range to another. The tr and y operators are identical.
=>	List separator; same as a comma.
` (backtick)	Runs the command between the two backticks and returns the STDOUT.

Operator	Description
->	Dereference. Usually used with object-oriented programs as CLASS->METHOD.
\	Reference.

Perl's Operator Hierarchy

Although using parentheses to group your operations is always safer, some programmers prefer to trust Perl's rules for deciding which operators are evaluated first. The following table lists the operators in order of their precedence. Those operators with the same ranking (they're shown on the same line in the list that follows), Perl evaluates them from left to right.

For example, the following statement

```
$a = 3 / 4 ** 2;
```

is interpreted as

```
$a = 3 / (4 ** 2);
```

because ** has higher precedence than / and is, therefore, evaluated first.

Operators are evaluated in the following order (lower numbers mean higher precedence):

1. ->
2. ++ --
3. **
4. ! ~ \ {unary +} {unary -}
5. =~ !~
6. * / % x
7. + - .
8. << >>
9. < > <= >= lt gt le ge
10. == != <= > eq ne cmp
11. &
12. | ^

13. &&

14. ||

15. .

16. ?:

17. = += -= *= and other operators that end in =

18. , =>

19. not

20. and

21. or xor

Perl's Functions and Statements

The following table lists all of Perl's functions and statements in alphabetical order. Note that the function arguments in the table represent the kind of argument that you would normally give to the function. For example, the abs function would take a number for its argument, thus it is shown as abs(*number*).

Name	Description
abs(*number*)	Takes the absolute value of the argument (that is, negative numbers are made positive).
accept (*newsockethandle, genericsickethandle*)	Accepts a connection on a socket.
alarm(*time*)	Sends the SIGALRM signal to the program after a specified number of seconds.
atan2(Y, X)	Returns the arctangent of Y/X.
bind(*socket, name*)	Assigns a name to an existing open socket.
binmode(*filehandle*)	Tells Perl to treat the file as a binary file. It has no function under UNIX or MacOS.
bless(*reference, package*)	Tells the item that is referred to in the reference that it is an object in the specified package. If the package is not specified, Perl uses the current package.

Name	Description
caller (*numberofstacks*)	Provides information on the stack of subroutine calls. The argument is the number of subroutine calls to unnest. With an argument, it returns a list with the package name, filename, line number, subroutine name, whether the subroutine has arguments, and whether the subroutine wants an array as its argument. Without an argument, caller returns just the first three list items, refer ring to the current subroutine.
chdir(*dirname*)	Changes the working directory of a program to a specified directory or, with no argument, changes the directory to the home directory of the user. Returns true if successful, false if it isn't (for example, if the directory doesn't exist).
chmod(*nummode*, *listoffiles*)	Changes the access permissions on one or more files. The first argument must be an octal file mode, such as 0777. The function returns the number of files successfully changed.
chomp(*stringvar*)	Removes the line ending from the end of a string variable, returning the number of characters deleted. If the last character is not a line-ending character, as defined in the special variable $/, nothing is removed. If $/ is two characters, both characters are removed. ***Note:*** This function changes the value of the variable. You can also use the function chomp(LIST), which removes the line ending from the end of each list item.
chop(*stringvar*)	Removes the last character from the end of the string variable, returning the character deleted. ***Note:*** This function changes the value of the variable.
chown(*userid*, *groupid*, *listoffiles*)	Changes the user and group ownership of one or more files. The userid and groupid must be numbers, not names. The function returns the number of files successfully changed.
chr(*number*)	Returns the character represented by the argument.

(continued)

Name	Description
chroot(*directory*)	Changes the root directory available to a program to the specified directory. The named directory becomes the root directory to the program, and the program cannot modify or see other directo ries above this one in the directory hierarchy.
close(*filehandle*)	Closes a file that was opened with the open function.
closedir(*dirhandle*)	Closes a directory that was opened with the opendir function.
connect(*socket*, *netaddress*)	Connects to another process using the specified socket.
continue { *block* }	Executes the block. The continue statement always follows other blocks because it is exe cuted when other blocks exit.
cos(*number*)	Returns the cosine of the number, expressed in radians.
crypt(*plaintext*, *salt*)	Encrypts the first argument using the salt para meter. This function is system dependent, so you may get varying results, depending on the operat ing system.
dbmclose(*array*)	Breaks the binding between the array and the DBM file that was associated with the array by an earlier dbmopen function.
dbmopen(*array*, *filename*, *mode*)	Begins the process of associating a hash with the named database. The mode is the octal file mode used to open the database. This function clears out any values already in the hash.
defined(*variable*)	Returns true if the variable has been defined (that is, if it has a valid string, numeric, or reference value). This function is useful for testing unde fined values returned under error conditions.
delete($array{key})	Removes a key and its value from a hash.
die(*text*)	Prints the text to the standard error output and terminates the Perl program. The program returns the value that was in the $! special variable.
do { *block* }	Executes the block and returns the value of the last expression in the block.

Name	Description
do(*filename*)	Executes the statements in the file and returns the value of the last expression in the file.
dump	Causes a core dump, if the operating system supports it. You can also specify a label, which the program will start from if you can recreate the core from the dump.
each(*array*)	Returns a two-item list (the key and the value) for the next value in the array.
endgrent	Resets the cycling through the group list begun by the getgrent function.
endhostent	Resets the cycling through the host list begun by the gethostent function.
endnetent	Resets the cycling through the network list begun by the getnetent function.
endprotoent	Resets the cycling through the protocol list begun by the getprotoent function.
endpwent	Resets the cycling through the password list begun by the getpwent function.
endservent	Resets the cycling through the server list begun by the getservent function.
eof(*filehandle*)	Returns true if the next read on the file handle would read off the end of the file.
eval(*expression*)	Causes Perl to execute the expression as though the expression were a Perl program. The expression can be one or more statements.
exec(*program*)	Causes the Perl program to stop and the program named in the argument to be run. The argument can be a list, in which case each item is passed as an element of the command line to be executed.
exists (*$array{$key}*)	Returns true if the specified key exists in the specified array.
exit(*number*)	Stops the program. The argument is used as the return value for the program.
exp(*number*)	Returns the number *e* raised to the power of the argument.

(continued)

Name	Description
fcntl(*filehandkle*, *function*, *scalar*)	Executes the UNIX fctl function for performing low-level file control.
File tests: -X FILENAME	Returns values based on the file. File tests include determining whether the file exists and how many bytes are in the file, and other tests.
fileno(*filehandle*)	Returns the numeric file descriptor of the handle given, or the undef value if the file is not open.
flock(*filehandle operation*)	Performs low-level file locking in UNIX.
for (*initexpr; testexpr; endexpr*) { *block* }	Executes the block repeatedly. The initial expression is evaluated first, followed by the test expression. If the test expression is true, the block is executed, and the end expression is evaluated. The test expression is then evaluated, and the loop continues.
foreach *variable* (*list*) { *block* }	Executes the block repeatedly. For each item in the list, the variable is set to the item's value and the block is executed.
fork	Starts a child process and returns its process ID number.
format NAME= FORMATLIST	Creates a format that can be used by the write function. The format list consists of lines that contain picture formats, lists of arguments, or comments.
formline (*picture, list*)	Formats a list of values according to the picture.
getc(*filehandle*)	Returns the next byte from the file, or a null string if you're at the end of the file. If called without an argument, it returns the next byte from the standard file input.
getgrent	Returns UNIX group information from the next line of the /etc/group file. The list returned has four items: the group name, the group password (encrypted), the group number, and a string of all the members' names.

Name	Description
getgrgid(*groupid*)	Returns information about the group, based on the group ID number. The list returned has four items: the group name, the group password (encrypted), the group number, and a string of all the members' names.
getgrnam(*groupname*)	Returns information about the group, based on the group's name. The list returned has four items: the group name, the group password (encrypted), the group number, and a string of all the members' names.
gethostbyaddr (*packedaddr*, *addrtype*)	Returns information about the host based on its address. The address argument is packed, probably with the pack('C4') function, and the address type is always 2 for Internet addresses. In scalar context, gethostbyaddr returns the host name; in list context, it returns the host name, a string of aliases, the address type, the length of the returned list of packed addresses, and a list of packed addresses.
gethostbyname	Returns information from the DNS about the host, based on its (*domainname*) domain name. In scalar context, gethostbyname returns the IP address, packed; in list context, it returns the host name, a string of aliases, the address type, the length of the returned list of packed addresses, and a list of packed addresses. You can unpack the IP address with the unpack('C4') function.
gethostent	Returns the next record from the /etc/ hosts file. It returns the host name, a string of aliases, the address type, the length of the returned list of packed addresses, and a list of packed addresses.
getlogin	Returns the current login name by querying the /etc/utmp file.
getnetbyaddr (*packedaddr*, *addrtype*)	Returns information about the network based on its address from the /etc/ networks file. The address argument is packed, probably with the pack('C4') function, and the address type is always 2 for Internet addresses. In scalar context, getnetbyaddr returns the network name; in list context, it returns the network name, a string of aliases, the address type, and the packed address.

(continued)

Name	Description
getnetbyname (*domainname*)	Returns information about the network based on its name from the /etc/networks file. In scalar context, getnetbyaddr returns the network name; in list context, it returns the network name, a string of aliases, the address type, and the packed address.
getnetent	Returns information from the next line in the /etc/networks file. In scalar context, getnetbyaddr returns the network name; in list context, it returns the network name, a string of aliases, the address type, and the packed address.
getpeername(*socket*)	Returns the socket address of the other end of a connection. The address returned is packed.
getpgrp(*processid*)	Returns the process group number for the given process number. Use an argument of 0 to indicate the current process.
getppid	Returns the process number of the parent process.
getpriority (*processkind, who*)	Returns the priority of a process.
getprotobyname (*protoname*)	Returns information about a protocol based on its name. In scalar context, the protocol number is returned. In list context, the items in the list returned are the protocol name, aliases for the name, and the protocol number.
getprotobynumber (*protonumber*)	Returns information about a protocol based on its number. In scalar context, the protocol name is returned. In list context, the items in the list returned are the protocol name, aliases for the name, and the protocol number.
getprotoent	Returns the next record from the /etc/ protocols file. In scalar context, the protocol name is returned. In list context, the items in the list returned are the protocol name, aliases for the name, and the protocol number.
getpwent	Returns user information from the next line of the /etc/passwd file. The list returned has nine items: the user name, the password (encrypted), the user number, the group number, the quota field, the comment field, the gcos field, the home directory, and the default shell. In scalar context, only the user name is returned.

Name	Description
getpwnam(*username*)	Returns user information for the specified user name. The list returned has nine items: the user name, the password (encrypted), the user number, the group number, the quota field, the comment field, the gcos field, the home directory, and the default shell. In scalar context, only the user number is returned.
getpwuid(*userid*)	Returns user information for the specified user number. The list returned has nine items: the user name, the password (encrypted), the user number, the group number, the quota field, the comment field, the gcos field, the home directory, and the default shell. In scalar context, only the user name is returned.
getservbyname (*servicename, proto*)	Returns information about a service based on its name. In scalar context, the port number is returned. In list context, the items in the list returned are the service name, aliases for the name, port number, and protocol name.
getservbyport (*port, proto*)	Returns information about a service based on its port number. In scalar context, the service name is returned. In list context, the items in the list returned are the service name, aliases for the name, port number, and protocol name.
getservent	Returns information from the next record in the /etc/services file. In scalar context, the service name is returned. In list context, the items in the list returned are the service name, aliases for the name, the port number, and protocol name.
getsockname(*socket*)	Returns the socket address of the local end of a connection. The address returned is packed.
getsockopt (*socket, level, optionname*)	Returns the socket option specified.
glob(*string*)	Returns a list of files matching the argument; the argument may have wildcard characters.

(continued)

Name	Description
gmtime(*time*)	Converts the given time into Greenwich Mean Time. In scalar context, this function returns a string that looks something like Sat Nov 23 20:07:47 1996 (in Perl 5 and later versions only); in list context, the items are: second, minute, hour, day of month, month (January = 0, February = 1, . . .), year, weekday (Sunday = 0, Monday = 1, . . .), day of the year (January 1 = 0, January 2 = 1, . . .), and standard time (true or false). With no argument, the function assumes the current time.
goto LABEL	Jumps to the named label. You can use an expression instead of a label name, and Perl interprets that expression into a label name.
grep(*block*, *list*)	Evaluates the block in Boolean context on each item of the list. In scalar context, it returns the number of times that the block evaluated true; in list context, it returns the list of items matched.
grep(*regexp*, *list*)	Searches for the regular expression in each item of the list. In scalar context, returns the number of times that the regular expression was found; in list context, returns the list of items matched.
hex(*string*)	Returns the number that interprets the string as hexadecimal digits.
if(*test*) { *block1* }	Executes the block if the test is true. The first block may be followed by else { BLOCK2 }. In this case, if the test is false, the second block is executed. The first block may also be followed by one or more instances of elsif { BLOCKn }, which acts the same as else if.
import(*classname*)	This class method exports the class name to the current module.
index(*string*, *substring*, *position*)	Returns the position of the first occurrence of a substring in the string, or −1 if the substring isn't found. If the position is specified, Perl starts looking from that position instead of from the beginning of the string.
int(*number*)	Returns the integer portion of the number.
ioctl (*filehandle*, *function*, *scalar*)	Executes UNIX's ioctl function for performing low-level input and output.

Name	Description
join(*separator*, *list*)	Returns a string that consists of the items in the list with the separator between each item. The separator is not added to the beginning or end of the resulting string.
keys(*array*)	Normally used to return a list of all the keys in the hash. In scalar context, it returns the number of elements in the hash.
kill(*signal*, *list*)	Sends the signal to the list of process IDs. The signal is either the signal number or the name of the signal, for example, HUP. The function returns the number of processes signaled.
last	Exits the innermost loop that is executing. You can also give an argument of a label, in which case Perl exits out to the loop with that label.
lc(*string*)	Returns the string in all lowercase characters.
lcfirst(*string*)	Returns the string with the first character changed to lowercase.
length(*string*)	Returns the length of the string.
link(*oldfile*, *newfile*)	Creates a new file that has a hard link to the old file. Returns true if successful.
listen(*socket*, *maxconn*)	Causes the system to allow connections on the socket. The system queues up to the number of connections specified.
local(*variables*)	Makes one or more variables local to the current block, subroutine, eval function, or file.
localtime(*time*)	Converts the given time into the local time. In scalar context, this returns a string that looks something like Sat Nov 23 20:07:47 1996 (in Perl 5 only); in list context, the items are: second, minute, hour, day of month, month (January = 0, February = 1, . . .), year, weekday (Sunday = 0, Monday = 1, . . .), day of the year (January 1 = 0, January 2 = 1, . . .), and standard time (true or false). With no argument, the function assumes the current time.
log(*number*)	Returns the natural logarithm (base *e*) of the number.

(continued)

Name	Description
lstat(*file*)	Returns information about the file. The argument can be either a file handle or a string with the file's name. If the file is a symbolic link, the information is about the linked-to file, not the link itself. The following items in the list are returned: the device number of the filesystem, inode number, file permissions (number), number of hard links to the file, user number of file's owner, group number of the file's owner, device identifier for special files, size of file, last access time, last modify time, last inode change time, preferred block size, and number of blocks allocated.
map { *block* } *list*	Returns a list of the block evaluated in list context for each item in the list. During evaluation, $_ is set to the list item being evaluated.
map(*expression*, *list*)	Returns a list of the expression evaluated in list context for each item in the list. During evaluation, $_ is set to the list item being evaluated.
mkdir(*dirname*, *permission*)	Creates a directory with the specified permissions (in octal). Returns true if successful.
msgctl(*id*,*command*, *argument*)	Sends a message using UNIX's mesgctl function.
msgget(*key*, *flags*)	Returns the message ID for System V IPC messages.
msgrcv(*id*, *variable*, *size*, *type*, *flags*)	Receives a message with the message ID.
msgsnd(*id*, *message*, *flags*)	Sends a message with the message ID.
my(*variables*)	Makes one or more variables local to the current block, subroutine, eval function, or file.
new(*classname*)	Constructs an object from the class. You can also specify a list after the class name as arguments passed to the constructor.
next	Causes the innermost loop to start again from the beginning of the loop. You can also include a label with the function, in which case Perl jumps to the beginning of the loop with that label.

Name	Description
no MODULE	Removes subroutine and variable names that were imported by the use function after the use function is called on the same module name.
oct(*string*)	Returns the number that is the string interpreted as an octal value.
open(*filehandle,* *name*)	Opens the named file or command and associates it with the given file handle. The characters at the beginning of the name determine whether the file is opened for input, output, or appending. In the case of a command, the location of the | charac ter in the command name determines whether the file handle is for reading or writing. The function returns true if the file or command is opened suc cessfully. Starting with Perl 5.6, the open function can take three arguments: open(FILEHANDLE, MODE, NAME). The mode is the prefix you would have added to the file name, such as > to indicate writing to a file.
opendir(*dirhandle,* *dirname*)	Opens the directory for reading and associates the directory handle with that directory.
ord(*string*)	Returns the ASCII value of the first character of the string.
our(*variables*)	Makes one or more variables local to the current block, subroutine, eval function, or file. Unlike my, our doesn't create a local variable.
pack(*template,* *list*)	Returns a string containing the items from the list put together using the template.
package NAME	Declares that the rest of the innermost block, sub routine, eval function, or file belongs to the specified package name.
pipe(*readhandle,* *writehandle*)	Opens a pair of pipes for use by other functions.
pop(*listname*)	Shortens the list by removing the last item, and returns that item. If the list is empty, it returns the undefined value. **Note:** The argument must be the name of a list, not an actual list.
pos(*variable*)	Returns the position in a variable where the last m//g associated with the variable left off.

(continued)

Name	Description
print(*filehandle, list*)	Sends a list to the file specified by the file handle and returns true if successful. Note that the argu ment is a list, not a scalar; therefore, variables that are arguments to print are evaluated in list context. The print function is more commonly written without parentheses.
print(*list*)	Sends the list to the standard file output and returns true if successful. The argument is a list, not a scalar; therefore, variables that are argu ments to print are evaluated in list context. The print function is more commonly written with out parentheses.
printf(*filehandle format, list*)	Formats a list using the format string, sends the resulting list to the file specified by the filehandle, and returns true if successful. ***Note:*** No comma appears after the file handle.
printf (*format, list*)	Formats a list using the format string, sends the resulting list to the standard file output, and returns true if successful.
push(*listname, items...*)	Adds the item(s) in the arguments after the first argument to the end of the list named in the first argument.
q/STRING/	Returns a string with no interpretation of the string's contents. This function is similar to using single quotes (' '), except that you can choose the quoting character.
qq/STRING/	Quotes a string, with interpretation of the string's contents. This function is similar to using double quotes (" "), except that you can choose the quot ing character.
quotemeta(*string*)	Returns the value of an argument with all the reg ular expression metacharacters back-slashed as necessary.
qw/STRING/	Returns the words in a string with no interpreta tion. Ignores differences in white space between words.
qx/COMMAND/	Returns the output of running a command. This function is similar to using the backtick character (`), except that you can choose the quoting character.

Name	Description
rand(*number*)	Returns a random number between 0 and the specified number (including 0 but not including the specified number). If no argument is given, it returns a random number between 0 and 1. The seed used for the random number is set with the srand function.
read(*filehandle, variable, length, offset*)	Reads the number of bytes from the file into the scalar variable. The function starts writing into the variable at the given offset, which is optional. The function returns the actual number of bytes read or 0 if you are already at the end of the file; the actual number may be less than the desired number if the function read off the end of the file.
readdir(*dirhandle*)	Reads the next entry from a directory. In scalar context, the function returns the next filename in the directory; in list context, the function returns the rest of the filenames.
readlink(*filename*)	Returns the name of the file pointed to by the sym bolic link in the filename given in the argument. If the named file is not a symbolic link or some other error occurs, the function returns the undefined value.
recv(*socket, variable, length, flags*)	Receives a message on the socket and puts it in the variable.
redo	Restarts the innermost loop without reevaluating the conditional test for the loop. You can also give an argument of a label, which causes Perl to restart the loop with that label.
ref(*variable*)	Returns true if the variable is a reference, other wise returns the null string. The value returned is a string indicating the type of reference.
rename(*filename, newname*)	Renames a file and returns true if successful. This function does not work across file systems on UNIX.
require(*filename*)	Executes the named Perl program provided that program has not already been executed.
require(*number*)	Stops the program if the Perl version number is lower than the argument.

(continued)

Name	*Description*
require(*packagename*)	Loads the package in the same way the use function does, except that the package is loaded while the program is running, not when it is compiled.
reset	Resets variables and single-match searches performed with the ?? operator.
reset(*string*)	Resets all variables that have a name starting with the letter in the string. If the string is more than one character, that string must be a range expressed with a hyphen, in which case all variables whose first letter starts with any letter in the given range are reset. Avoid using this function.
return(*list*)	Returns the specified value from a subroutine. If the subroutine is in scalar context, the first item in the list is returned; if the subroutine is in list context, the entire list is returned.
reverse(*list*)	Returns a list in the reverse order of the argument.
rewinddir(*dirhandle*)	Sets the position of the next readdir function to the beginning of the directory.
rindex(*string, substring, position*)	Returns the position of the last occurrence of the substring in the string, or −1 if the substring isn't found. If the position is specified, Perl starts looking from that position instead of from the beginning of the string.
rmdir (*directoryname*)	Removes the directory provided the directory is empty.
scalar(*expression*)	Forces an argument to be evaluated in scalar context. This function is useful if the expression may be a list and you don't want the expression to be evaluated in list context.
seek(*filehandle, position, relative*)	Sets the position of the file pointer for the file. The value of the third argument specifies the relative position of the file pointer: 0 means it's relative to the beginning of the file; 1 means it's relative to the current position; and 2 means it's relative to the end of the file. The function returns true if successful.
seekdir(*dirhandle, position*)	Sets the position for the readdir function.

Name	*Description*
select(*filehandle*)	Selects the file handle to be used by the print and write functions if no file handle is specified in them. The function returns the file handle that was in use before the function was called. If you do not give an argument to the function, it simply returns the file handle being used.
select(*readbits, writebits, exceptionalbits, timeout*)	Tells you which of your file descriptors are ready to do reads or writes, or are reporting an exceptional condition.
semctl(*id, semnum, command, argument*)	Controls semaphore messages on systems that support semaphores.
semget(*key, nsems, flags*)	Returns a semaphore ID on systems that support semaphores.
semop(*key, opstring*)	Performs semaphore operations on systems that support semaphores.
send(*socket, message,flags,to*)	Sends a message to the socket.
setgrent	Causes the next call to getgrent to start read ing from the top of the /etc/groups file.
sethostent	Causes the next call to gethostent to start reading from the top of the /etc/hosts file.
setnetent	Causes the next call to getnetent to start read ing from the top of the /etc/networks file.
setpgrp(*processid, processgroup*)	Sets the process group for the process specified in the first argument.
setpriority (*processkind, who, priority*)	Sets the priority for a process, a process group, or a user.
setprotoent	Causes the next call to getprotoent to start reading from the top of the /etc/protocols file.
setpwent	Causes the next call to getpwent to start read ing from the top of the /etc/passwd file.
setservent	Causes the next call to getservent to start reading from the top of the /etc/services file.

(continued)

Name	Description
`setsockopt(socket, level, optionname, optionval)`	Sets an option on the socket.
`shift(listname)`	Shortens the list by removing the first item, and returns that item. If the list is empty, it returns the undefined value. **Note:** The argument must be the name of a list, not an actual list.
`shmctl(id, command, argument)`	Controls shared memory on systems that support shared memory.
`shmget(key, size, flags)`	Returns the shared memory ID on systems that support shared memory.
`shmread(id, variable, position, size)`	Reads from shared memory on systems that support shared memory.
`shmwrite(id, string, position, size)`	Writes to shared memory on systems that support shared memory.
`shutdown (socket, how)`	Closes the socket.
`sin(number)`	Returns the sine of the number, expressed in radians.
`sleep(number)`	Causes the program to sleep for a specified number of seconds. If no argument is given, the program sleeps until it receives a `SIGALRM` signal from some other program. The function returns the actual number of seconds slept.
`socket(socket, domain, type, protocol)`	Opens a socket and returns true if successful.
`socketpair(socket1, socket2, domain, type, protocol)`	Creates a pair of sockets and returns true if successful.
`sort { block } list`	Returns a list of the items in the list argument sorted using the comparison specified in the block. The block compares two variables, $a and $b, and the comparison determines how the sorting is done.
`sort(list)`	Returns a list of the items in the argument sorted in ascending string order.

Name	Description
sort SUBROUTINE-NAME	Returns a list of the items in the LIST list argument sorted using the comparison specified in the subroutine. The subroutine compares two variables, $a and $b, and the comparison determines how the sorting is done.
splice(listname, removeoffset, removenumber, addlist)	Returns a list that is the named list with the specified number of items removed from the specified offset, with the list in the fourth argument added at the offset. **Note**: The first argument must be the name of a list, not an actual list.
split(/pattern/, string, limit)	Returns a list that consists of a string split at each point where the pattern matches a substring of the full string. If a limit is specified, only that limited number of items is returned, with the last item being the remainder of the string after the initial segments are split out; if no limit is specified, any number of items can be returned. In scalar context, the function returns only the number of items that would have been returned in list context. If the pattern contains parentheses, the delimiter matched in each set of parentheses is returned interspersed with the other list items.
sprintf(format, list)	Formats a list using the format string and returns the resulting list.
sqrt(number)	Returns the square root of the argument.
srand(number)	Sets the seed value for the rand function to the number specified. If you do not specify an argument, Perl uses the time function as the argument.
stat(file)	Returns information about a file. The argument can be either a file handle or a string with the file's name. If the file is a symbolic link, the information is about the link itself, not the linked-to file. The following items in the list are returned: the device number of the file system, inode number, file permissions (number), number of hard links to the file, user number of file's owner, group number of the file's owner, device identifier for special files, size of file, last access time, last modify time, last inode change time, preferred block size, and number of blocks allocated.

(continued)

Name	Description
study(*scalar*)	Carefully examines a string in order to speed up later searches on that string.
sub NAME { *block* }	Defines a subroutine. You also include a prototype for calling the subroutine between the name and the block. If you do not specify a block, Perl notes that the name exists when it interprets your program.
substr(*string*, *offset*, *length*)	Returns a string that is a substring of the first argument. The substring starts at the specified offset and is of the specified length, if possible. If the offset is negative, the offset is from the end of the string instead of from the beginning. If you do not specify a length, everything from the offset to the end of the string is returned. This function can also be used on the left side of an assignment, in which case the string must be a string name, and the contents of the string will change.
switch(*variable*) { case(*value1*) { *block1* } case(*value2*) { *block2* } ... }	Picks which block to run based on the value of a variable. Each case statement gives a value that is tested against the variable, and the first case statement that matches is executed. This command was introduced in Perl 5.8, and a program using it must first contain the statement use Switch.
symlink(*oldfile*, *newfile*)	Creates a new file that has a symbolic link to the old file. Returns true if successful.
syscall(*callname*, *list*)	Executes the specified system call, using the list as arguments.
sysopen(*filehandle*, *filename*, *mode*)	Opens the file using system-level calls.
sysread(*filehandle*, *variable*, *length*, *offset*)	Reads from the file using system-level calls.
system(*command*)	Runs a command and waits for the command to finish. The function returns the exit status of the program multiplied by 256.
syswrite(*filehandle*, *variable*, *length*, *offset*)	Writes to the file using system-level calls.

Name	Description
tell(*filehandle*)	Returns the file position keeper of the specified file.
telldir(*dirhandle*)	Returns the directory position keeper of the speci fied file.
tie(*variable, newpackagename, list*)	Associates a variable with a particular package so that calls to the package are reflected in the variable.
tied(*variable*)	Returns a reference to the object that is tied to the variable.
time	Returns the current time, which is the number of nonleap seconds from the time specified as the "beginning of time" for the operating system.
times	Returns a list of the amount of CPU seconds used. The items in the list include the number of sec onds for user instructions for this process, system instructions for this process, user instructions for child processes, and system instructions for child processes.
truncate(*filehandle, length*)	Shortens the file to the specified length.
uc(*string*)	Returns the string in all uppercase characters.
ucfirst(*string*)	Returns the string with the first character changed to uppercase.
umask(*mode*)	Sets the UNIX umask value for the current process.
undef(*variable*)	Undefines the value of the variable or sets the value of the variable to the undefined value.
unless(*test*) { *block1* }	Executes a block if the test is false. The first block may be followed by else { BLOCK2 }. In this case, if the test is true, the second block is exe cuted. The first block may also be followed by one or more instances of elsif { BLOCKn }, which acts the same as else if.
unlink(*filenames*)	Deletes the files in the list and returns the number of files deleted.
unpack(*template, string*)	Returns a list of items that is the string examined using the template (the first argument to the function).

(continued)

Name	*Description*
unshift(*listname*, *list*)	Adds the items of the list in the second argument to the beginning of the list named in the first argument.
untie(*variable*)	Unbinds a variable from a package.
until(*test*) { *block* }	If the test returns false, Perl executes the block and redoes the test in order to determine whether to execute the block again.
use MODULE	Imports semantics from a module into the current package. You can also specify a list of arguments for the module. Perl's pragmas are also implemented with this function.
utime(*accesstime*, *modtime*, *filenames*)	Changes the access time and modification time on the named files. The function returns the number of files successfully changed.
values(*array*)	Returns a list of the values in the hash.
vec(*string*, *offset*, *numbits*)	Returns the value of the element of the string that is the number of bits wide, starting at the specified offset.
wait	Waits for a child process to terminate.
waitpid(*pid*, *flags*)	Waits for the specified child process to terminate and returns true when the process is dead.
wantarray	Returns true if the current subroutine is looking for a list value or false if it is looking for a scalar value.
warn(*list*)	Sends a list to the standard error output.
while(*test*) { *block* }	If the test returns true, Perl executes the block and redoes the test to determine whether or not to execute the block again.
write(*filehandle*)	Writes text formatted with the format function to the specified file.

Perl's Special Variables

In the following section, I describe Perl's special variables. Don't be surprised if the descriptions are somewhat puzzling at this point. Only a few of the special variables are useful for novice and intermediate Perl programmers.

General-purpose variables

Variable	Description
$_	The default input to many functions and operations. Most useful with the while(<*filehandle*>) construct described in Chapter 10.
$/	The input record separator. The default depends on the operating system.
$[	Index of the first element in a list. The index is normally 0 (and you really shouldn't change it), but some people insist that the first item of a list should be numbered as 1.
$|	Forces automatic flushing to the selected file handle if this variable is set to true. If false (the default), output to the selected file handle will only be done when the operating system feels like it or when the file is closed.
$]	The version of Perl.
$0	The name of the file containing the Perl program being run.
$^T	Time at which this program started running.
$.	The input line number of the last file handle read.
$ARGV	Name of the current file, when using <ARGV>.
@ARGV	Command-line arguments for the program.
@INC	List of directories in which Perl looks for programs named in the do, require, and use functions.
%INC	The files that have been used by do and require. Each key is the filename specified, and each value is the full path to the found file.
%ENV	Operating system environment variables.

Variables that relate to errors and return values

Variable	Description
$!	The current system error number or string.
$?	Status returned by the last `system` function, ` (backtick) command, or	(pipe). This value is actually 256 times the number returned from the process.
$@	Error message returned by the last `eval` function.

Special variables for regular expressions

Variable	Description
$&	The text matched by the last successful pattern match in a regular expression.
$'	The text preceding the last successful pattern match in a regular expression.
$'	The text following the last successful pattern match in a regular expression.
$+	The text that matched the last successful bracketed pattern in a regular expression.
$digit	The text matched by the set of parentheses in a regular expression. The digit corresponds to the number of the matched set.

Variables that relate to processes

Variable	Description
$$	The Perl program's process number.
$<	The real userid of this process.
$>	The effective userid of this process.
$(	The real groupid of this process.
$)	The effective groupid of this process.

Variables for formats

Variable	Description
$%	Current page number.
$-	Number of lines left on the current page.
$=	Page length.
$~	Name of the report format.
$^	Name of the top-of-page format.
^L	Text that a format puts out when doing a form feed.
$:	Text after which a string may be broken for format continuation fields.
$^A	Contents of the accumulator of format lines.

Miscellaneous variables

Variable	Description
$,	Output field separator, which is printed between each item in the list that is output by print.
$\	Output record separator, which is printed at the end of the list that is output by print.
$"	List separator placed between each item in a list if the list is interpreted in double-quotes, such as "@a".
$;	Separator placed between subscripts of multidimensional arrays.
$^D	Debugging flags.
$^F	Maximum system file descriptor.
$^H	Internal compiler hints.
$^I	In-place edit extension.
$^O	Name of the operating system for which Perl was compiled.
$^P	Internal flag for the debugger.
$^W	Value of the warning switch.

(continued)

Variable	Description
$\$^X$	Name that the Perl binary was compiled as.
@F	Holds the results of the -a command-line option.
%SIG	Signal handlers.

Perl's Predefined File Handles

File Handle	Description
ARGV	Iterates over the filenames in @ARGV.
STDERR	Standard error output.
STDIN	Standard file input.
STDOUT	Standard file output.
DATA	Anything that follows a token __DATA__ in a program.
_	Cache for the stat and lstat functions and file test operators.

Index

• *p* •

FOR DUMMIES

The easy way to get more done and have more fun

FOR DUMMIES®

A world of resources to help you grow

HOME, GARDEN & HOBBIES

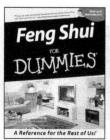

Feng Shui For Dummies
0-7645-5295-3

Gardening For Dummies
0-7645-5130-2

Guitar For Dummies
0-7645-5106-X

Also available:

Auto Repair For Dummies
(0-7645-5089-6)

Chess For Dummies
(0-7645-5003-9)

Home Maintenance For Dummies
(0-7645-5215-5)

Organizing For Dummies
(0-7645-5300-3)

Piano For Dummies
(0-7645-5105-1)

Poker For Dummies
(0-7645-5232-5)

Quilting For Dummies
(0-7645-5118-3)

Rock Guitar For Dumm
(0-7645-5356-9)

Roses For Dummies
(0-7645-5202-3)

Sewing For Dummies
(0-7645-5137-X)

FOOD & WINE

Cooking For Dummies
0-7645-5250-3

Cookies For Dummies
0-7645-5390-9

Wine For Dummies
0-7645-5114-0

Also available:

Bartending For Dummies
(0-7645-5051-9)

Chinese Cooking For Dummies
(0-7645-5247-3)

Christmas Cooking For Dummies
(0-7645-5407-7)

Diabetes Cookbook For Dummies
(0-7645-5230-9)

Grilling For Dummies
(0-7645-5076-4)

Low-Fat Cooking For Dummies
(0-7645-5035-7)

Slow Cookers For Dum
(0-7645-5240-6)

TRAVEL

Italy For Dummies
0-7645-5453-0

Hawaii For Dummies
0-7645-5438-7

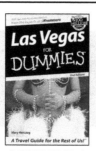

Las Vegas For Dummies
0-7645-5448-4

Also available:

America's National Parks For Dummies
(0-7645-6204-5)

Caribbean For Dummies
(0-7645-5445-X)

Cruise Vacations For Dummies 2003
(0-7645-5459-X)

Europe For Dummies
(0-7645-5456-5)

Ireland For Dummies
(0-7645-6199-5)

France For Dummies
(0-7645-6292-4)

London For Dummies
(0-7645-5416-6)

Mexico's Beach Resorts Dummies
(0-7645-6262-2)

Paris For Dummies
(0-7645-5494-8)

RV Vacations For Dumm
(0-7645-5443-3)

Walt Disney World & Or For Dummies
(0-7645-5444-1)

Available wherever books are sold. Go to www.dummies.com or call 1-877-762-2974 to order direct.

FOR DUMMIES®

Plain-English solutions for everyday challenges

COMPUTER BASICS

0-7645-0838-5

0-7645-1663-9

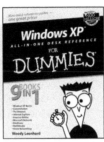

0-7645-1548-9

Also available:

PCs All-in-One Desk Reference For Dummies (0-7645-0791-5)

Pocket PC For Dummies (0-7645-1640-X)

Treo and Visor For Dummies (0-7645-1673-6)

Troubleshooting Your PC For Dummies (0-7645-1669-8)

Upgrading & Fixing PCs For Dummies (0-7645-1665-5)

Windows XP For Dummies (0-7645-0893-8)

Windows XP For Dummies Quick Reference (0-7645-0897-0)

BUSINESS SOFTWARE

0-7645-0822-9

0-7645-0839-3

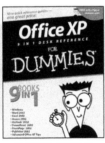

0-7645-0819-9

Also available:

Excel Data Analysis For Dummies (0-7645-1661-2)

Excel 2002 All-in-One Desk Reference For Dummies (0-7645-1794-5)

Excel 2002 For Dummies Quick Reference (0-7645-0829-6)

GoldMine "X" For Dummies (0-7645-0845-8)

Microsoft CRM For Dummies (0-7645-1698-1)

Microsoft Project 2002 For Dummies (0-7645-1628-0)

Office XP For Dummies (0-7645-0830-X)

Outlook 2002 For Dummies (0-7645-0828-8)

Get smart! Visit www.dummies.com

- **Find listings of even more *For Dummies* titles**
- **Browse online articles**
- **Sign up for Dummies eTips™**
- **Check out *For Dummies* fitness videos and other products**
- **Order from our online bookstore**

Available wherever books are sold. Go to www.dummies.com or call 1-877-762-2974 to order direct.

FOR DUMMIES

Helping you expand your horizons and realize your potentia

INTERNET

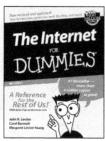

The Internet FOR DUMMIES

0-7645-0894-6

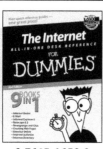

The Internet ALL-IN-ONE DESK REFERENCE FOR DUMMIES

0-7645-1659-0

eBay FOR DUMMIES

0-7645-1642-6

Also available:

America Online 7.0 For Dummies
(0-7645-1624-8)

Genealogy Online For Dummies
(0-7645-0807-5)

The Internet All-in-One Desk Reference For Dummies
(0-7645-1659-0)

Internet Explorer 6 For Dummies
(0-7645-1344-3)

The Internet For Dummie Quick Reference
(0-7645-1645-0)

Internet Privacy For Dumm
(0-7645-0846-6)

Researching Online For Dummies
(0-7645-0546-7)

Starting an Online Busine For Dummies
(0-7645-1655-8)

DIGITAL MEDIA

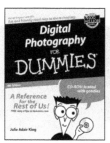

Digital Photography FOR DUMMIES

0-7645-1664-7

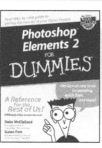

Photoshop Elements 2 FOR DUMMIES

0-7645-1675-2

Digital Video FOR DUMMIES

0-7645-0806-7

Also available:

CD and DVD Recording For Dummies
(0-7645-1627-2)

Digital Photography All-in-One Desk Reference For Dummies
(0-7645-1800-3)

Digital Photography For Dummies Quick Reference
(0-7645-0750-8)

Home Recording for Musicians For Dummies
(0-7645-1634-5)

MP3 For Dummies
(0-7645-0858-X)

Paint Shop Pro "X" For Dummies
(0-7645-2440-2)

Photo Retouching & Restoration For Dummies
(0-7645-1662-0)

Scanners For Dummies
(0-7645-0783-4)

GRAPHICS

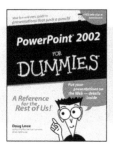

PowerPoint 2002 FOR DUMMIES

0-7645-0817-2

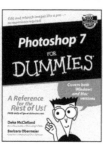

Photoshop 7 FOR DUMMIES

0-7645-1651-5

Macromedia Flash MX FOR DUMMIES

0-7645-0895-4

Also available:

Adobe Acrobat 5 PDF For Dummies
(0-7645-1652-3)

Fireworks 4 For Dummies
(0-7645-0804-0)

Illustrator 10 For Dummies
(0-7645-3636-2)

QuarkXPress 5 For Dumm
(0-7645-0643-9)

Visio 2000 For Dummies
(0-7645-0635-8)

Available wherever books are sold. Go to www.dummies.com or call 1-877-762-2974 to order direct.